More

...erstanding

Moving Globally

Joy I. Butler, EdD
The University of British Columbia

Linda L. Griffin, PhD
University of Massachusetts, Amherst

Editors

Human Kinetics

Library of Congress Cataloging-in-Publication Data

More teaching games for understanding : moving globally / Joy Butler and Linda Griffin.
    p. cm.
  Includes bibliographical references and index.
  ISBN-13: 978-0-7360-8334-8 (soft cover)
  ISBN-10: 0-7360-8334-0 (soft cover)
 1. Sports--Study and teaching. 2. Physical education and training--Study and teaching. 3. Student-centered learning. I. Butler, Joy. II. Griffin, Linda L., 1954-
  GV361.M73 2010
  796.07'7--dc22

                                2010002428

ISBN-10: 0-7360-8334-0 (print)
ISBN-13: 978-0-7360-8334-8 (print)

The Web addresses cited in this text were current as of January 27, 2010, unless otherwise noted.

Acquisitions Editor: Scott Wikgren; **Managing Editor:** Amy Stahl; **Assistant Editors:** Elizabeth Evans, Anne Rumery, Rachel Brito, and Casey A. Gentis; **Copyeditor:** Joy Wotherspoon; **Indexer:** Betty Frizzéll; **Permission Manager:** Dalene Reeder; **Graphic Designer:** Fred Starbird; **Graphic Artist:** Kathleen Boudreau-Fuoss; **Cover Designer:** Keith Blomberg; **Photographer (cover):** © Human Kinetics; **Photographer (interior):** © Human Kinetics, unless otherwise noted. Photos courtesy of Karin McKenna (p. 49); James Mandigo (pp. 69, 73, 76, 77, 81, and 83); AVAVA (p. 121); Brand X Pictures (p. 171); Dianna Bandhauer (p. 209); Daniel Memmert (p. 231); Deborah J. Karson (p. 245); **Photo Asset Manager:** Laura Fitch; **Photo Production Manager:** Jason Allen; **Art Manager:** Kelly Hendren; **Associate Art Manager:** Alan L. Wilborn; **Illustrator:** Alan L. Wilborn; **Printer:** Versa Press

Printed in the United States of America   10 9 8 7 6 5 4 3 2 1

The paper in this book is certified under a sustainable forestry program.

Human Kinetics
Web site: www.HumanKinetics.com

United States: Human Kinetics
P.O. Box 5076, Champaign, IL 61825-5076
800-747-4457
e-mail: humank@hkusa.com

Canada: Human Kinetics
475 Devonshire Road Unit 100,
Windsor, ON N8Y 2L5
800-465-7301 (in Canada only)
e-mail: info@hkcanada.com

Europe: Human Kinetics
107 Bradford Road, Stanningley,
Leeds LS28 6AT, United Kingdom
+44 (0) 113 255 5665
e-mail: hk@hkeurope.com

Australia: Human Kinetics
57A Price Avenue, Lower Mitcham,
South Australia 5062
08 8372 0999
e-mail: info@hkaustralia.com

New Zealand: Human Kinetics
P.O. Box 80
Torrens Park, South Australia 5062
0800 222 062
e-mail: info@hknewzealand.com

E4824

Contents

Foreword:
Revisiting the TGfU Brand

Len Almond

In the late 1970s and early 1980s, educators were concerned that children did not experience the thrill of playing games and very few understood anything about games. In the same way, many believed that neither children nor adults understood the games they were playing. As a consequence of these observations, a different approach was developed to teach children games through other games. The introductory games were representations of the real game with simplified rules that all children could play right away. This approach became known as Teaching Games for Understanding (TGfU).

As a result of inviting many practitioners and lecturers to explore this approach, a series of papers (Bulletin of Physical Education, 1982) and a book titled *Rethinking Games Teaching* emerged (Thorpe, Bunker, & Almond, 1986). Since this time, hundreds of publications, conference presentations, and workshops have been developed to discuss and debate TGfU. A number of national coaches have adopted the rationale for TGfU in the United Kingdom, but the practice has mainly been embraced in other countries. In addition, an approach for all sports has emerged called *Play Practice* (2001), which guides practitioners through teaching games and goes beyond TGfU in important ways. Although TGfU was enshrined in the 1990s in the first UK national-curriculum recommendations for physical education, the rationale seems to have passed by practitioners without any major effect. TGfU currently thrives in only a few areas where practitioners are faithful to its original approach.

I would like to suggest that pedagogy in physical education needs to be a central theoretical and practical issue if we are to develop a more informed vision of the potential of physical education in the lives of all children and young people. In this piece, I would like to use TGfU as the basis for generating a debate about pedagogy. It is short because my motive is to generate debate and criticism and to encourage practitioners and teachers to explore the relevance of TGfU for today's children.

I would like to propose that we revisit TGfU in a different format to enable today's teachers to explore the relevance of a rebranded TGfU and to start to rethink its relevance. One of the major strengths of TGfU, its pedagogical approach, was never spelled out in more precise terms.

Therefore, I would like to suggest that we explore TGfU as an approach with a number of key pedagogical principles.

Pedagogical Principles

1. All games need to be represented in their simplest form to enable all children to play and learn the game. How can games be represented to all children?

At the 1984 Olympic Congress in Oregon, a paper titled A Change in Focus for the Teaching of Games proposed four fundamental aspects of games curriculum:

- Sampling
- Modification – representation
- Modification – exaggeration
- Tactical complexity

However, these fundamental aspects represent two quite discrete concepts. First, a curriculum decision (a sampling of the richness of all games) determines which games we should teach and why. Second, pedagogical decisions about modification (representation, exaggeration, and tactical complexity) determine the order in which games should be taught. Should some games be taught earlier, as in the case of building toward more complex games?

These pedagogical decisions represent the most significant features of TGfU thinking. The team (Dave Bunker, Rod Thorpe, and Len Almond) believed that we needed to modify adult versions of a game and to represent them in their simplest form in order to reduce the problems and demands faced by children. Modification involved changing rules, playing areas, and time frames and increasing the size of implements or balls to suit the needs of children and to reduce the technical demands. Exaggeration was used to illustrate the primary rules of the game and to highlight the tactical problems of the game. Bruner's spiral curriculum and theory of instruction (motivation, representation, structure, and sequence) were the inspirations for this development.

In this way, the team believed that we could make all games amenable to all children and attractive enough to sustain their interest and stimulate further participation both in and out of school. We could encourage more practice, which would improve game techniques and help children increase their level of activity and enjoyment.

2. All games need to be shaped in order to progress and develop. At the same time, they must also address the different needs of children in a developmentally appropriate format. How can we shape games?

When Margaret Ellis (1986) used the term shaping games, she meant basic modification. More recently, Alan Launder used the terms shaping play, focusing play, and enhancing play in a pedagogical sense in his book, *Play Practice* (2001). His use of the term shaping is important because its goes beyond representation and basic modification of TGfU. The ideas he uses merit close scrutiny: creating appropriate learning opportunities, changing games, and meeting the needs of different students. His forthcoming rewrite of *Play Practice* should illuminate the second pedagogical principle.

3. In order to understand games and make intelligent decisions during play, both children and teachers need to acquire and develop what one could call games sense. What does games sense entail?

The term games sense emerged in Australia, where it was used to make the game the focus for developing tactical and strategic thinking. In this approach, the teacher or coach becomes a facilitator, creating situations for players to find solutions to game problems themselves. This is a very specific use of games sense.

However, I believe that games sense should be used in a different way. Games sense represents a whole mind-set in which players accumulate the wisdom to make intelligent decisions about their play. There is huge potential here. I believe that the characteristics of games sense need to be articulated because they represent a key pedagogical principle that needs to be nurtured and cherished. Games sense enables participants to enhance their understanding of games and to appreciate their own potential to excite and challenge themselves. I believe that this notion is a worthy target for creative thinking, a sharing of ideas, and the emergence of an important dimension of a revised TGfU. Perhaps we should consider some of the following goals:

- Comprehending the shape and flow of the games
- Understanding the available options quickly and decisively
- Understanding the location of other players on the team and anticipating the type and direction of their future movements
- Identifying how the team links together and copes with changeovers
- Understanding which roles individual players have during times of offense, defense, and neutrality
- Understanding how the opposition plays
- Developing positional sense

4. If they are to teach games to all children, teachers need what I call a pedagogy of engagement. What does this entail? This fourth pedagogical concept was originally missing from TGfU because we failed to articulate

it in detail, assuming that the concept of engagement would be part of teachers' training and skill set. Teachers must learn to achieve the following goals:

- Reach out to children
- Connect with them
- Engage them constructively
- Draw out their confidence and potential
- Stretch their capabilities

These competences can be practiced and learned to build up a whole repertoire of teaching skills that will help instructors in their games teaching.

Conclusion

In summary, I have attempted to identify four pedagogical principles within a TGfU framework that need to be considered in the development of teaching games. I believe that play practice challenges our thinking about shaping games and provides another dimension to TGfU. With critical analysis and application of its characteristics, games sense may well be the key to the idea of intelligent performance in a game. Finally, I have introduced a pedagogy of engagement which complements TGfU.

I hope to stimulate debate and reawaken interest among practitioners of TGfU. Although this approach has the power to transform games teaching, it needs to be presented in a format that allows practitioners to recognize its significance. The next stage is to provide practical illustrations of TGfU that all teachers can use.

References

Ellis, M. (1986). Modifications of games. In R. Thorpe, D. Bunker, & L. Almond (Eds.), *Rethinking Games Teaching*. Loughborough, UK: University of Technology.

Launder, A.G. (2001). *Play practice: The games approach to teaching and coaching sports.* Champaign, IL: Human Kinetics.

Thorpe, R., Bunker, D., & Almond, L. (Eds.). (1986). *Rethinking games teaching.* Loughborough, UK: University of Technology.

Preface

Rod Thorpe • David Bunker

We have always been surprised that the TGfU model has attracted such a great deal of interest. Perhaps it is not surprising when one considers the slow evolution of the approach and the field testing it received. It seems to tick many boxes for many people. Although it was first developed for implementation into the physical-education (PE) curriculum, TGfU has subsequently been embraced by programs as varied as games-based activities taught by inexperienced teachers and beginning coaches for children under age 11 (Playsport[1]) and coaching of elite players by experienced coaches (Games Sense[2]).

Both of us changed our teaching as physical educators in the late 1960s. At college, we had been taught to follow a lesson plan of "warm up, skill, game," but this approach did not seem to be the answer. This being said, many of the ideas presented by our lecturers, such as concepts from educational gymnastics and modified games, influenced this change. As lecturers and preparing teachers in the early 1970s, we observed games lessons that followed the traditional pattern and noted any failure to meet a number of intended learning outcomes. We began to evolve the TGfU model with our students, local teachers, and other members of the Loughborough staff. It is worth noting that when the model was presented to some teachers, they responded by saying, "Thank you for that. I was doing something similar, as I was not satisfied with traditional games lessons, but could not rationalize or explain quite what I was doing." Real impetus came when Len Almond, a curriculum developer, joined the staff and convinced us that the ideas we were working with, grounded in skill acquisition and social psychology, needed to be articulated in a more coherent framework in order to inform games teaching. Len not only brought his own ideas to the development of this framework but also encouraged us to test our ideas with other colleagues working in the UK. As an executive member of AIESEP (Association Internationale des Écoles Superieures d'Education Physique or International Association for Physical Education in Higher Education), he proposed that we promote these ideas to a wider international audience.

We present this short résumé of the development of TGfU to reinforce our belief that when people work together, great progress can be made. Students make their critical input; the barriers between teachers, coaches, and researchers break down as each informs the other In a fruitful exchange of ideas. TGfU conferences facilitate this progress, since individuals who represent these groups are invited to make their contributions. This process is both rewarding and exciting, but we suggest that this exchange should be transferred from the conference room into practical situations.

Writing this foreword presents us with an opportunity to reflect on our past practices as teachers, coaches, and researchers who have developed the precepts of TGfU. We are reassured by the unanimous view that the learner is all important, that the teacher or coach will no longer be expected to control highly structured sessions based upon correct techniques, and that the teacher or coach will not be expected to throw a ball into the mix and let a game continue unfettered.

It is not surprising, given current customs and practices, that our apparent disregard for technique and skill execution has received some criticism. It is not that we consider skill as unimportant, quite the contrary (see later), but skill depends on the learning situation, a contextualized game form, which is a key component of the TGfU model. From our perspective, practitioners have not given enough thought to game form and researchers have tended to pass it by when writing about learning theory. We welcome the fact that small-side games have become an established feature of games-based activity, but rarely have we seen games in which five players pit their wits against three others in an invasion game, or one plays two in a net-court game. These games challenge all the participants and help prevent situations in which the best players tend to take over in small-side games of three on three or four on four.

We feel that more time needs to be given to game appreciation, which shapes a game by setting out rules and the means by which goals, points, and touchdowns are scored. At the same time, we must make sure that students understand the rules and are playing the game we want them to play. We will need to make modifications to the game and changes to the rules as a game develops, but we must not forget that we may need to change a rule to make the game easier in order for individuals to progress. A situation might occur in which an individual or team exploits a particular tactic, demonstrating good game understanding, but in so doing, spoils the game. The opposition may demand a new rule! Youngsters frequently change rules in the games they play, saying, "That's not fair, you can't do that." Indeed, this is how our traditional games develop, with continual changes to rules to make the game better. With more thought given to game form and game appreciation, there is an excellent chance that a good game will result, learning will take place, and that stated learning objectives will be achieved.

The most disappointing reaction from teachers to the TGfU approach is that it is difficult, requiring the ability to select and modify games to suit the needs of the moment and an in-depth knowledge of the principles of play across the games spectrum. But why should this not be required of professionals responsible for the physical education and sport education of young people? Is it any wonder that physical education as a subject on the school curriculum still lacks credibility for many?

A positive outcome of the TGfU approach has been to draw attention to the importance of developing tactical awareness in games playing. As we all know, games present problems to participants no matter what their age, ability, and experience. Therefore, it seems logical for the teacher or coach to take a problem-solving approach, to ask the right questions, and to help the players search for solutions by drawing from their involvement in the game form. We must recognize that when players are heavily involved in the game, they may not have time to think and, of course, when they are part of a team, they have no time to work out solutions. We should build time to think into our sessions.

One such example, often forced on the teacher or coach by a shortage of space, is when two 4v4 games are going on while another team waits in the wings. Much of our teaching takes place with the students not on court, as we use questions to direct their attention and prompt facets of play that they might try to implement when they are on court. In this manner, they find ways to score a goal, win a point, hit a run, and stop opponents from scoring. To be sure, the answers are found in core principles, whether creating or denying space, working with the construct of time, or responding to the moment when possession is lost, handed over, or regained. We should be mindful, particularly with the young, not to become too sport specific when seeking to developing tactical awareness, and should remember that much can be learned from the application of principles in other sports. Why not select one such principle, say depth, and work in a practical situation to apply this concept to different games (in game form) and to break out games such as soccer-rounders? Importantly, a principles approach makes it possible for teachers and others involved in sports development to achieve a broad-based games education. More specifically, greater tactical awareness makes more than one option available to students and requires them to decide what they will do.

There is little doubt that two outcomes of the approach, decision making and empowerment, made it attractive to the coaching world in the 1990s. As knowledge of the physical elements (conditioning, nutrition, and biomechanical analysis) became more refined, many realized that the development of decision making, based on reading the environment and selecting a response that works for individual students, had been largely neglected. Indeed, observation of tactical teaching and coaching seemed to rely on telling players what to do in given situations, rather than challenging them to find out. This is one reason why, when we ask tactical questions, we will often say, "Don't tell me; show me." We do not want a logical, verbal answer; we want to see a movement response to a situation that must have already been perceived.

We feel that many of the most creative players in a range of sports come from countries where coaching is absent or minimal. Their playful activity, forced on them by circumstances, encourages a broad range of personally developed responses. Making decisions at a high level of performance is virtually reflexive, since responses often occur at speeds that do not allow time to consider. We argue that decision making should be developed throughout a child's games education, and that the key to doing this, once again, is to design games that are challenging. Leave the youngsters alone to play; structure and order can come later.

It has always annoyed us when people have said that we don't teach skill in TGfU or when they have failed to teach skills, used TGfU as an excuse. The model has always addressed the importance of skill. Current thinking about skill acquisition supports the notion that it is best developed in circumstances that most closely resemble the situation in which they will be used. Indeed, what we did in the past was teach technique—a movement in isolation. Becoming skillful requires practice, and we are again forced to recognize the value in presenting carefully designed games. These games challenge players tactically and technically. The skill to be used will be individually assessed. If the game is enjoyable and offers many chances to use the skill, the players will have a lot of turns. We know that observational learning is a powerful form of learning; demonstration by the teacher or coach may be useful in learning a skill. However, structuring sessions to allow students to play with and against their more highly skilled peers helps them develop, in many cases, a more powerful image of themselves. Models similar to observation are most effective. A major advantage of this incidental learning is that the observer does not have to copy a skill, but can do so if needed. That being said, we believe there are times to teach skill more directly, but no single input would be suitable for most teachers and coaches, who deal with large groups of mixed-ability players. This type of teaching cannot be a class activity. If players are involved in small-sided, challenging games, they can be left to play. This means the teacher or coach can extract players with similar skill requirements and can spend some time with them. Of course, in doing so, we are back to our basic premise that a class or group is made up of individual players; we have to find ways of meeting their needs. There is no single right way to teach or coach, but we feel that TGfU works to meet the needs of the individual student and provides the opportunity for all to engage with games.

Readers of the book will be impressed by the breadth, depth, and quality of the essays drawing upon TGfU, which range in topic from video gaming to TGfU's connections to physical literacy, and from teaching games to elementary children to TGfU as a coaching methodology. There is little doubt that TGfU is in great health and good hands, and that all involved can look to the future and to the next international conference in 2012. Having said this, we should come back to earth and not lose sight of the reasons why TGfU came into being in the first place: to motivate young people to be interested and involved in games, to be more engaged in their own learning, to develop their knowledge of games, and to understand the causes and consequences of their games activity.

Endnotes

[1]In the early 1990s, Rod produced a series of progressive games while working with a research assistant, Ben Tan, on sports. These were simply presented on cards designed to lead a parent or beginning coach through a play approach to games. He recognized that this method provided an excellent starting point for inexperienced teachers (as well as a starting point for TGfU). Initially called Playsport, this method was the basis for the development, by the Youth Sports Trust (UK), of the TOP play programs.

[2]In 1992, Rod received a Winston Churchill Travelling Fellowship to look at Mini Games in Australia and New Zealand. His critique of these, although mainly positive, led to his invitation back to Australia to develop TGfU ideas in the coaching domain. The outcome was Games Sense.

Acknowledgments

Never doubt that a small group of thoughtful, committed citizens can change the world; indeed, it's the only thing that ever has.

— Margaret Mead

We would both like to acknowledge the entire international TGfU community for sharing their passion and enthusiasm for moving this approach along its path. We hope that we will continue to learn as a global community. We would also like to thank all the authors for their commitment to their work, for meeting timelines, and for working meticulously and thoughtfully on their chapters along the way.

In particular, we would also like to acknowledge University of British Columbia graduate students, Ileana Costrut and Fiona Hough from the department of Curriculum and Pedagogy, for thoughtfully and carefully editing early chapter drafts and for diligently organizing authors' permission forms, biographies, and photographs.

PART

I

TGfU Movement in an International Context

Introduction

Joy I. Butler, EdD • Linda L. Griffin, PhD

This book is a collection of essays written by teacher educators with a passion for sharing knowledge, research, and insights about the Teaching Games for Understanding (TGfU) approach. The intended audience for this collection is teacher educators and graduate and undergraduate students in physical education and sport pedagogy as well as practicing teachers and coaches interested in helping students and players to become better games players.

All our authors presented at the Fourth International TGfU Conference, which provided an arena for a restatement of the importance of games as a learning process. The conference was held in May 2008 at the University of British Columbia (UBC) in Vancouver, Canada. The next seminar will begin the newly adopted four-year cycle in 2012 in the United Kingdom and will be hosted by Loughborough University in Leicestershire. This event will mark the 30th anniversary of the seminal TGfU paper written by Bunker and Thorpe in 1982.

TGfU has become a significant movement in physical education worldwide. The 2008 TGfU conference was attended by 355 participants (150 teachers, 40 coaches, 40 graduate students, and 125 researchers and teacher educators) who represented 26 countries from 6 continents. Over 90 presentations, including 22 practical sessions, took place at the conference. The 2008 conference was able to achieve a more desirable balance in research, theory, and practice. The planning committee spent a great deal of energy targeting the K-12 schools, coaching organizations, and their networks.

This book represents and reflects on the spirit of the TGfU movement as it was communicated at the 2008 conference. The following reflect growing trends:

1. Strong and evolving international networks generated by regular international seminar conferences (every four years) and one-day symposia and workshops before the AIESEP Congress. These also occur every four years but are spaced evenly between the TGfU seminar conferences, thereby producing international venues every two years.

2. An organizational structure that supports conference planning and promotion in the form of a TGfU task force, extant from 2002 to 2008, which has since evolved into a special interest group of AIESEP.

3. Five books, online proceedings, and three special journal editions (*Physical Education and Sport Pedagogy* and two editions of *Health and Physical Education Journal*) related to conference proceedings.

The TGfU conferences, organization, and subsequent publications have resulted in the following:

- Sharing ideas and expertise between coaches and teachers regionally, nationally, and internationally
- Enabling structures to integrate research, theory, and practice in the same venue as well as exploring commonalities and differences within each major discipline of study—research, theory, and practice
- Communicating philosophical and sociological interpretations of TGfU worldwide

Almost three decades after the Bunker and Thorpe article (1982) outlined a model for the teaching of games in secondary schools, teachers and coaches are embracing the notion that the TGfU philosophical underpinnings align more closely with humanistic, child-centered, and constructivist ideals. Motor development research tells us that there is a sensitive time for learning new skills and concepts quickly and efficiently. Perhaps there is a similar period in which a profession can effectively respond to a new curricular approach. It takes time for the necessary examination of the merits and demerits of a new approach and for a comparison of the new and old assumptions. As teachers begin to understand that the approach offers cross-curricular connections, sound pedagogical logic, and efficient integration with the mission and goals of schools, then the time has come for TGfU legitimacy.

The TGfU movement is experiencing what we hope is the period before its peak. Once the approach becomes a common part of teachers' repertoires, it will have served its purpose: to improve the teaching and learning of games. TGfU has provided many of us with a catalyst for discussing the nature of good teaching, coaching, and learning, allowing us to consider the values and beliefs that underpin such approaches and their place in both physical and general education. In the process of considering a new approach such as TGfU, teachers and coaches have been led to consider their existing frameworks for conceptualizing games and to reflect on how their values and beliefs structure the way they teach and think about students' ability.

If TGfU is to become a movement that will broaden the scope of the physical education and coaching ethos, it must be anchored in sound research through a community of inquiry focused on the exploration of ideas. The curriculum and pedagogy department chair at UBC, Dennis Sumara, gave a rousing speech in support of the conference's goals and the need for education in general to go in this direction. Likening the TGfU movement to that of the whole language movement (WLM) of the 1980s, he cautioned TGfU advocates to avoid the mistakes of the WLM and to anchor TGfU in sound research. We believe that TGfU has built a strong community of practice that has led to the development of an international organization. We hope that this organizational structure can support research collaborations through global networks, connect research with practice, and maintain and promote TGfU international conferences.

The international TGfU task force's evolution into the first special interest group (SIG) of the Association Internationale des Écoles Superieures d'Education Physique (AIESEP) is a vital first step. This SIG and its alliance to AIESEP will help to sustain interest and ensure the maintenance of high-level research into the teaching and learning of sport-related games as they relate to TGfU.

The original TGfU task force was formed after the first TGfU conference. At a crowded town meeting, the conference organizers asked the international delegates where they thought they wanted to go from that point. The response was a resounding endorsement of Butler's proposal that an international committee be established to harness the groundswell of energy evident at the conference. A proposal for the task force was welcomed by AIESEP, and a meeting was held at the 2002 AIESEP Congress. A group of 10 members were elected to this task force, and ultimately the group created spaces for 2 more seats to obtain broader international coverage, encompassing 5 continents and 12 countries. Those members were Minna Blomqvist (Finland), Ross Brooker (Australia), Joy I. Butler (chair, USA), Keh Nuit Chin (Taiwan), Jean-Francis Gréhaigne (France), Linda L. Griffin (USA), Lynn Kidman (New Zealand), Raymond Liu Yuk-kwong (Hong Kong), James Mandigo (Canada), Robert Martin (USA), Elaine Musch (Belgium), and Steven Tan (Singapore).

The mission statement of the TGfU task force was written in 2002 (identified in bold) and the rest was developed by the TGfU SIG in 2009.

The mission of the AIESEP TGfU special interest group is to establish a globally representative group of institutions and individuals committed to the promotion and dissemination of scholarly inquiry around ways of knowing, learning and teaching through games-centered approaches. One of our major goals is to broaden international cooperation and understanding among teachers, coaches, researchers, students and institutions of the world through best practice, critical educational and research collaborations and exchanges. This group will allow us to address global challenges such as language, terminology, practical interpretations, philosophical and theoretical differences, and the dissemination of information through national and international organizations.

Table I.1 summarizes the task force's objectives, action plan, results, and future plans. At the 2006 AIESEP Congress in Finland, it was decided at the TGfU task force meeting that the movement had become large enough to handle a general membership with an executive group to help conduct affairs of the membership. AIESEP agreed to take on its first special interest group, and the policies and election process were developed. The transition of task force to SIG was formalized at the TGfU conference in Vancouver. Currently, the SIG executive committee consists of five members (past chair Joy I. Butler, chair Dinant Roode, chair-elect Tim Hopper, secretary Steve Harvey, treasurer James Mandigo) and began Skype meetings in January 2009. The final column of the table outlines the work that the SIG executive board has started as a strategic planning process.

With an increase in research efforts since the first conference in 2001, this book offers an opportunity for authors to examine the developments of TGfU from a broader theoretical basis than in the first book (i.e., postmodern, complexivist, and postcolonial perspectives) and with a wider research application. As part of striving toward a state where TGfU is no longer needed, the common thread weaving through this publication is a critical examination of the ways in which TGfU embodies big ideas and such different ways of knowing and being in our discipline of physical education and sport pedagogy. We believe that the movement has created a platform for critical discourse about new ideas and responses to challenges concerning pedagogical practice. Postmodern, poststructural, and postcolonial perspectives have allowed us to move away from reductionist positions and afford strong theoretical and empirical foundations from which we can address questions associated with the production of knowledge, the formation of values, and an understanding of embodiment.

Guiding Questions for Authors

The following questions served as a guide to all the authors:

- How does the TGfU approach influence pedagogical and curricular practices?
- What is the epistemological and ontological basis for TGfU?
- In what directions should TGfU research go?
- When will TGfU have served its purpose?

Table I.1   TGfU Task Force's Objectives, Action Plan, Results, and Future Plans

	Objectives	Action plan	Results	Special interest group's future plans
1	Disseminate scholarly information	• Establish a Web site • Establish registry of interest members	• www.tgfu.org • Development of SIG membership established in 2008: AIESEP	• Updates on Web site • Discussion groups • Post resources
2	Coordinate collaborative research	Organize regular conferences	• One-day pre-AIESEP Congress TGfU workshop (every 4 years) starting in Finland in 2006 • Seminar conferences every 4 years starting in 2008	• Connect with 2010 AIESEP Congress organizers (La Coruna) • Support UK 2012 conference team
3	Publish proceedings	Paper form and online	Set of 3 books published and 1 online proceeding	• Two books due in 2009 based on 2008 conference • Establish for 2012
4	Promote international dialogue	• Organize regular conference and 1-day seminars • Discussion time built into all presentations	Seminar conferences: 2001 United States, 2003 Australia, 2005 Hong Kong, 2006 Finland, 2008 Canada	• Seminar conferences: 2010 Spain, 2012 United Kingdom • Blogs to be established on Web site
5	Establish teaching programs	Develop links to national organizations	Initial discussions in Canada and United States	Funding through grants: connect liaison members to the national professional bodies
6	Review and reflect on philosophy, theory, and research	Create town meetings	Numerous articles published	Mission statement, goals, and action plan being revised

- How does TGfU serve as a catalyst or forum for the major issues facing physical education?
- What are the facilitators and inhibitors of a TGfU approach?

Structure of This Book

TGfU started with that altruistic desire of most committed teachers: improved student learning. David Bunker and Rod Thorpe combined this central passion with a critique of the UK school system and its tendency to turn off students and produce ineffective games players. Len Almond's expertise in curriculum development and alignment with social psychology enabled him to create a robust curriculum framework. All three were classic action researchers who engaged teachers and themselves in the very act of their own change. What started as a good idea in the vicinity of Loughborough University, where they first explored the approach, has reached much wider orbits around the world, changing the way that practitioners think about the place of games within their PE programs and the way that games are learned and taught. In other words, what started with physical educators concerned about the inadequate experiences of their learners has turned into a global force to be reckoned with.

The preface **(Rod Thorpe and David Bunker)** and foreword **(Len Almond)** reflect on whether the TGfU model, as they envisioned it in its inception in the 1980s, has retained its tenets after teachers and coaches have applied the model to their practice. They share some of the issues that have arisen over the years. In essence, they question whether sufficient thought has been given to contextualizing learning in a game form and what makes a good game. They guard teachers against thinking that the TGfU model is an excuse for the teacher or coach to throw a ball into the mix and let them play, or that it is a reason to be in control of highly structured sessions. The ongoing debate about development of techniques and skills is also discussed in the context of the literature available on skill acquisition.

Part I: TGfU Movement in an International Context

Joy I. Butler and Linda L. Griffin map out the journey the TGfU movement has taken since the ideas were first conceived and mapped out by Bunker, Thorpe, and Almond in the 1980s. In this introduction, Butler and Griffin give the context for TGfU moving globally.

Raymond Liu Yuk-kwong, retired from the Hong Kong Institute of Education and the director of the third conference held in 2005, examines the effects and influence of their work in Asian countries. In chapter 1, Liu Yuk-kwong analyzes how TGfU has been received in seven Asian countries (Hong Kong, mainland China, Singapore, Taiwan, Japan, Macau, Korea).

Liu Yuk-kwong analyzes the current situation in each country and makes some recommendations that will improve the research and application of TGfU in future developments. While there is ample literature published in Western countries such as the United States, Australia, and New Zealand, much less has been published in Asia, making this a key component of our consideration of the global impact of the approach.

Part II: Research: Reexamination

Chapters 2 and 3 describe research and call for a reexamination of TGfU research through the lenses of five authors. In chapter 2, **Judith Rink** reviews the research on TGfU from learning perspectives. She first defines the processes of learning inherent in the approach and the assumptions about the role of the learner inherent in these processes; second, she examines the implications of dynamical systems theories of learning as a framework for support of the approach. Third, she examines the contradicting theories on the development of expertise.

In chapter 3, **Connie S. Collier** and coauthors **Judy Oslin, Daniel Rodriguez,** and **David Gutierrez** describe their research into models of sport and games education and their experiences in teaching teachers to use models of sport and games education. Their study examines the teaching and learning in sport and game units involving four teachers with varying levels of experience, grade levels, and teaching contexts. The notion of pedagogical content knowledge (PCK) serves as a central tenet in examining the four teachers' version of sport and games models. The authors' findings suggest that the teachers value certain aspects of the public theories defined in the textbooks and formal teacher preparation curricula and develop unique interpretations of the models representative of their students' needs, their personal beliefs about sport and games, and their teaching contexts.

Part III: Theory: Understanding, Learning, and Complexity Thinking

Chapters 4 through 8 consider the big ideas embedded in TGfU. These include the various ways of knowing and being implicit in our physical education and sport pedagogy and their relationship to the conceptual framework of TGfU. Over the past three decades, the TGfU movement has created a platform for critical discourse about these new ideas and responses to challenges concerning pedagogical practice. Postmodern, poststructural, and postcolonial perspectives have allowed us to move away from reductionist positions and afford strong theoretical and empirical foundations from which we can address questions associated with the production of knowledge, the formation of values, and an understanding of embodiment.

> A curriculum theory is based on assumptions about society, human beings, and education. . . . The basic assumptions of a curriculum theory are a form of ideology and understanding curriculum as praxis requires examination of these assumptions. (Jewett, Bain, & Ennis, 1995, p. 14)

In chapter 4, **James Mandigo** and **John Corlett** present an analysis of the purpose of TGfU: how it connects to the recent UN focus on the new decade in literacy and how it is defined by the physical. Understanding how to play games with poise, confidence, and enthusiasm is part of being physically literate. Mandigo and Corlett discuss how, through a TGfU approach, students are more likely to attain knowledge and understanding of common rules and strategies, apply technical and tactical skills across a variety of games, and experience positive motivational states for themselves and others within and outside of games. This, they argue, facilitates the attainment of physical literacy and ultimately the healthy development of youth.

In chapter 5, **Rebecca J. Lloyd** and **Stephen Smith** bring a vitality approach to games and sport as they encourage learners to think in and through the motions of the activity. Their theory is that such an approach to games and sport brings the kinesthetic experience of movement to the fore. Understanding how to play and knowing what tactics to use become derivative of knowing kinesthetically why one is playing and what movements are called for in making the motions of play as poised, balanced, connecting, flowing, and fitting as possible. When games and sports are taught this way, the authors believe, students and teachers alike better understand the intrinsic, expressive, connective, life-enhancing qualities of movement.

In chapter 6, **Brent Davis** and **Dennis Sumara** begin a trilogy of chapters that describe more recent theoretical frameworks for TGfU. Their chapter is framed by an assumption that teachers are always and already working to affect individual understanding and collective action simultaneously. They focus on one of complexity theory's main elements: enabling constraints, which support the sorts of tasks and structures that enable both individual and collective learning. Although *enabling constraints* might sound like an oxymoron, the phrase flags a necessary tension rather than a contradiction. Complex unities are simultaneously rule bound (constraining) and capable of flexible, unanticipated possibilities (enabling). The pedagogical intent of enabling constraints is to investigate established knowledge while engaging in a process of establishing knowledge.

The concept of enabling constraints segues nicely into the focus of chapter 7, written by **Tim Hopper** and **Kath Sanford,** which considers complexity thinking as a way of helping us to consider more physically, emotionally, and socially meaningful perspectives to inform learning in PE. The challenge in teaching games is to enable learners to access game play so that they are invested in playing again and again. The authors draw on two examples of learning in game play. The first involves an alternative type of game play using video games. This provides a perspective on the learning that happens through engaging in a virtual world that adapts to the players and teaches the players skills that lead to more advanced game play. The second example is based on a lesson using the TGfU approach and illustrates the teacher's role in guiding learners to read game play and to adapt the game as they refine their capacity to engage in the game structure. Both examples inform us about the learning processes, which give ownership to the players by allowing them to reinvent game play and adapt the game to their own abilities and those of their coplayers.

Chapter 8, written by **Brian Storey** and **Joy I. Butler,** uses complexity thinking as a theory to frame the learning processes involved in TGfU. The authors explore language for describing games learning as a complex adaptive process that reconceptualizes the purpose of teaching games. Simply put, the game does not produce only winners and losers; rather, we see players and learners. The authors draw from an ecological perspective to understand the learner, the learning environment, and the teacher's role. The study of complex adaptive systems in education allows the authors to view players as biological systems, nested in a set of interactions that constitute a game localized in time and place and within the living history of the participants. Each game is also nested in our complex sociopolity that projects values into the games curriculum and pedagogy while being reflected back by the games as they are played out. To capture the importance of game thinking to the broader sociopolitical background, the authors present a philosophical understanding of the game as a metaphor and its implications for games teaching.

Part IV: Practice: Assessment, Coaching, Elementary and Secondary Teaching

Chapters 9 through 14 explore various forms of practice in TGfU with foci on assessment, coaching, and teaching at the elementary and secondary levels. In chapter 9, **Jean-François Richard** examines the critical role that assessment plays in the teaching–learning process in TGfU. He examines the efficacy of authentic assessment instruments such as the Game Performance Assessment Instrument (GPAI) and the Team Sport Assessment Procedure (TSAP) as ways to help learners analyze the construction of game performance and build authentic, meaningful, and durable learning.

TGfU is an approach used widely at all levels in athletic practice. In chapter 10, **Lynn Kidman** and **Bennett J. Lombardo** offer the first of two chapters on the application of TGfU to coaching. Like many of the authors in this book, Kidman and Lombardo reexamine the purpose of playing games and the learning–teaching–coaching dynamic. They draw out the benefits of using a humanistic coaching approach such as TGfU, which positively influences self-esteem, self-direction, and independence and creates opportunities to express moments of joy and supreme well-being.

Chapter 11, by **Adriano De Souza** and **Steve Mitchell,** provides a bridge between the coaching focus and the global perspective that TGfU had taken on since the first international conference in 2001. They suggest that TGfU is more prevalent in public school physical education programs than in coaching programs. The authors look more closely at the use of TGfU as a coaching methodology in the United States, Brazil, the United Kingdom, Canada, and Australia. They investigate the reasons for the adoption or nonadoption of TGfU in coaching contexts, and then examine the impact of TGfU on coaching practices and player performance.

Inez Rovegno describes in chapter 12 how the original TGfU framework designed for secondary schools can be considered and used for elementary children. Basing her ideas on current research, Rovegno offers suggestions about what elements of the framework can be similar and what might need to be different when considering progression, meaning, and relevance at each elementary level. Inez uses Laban's analysis of movement and its movement concepts as a means of identifying ways to vary skills presented so that they become open, gamelike, and tactically useful. Inez suggests that game appreciation is a priority for elementary children as they approach tactics and skills. This is a useful chapter for teachers who are looking for ways to teach game structures, rules, and boundaries so that children understand them and find them relevant. It's also a framework for breaking down and progressively teaching the thinking skills, social skills, and affective aspects of games that are necessary content at the elementary level.

Daniel Memmert explores in chapter 13 the possibility of elementary children being able to be creative in game play, despite the enormous amount of information they need to absorb in order to simply participate. Memmert leads us through areas of focus that a coach or teacher should attend to when teaching players to identify tactical solutions and be tactically creative. Memmert outlines his theoretical framework for the development of tactical creativity in team sport and describes its implementation with elementary children. The framework distinguishes between a macro (content) level and a micro (method) level. The former points toward the natural (noninfluenceable) or organizable environmental conditions (macro rules) and the latter toward the methodical accents in the respective training units (micro rules) that can be steered by the teacher. Through the three micro rules, Memmert suggests that players can learn to perceive, use, and learn better alternative solutions for unexpected situations in game play.

In chapter 14, **Kath Howarth**, **Jennifer L. Fisette**, **Michele Sweeney**, and **Linda L. Griffin** integrate Laban's movement concepts as a way to unpack (deconstruct) tactical problems in invasion games. When one examines old material through different language, new ideas start to emerge. The authors take an in-depth look at invasion games through larger concepts such as time, space, flow, tempo, and risk. For example, one of the tactical problems in invasion games is to maintain possession of the ball. Though we understand the specific on-the-ball skills and off-the-ball movements related to each specific game, there are still questions we have to consider:

- How do we unpack this tactical problem for the learner?
- How do we shape games appropriately for each level of learner?
- What sequence of concepts will be most efficient in helping learners increase their tactical awareness?

Conclusion

The authors of this book have shared their passion for games teaching and learning and, most important, their commitment to and concern for improving the learning experiences of youth in sport-related games as a way to facilitate the development of decent human beings. Throughout this book, you will read about new concepts to describe the learning–teaching–coaching process that allows the TGfU community and beyond to be open to new ideas and set aside old baggage. A few of the chapters highlight Laban and various movement education concepts, which bring us back full circle to the roots of constructivist learning. Authors make connections between theory and practice, providing a praxis orientation theme to this book.

TGfU is a global movement, and this is a point of pride. As editors of this book, we hope that the community can keep learning and growing through our multiple ways of knowing and collaborating. We also want teachers and coaches worldwide to know that they are welcome to join the movement at any time.

References

Jewett, A.E., Bain, L.L., & Ennis, C.D. (1995). *The curriculum process in physical education.* Dubuque, IA: Brown.

Asian-Pacific Perspectives on Analyzing TGfU

Raymond Liu Yuk-kwong, PhD

The mission of the International Association for Physical Education in Higher Education (Association Internationale des Écoles Superieures d'Education Physique; AIESEP) TGfU Special Interest Group is to establish a globally representative group of institutions and individuals committed to the promotion and dissemination of scholarly inquiry. One of our major goals is to broaden international cooperation and understanding among teachers, coaches, researchers, students, and institutions of the world through best practice, critical educational, and research collaborations and exchanges. This group will allow us to address global challenges, such as language, terminology, practical interpretations, philosophical and theoretical differences, and the dissemination of information through national and international organizations.

— *Joy I. Butler, Chair of the TGfU task force, 2002-2008*

This movement has spread to Europe, the United States, Australia, New Zealand, and Asia (Hong Kong, mainland China, Singapore, Taiwan, Macau, Japan, and Korea). An obvious phenomenon can be observed: ample literature has been published by scholars from western countries, including the United States, Australia, and New Zealand. The investigations are mostly related to students' learning performance, enjoyment, decision making, and tactical awareness. It seems that such influence is not as great in Asia as in the countries previously mentioned. The intention of this chapter is to analyze the current situation of Teaching Games for Understanding (TGfU) in the Asian-Pacific region and to make recommendations for future development.

Beginnings of Teaching Games for Understanding

TGfU was first developed in 1982 by David Bunker and Rod Thorpe at Loughborough University in the United Kingdom. Discontent with skill-based approaches originally started in the early 1960s when Alan Wade, a physical-education lecturer at Loughborough College of Education, dissatisfied with how games were being taught, began to look at the central features of games. He tried to analyze them and developed a framework of common elements for a games curriculum. Later, he made contact with Charles Hughes at the football association, where he developed and published the principles of play notion. This notion had a direct influence not only on Wade but also on his colleagues, Eric Worthington and Stan Wigmore. They suggested that games skills should be taught through the principles of play. Some of these ideas were formalized in *The F.A. Guide to Training and Coaching* (Wade, 1967), through which the development of small-side games became the vehicle for the transmission of game skills.

While Thorpe and Bunker were students at Loughborough, being influenced by Wade, Worthington, and Wigmore, they began to consider the benefits of small-sided games and games skills through principles of play. After graduation, Thorpe and Bunker became more concerned as they observed a skill-based approach to games teaching in most schools. They indicated that their children seemed to be getting nowhere, showing little progress and interest in the games lessons (Thorpe and Bunker, 1986).

In 1968, Rod Thorpe, who worked as a physical-education lecturer at Loughborough College, was invited by Worthington to adapt tennis equipment for less-able children. Thorpe began to develop this work and moved away from skill-based lessons toward an approach that included the concepts of space, attack, and defense. Thorpe was also influenced by educational gymnastics, which was very popular in the 1960s and 1970s. He recognized that the rationale for this approach, teaching gymnastics by posing problems for children to solve in their own way and at their own level, fit well with the ideas being presented by cognitive psychologists and educationalists. However, its weakness was that teachers found it difficult to set appropriate and challenging problems, which resulted in lessons that were poorly presented. Thorpe felt that games were a more appropriate vehicle for these ideas. In 1972, Bunker, a physical-education lecturer at Loughborough, also became disenchanted with the skill-based approach to games teaching and introduced the principles of play as core elements in his games lectures.

After teaching at Loughborough College for several years, both Bunker and Thorpe (1983) observed that the skill- and drill-based method of teaching, which tended to concentrate on specific motor responses, failed to account for the contextual nature of games. They believed that unlike other sports activities in the physical-education curriculum, the teaching of games should present questions, such as "What to do?" and "When to do it?" and not just "How is it done?" They believed that if the emphasis was shifted to tactical considerations in a game, children would find games interesting and challenging as they learned to make correct decisions based on tactical awareness. Children would begin to be aware of the need for particular techniques if those skills were required in the game situation.

In 1976, Thorpe's teaching of badminton impressed Len Almond with the way that teachers were asked to think about games. He was able to integrate TGfU with his interest in evaluating teaching. At the same time, Thorpe began to consider implementing the principles of play into games teaching and introduced the ideas to students in New Zealand. The results from his work were positive and encouraging. He recognized that this approach would have an effect on games teaching in schools. At the same time, Williamson (1982), a physical-education advisor for Suffolk, completed some work on questioning the common practice of teaching games, even questioning the games that were being taught. After exchanging and sharing ideas, Almond, Thorpe, Bunker, and Williamson thought that the time was right to ask instructors to rethink their teaching of games. They began to disseminate these ideas in summer schools and in courses with teachers, working with local-education authorities throughout England *(Coventry Teachers,* 1986).

Many teachers responded in a positive manner, while others were critical, stating that TGfU was not a new concept. There were two major critiques. The first was that if technique was not emphasized, then children would not be able to play the game. Thorpe and Bunker countered that techniques were taught; however, they were not the central aim of the lesson and were solely related to the learners' need to develop as games players. Thorpe and Bunker believed that if the game was breaking down because of technical problems, the teacher needed to change the game.

The second critique was that, like the skill-based approach, TGfU also adopts mini and small-sided games. Thorpe and Bunker (1983) argued that in the skill-based approach, small-sided games helped develop techniques and skills. In TGfU, however, lessons focused on modified small-sided games as principles of play, representing them in each game form.

*S*ince the introduction of TGfU at the PreOlympic Conference in Eugene, Oregon, United States in 1984 (Thorpe, Bunker, & Almond, 1984), this innovation has attracted great attention and has opened up a number of discussions in the United States and Europe.

Since the introduction of TGfU at the PreOlympic Conference in Eugene, Oregon, United States in 1984 (Thorpe et al., 1984), this innovation has attracted great attention and has opened up a number of discussions in the United States and Europe. Subsequently, many articles and workshops have been published and conducted across the world.

In order to arrive at the objective of this chapter, I have selected seven Asian countries and regions which are familiar with TGfU, including Hong Kong, mainland China, Singapore, Taiwan, Macau, Japan, and Korea. I will review and analyze the current TGfU situation for each of them. Finally, I will make an overall recommendation for future development.

Hong Kong

Hong Kong is a bilingual region (Chinese and English), with the majority of people using Chinese for communication. Before 1997, the sovereignty of Hong Kong belonged to the British. Physical-education (PE) teaching in Hong Kong can be termed as sports-oriented and technique-based. Since the 1960s, PE teaching in Hong Kong has been greatly influenced by the British. Game teaching relied heavily on techniques, and little time was spent learning how to play the game. This is evident in the PE syllabus (PE Section, 1964; Curriculum Development Committee, 1974, 1988, 1995), which suggests a series of techniques to be taught in games lessons. For instance, in badminton, the suggested skills and techniques include the long service, the overhead clear, and the forehand drive. In a unit of eight badminton lessons, PE teachers allocate about six lessons for teaching the preceding techniques and two lessons for rules and competitions. The games lesson is highly structured, with an emphasis on teaching techniques.

Liu (1994) conducted a survey to investigate which approaches PE teachers use during games lessons in school, what they think of TGfU, and if they are willing to accept new teaching approaches. A survey of six questions was randomly distributed to 155 PE teachers in 75 secondary schools. Findings indicated that 144 PE teachers (92.9 percent) used the technique-based approach in games teaching and 47 PE teachers (30.3 percent) found using the technique-based approach difficult; however, 87.1

percent of the PE teachers showed a strong willingness to implement a new teaching approach.

TGfU first arrived in Hong Kong in 1994. An article was published in the *Primary-School Education Journal,* inviting PE teachers to rethink their games teaching (Liu, 1994). In the following years, the government and teacher-training institute organized workshops on TGfU, which resulted in its incorporation into the syllabus for preservice PE teachers at Hong Kong's teacher-training institute. After receiving requests from PE teachers, Thorpe was invited by the Hong Kong Institute of Education to conduct two different workshops for approximately 300 PE teachers in 1996 and 1997. In the workshops, Thorpe demonstrated how to put the TGfU concept into real games lessons. The teachers' feedback was very encouraging and positive. At the same time, they also requested some Chinese references about TGfU.

> *TGfU first arrived in Hong Kong in 1994. In the following years, the government and teacher-training institute organized workshops on TGfU, which resulted in its incorporation into the syllabus for preservice PE teachers at Hong Kong's teacher-training institute.*

In order to draw the attention of more PE teachers, several TGfU articles on teachers' reactions, students' enjoyment, and assessment were subsequently published in a local PE Journal (Liu, 1996; Liu & Thorpe, 1997). Additionally, TGfU presentations were made at an international level, including the 1997 AIESEP conference in Singapore.

In 2000, to support the requests that PE teachers raised after Thorpe's workshops, a Chinese research project for writing different lesson plans for ball games was funded. A core group of four PE lecturers and six experienced PE teachers was formed to prepare the lesson plans. Finally, a Chinese TGfU book titled *Games Teaching – Teaching Games for Understanding* was published in 2002 (Liu, 2002). This was the first TGfU publication for the Chinese community.

To keep up with current TGfU information, it is necessary to build a link with international scholars. After attending the first international TGfU conference, Hong Kong became a member of the TGfU task force, showing great interest at the annual general meeting in hosting the third international TGfU conference in 2005.

In 2004, a survey was conducted to investigate the effectiveness of TGfU in Hong Kong after 10 years of promotion (Liu & Cheung, 2005). The results indicated that 62 percent of PE teachers understood what TGfU is, and 29 percent had adopted TGfU for their ball-games lessons. Some didn't adopt it due to insufficient knowledge (33 percent), little experience (39 percent), and insufficient facilities (13 percent). Additionally,

89 percent of PE teachers were willing to accept and apply TGfU in their teaching in the future.

In 2005, the third international TGfU conference was organized by the Hong Kong Institute of Education. A proceeding titled *Teaching Games for Understanding in the Asia-Pacific Region* was published in 2006, which consisted of 12 English articles and two Chinese articles. Hong Kong has contributed three English papers related to preservice-teacher training, soccer, and the teaching of Tae Kwon Do (Li & Cruz, 2005; Kam, Li, & Cruz, 2005; Liu & Cheung, 2005).

In 2006, owing to the usefulness of the Chinese TGfU book, I was approached and invited by the Beijing Normal University in mainland China to reprint it for dissemination (Liu & Yen, 2006). In the next two years, I was invited by the PE section of the Hong Kong Education Bureau to conduct TGfU workshops and a seminar related to education reform in the summer-school program. A proceeding was published for dissemination to each school by the end of 2008. Since 1997, I have also been invited to conduct TGfU workshops and presentations in mainland China, Taiwan, and Macau.

Since 1994, I have disseminated the TGfU approach and have conducted research with PE teachers in Hong Kong. In 2005, a survey was conducted by Liu and Cheung to investigate the effectiveness of dissemination in the past 10 years with positive results.

At present, TGfU is not only taught in the Hong Kong Institute of Education. It has also been used in the Chinese University of Hong Kong to train PE teachers. This might mean that more preservice PE teachers in Hong Kong will have the opportunity to learn about TGfU. TGfU has also become a recurring thesis topic for students in the postgraduate PE program.

Mainland China

From the 1950s onward, the PE culture in mainland China was mostly inherited from Russia. The teaching focused on drilling techniques and required children's absolute obedience during lessons. Comparatively, mainland China follows these concepts more closely than Hong Kong does. That kind of practice remained unchanged until the year 2000 when education reform (Mao, 2003) was enforced, which had a strong effect on the PE curriculum and pedagogy.

In 1997, Hong Kong returned to mainland China; this was also the year that TGfU was introduced there. Thorpe was invited by the Education Commission of China and Suzhou University in mainland China to conduct a TGfU workshop for approximately 40 PE lecturers who were teaching ball games in different provinces. Before the workshop, an article inviting PE instructors to rethink their teaching was published in the *China*

Physical Education Journal (Liu & Yang, 1997). The next year, the Beijing Normal University in mainland China again invited Thorpe to conduct a second TGfU workshop.

In general, the feedback from the surveys conducted after these two workshops was positive and encouraging. More than 70 percent of participants showed support for this new approach and planned to introduce it in their lectures. About 20 percent of participants had doubts on this approach because of the lack of technique being taught. In addition, many questions were raised during the discussion sessions. Except for a few TGfU articles related to the teaching of athletics, ball games, and martial arts (published in the *China Journal of PE* in 1998 and 2000), no further development in publications was observed after these two workshops. This situation might be due to the fact that the PE lecturers attending the workshops did not fully understand the concept of TGfU.

In 2000, China implemented education reform, which had a great effect on PE teaching. New teaching approaches were advocated, such as the discovery approach, the creative approach, and the TGfU approach (Mao, 2003). To facilitate PE teachers' understanding of TGfU, the Beijing Normal University reprinted the Chinese TGfU book titled *Games Teaching – Teaching Games for Understanding* (Liu, 2002). It was also used as a reference book for PE students in universities in mainland China. Since then, very few papers have been published on TGfU, either in local PE journals or in international journals from mainland China. This is mostly due to the language barrier. Scholars faced great difficulties in writing papers in English for submission to the international journals.

Although TGfU was launched in mainland China in 1997, no concrete evidence of any progress exists. The majority of PE teachers continue to adopt the didactic, or drilling, approach to teaching games. One crucial problem is that PE teachers in mainland China have difficulty accessing the updated TGfU information, which is all written in English. They lack the support and network to get advice from experts.

The concept of TGfU may have been misinterpreted or slightly modified to suit the culture of mainland China. Mao (2003) of the Beijing Normal University is a key figure in PE curriculum and teaching. He writes a few paragraphs in his book

The concept of TGfU may have been misinterpreted or slightly modified to suit the culture of mainland China. Mao (2003) of the Beijing Normal University is a key figure in PE curriculum and teaching. He writes a few paragraphs in his book (2003), explaining his view on TGfU and advocating for students to aim for understanding in order to learn activities.

(2003), explaining his view on TGfU and advocating for students to aim for *understanding* in order to learn activities.

He outlines that a helpful relationship exists between *understanding* and *not understanding* during the learning process for different activities, particularly while learning difficult techniques. He separates sport activities, such as swimming and gymnastics, from skill activities, such as running, jumping, and throwing. Since swimming and gymnastics involve difficult techniques, he perceives that it is more effective for students to learn by understanding these two activities before breaking down their skills. On the other hand, running, jumping, and throwing can be learned without understanding them fully because the techniques for these three activities are simple. Therefore, students do not need to break down the skills during learning. We are delighted that a big move has been made from the didactic approach, but we notice that a great emphasis on learning techniques still exists.

In the past two years, I was invited by the PE section of the Henan province of mainland China to conduct three TGfU workshops for more than 1500 PE teachers, who would in turn disseminate the information to colleagues in their schools. Although no formal survey was conducted by the organizing committee, I observed that participants actively raised questions at the end of the workshops in discussions related to the implementation of TGfU in lessons. The feedback was encouraging and the workshops were received very well.

In March of 2010, I conducted a TGfU presentation for postgraduate PE students at South China Normal University. Similar presentations and workshops are expected to be organized in other provinces; eventually, TGfU will be disseminated across mainland China in the future.

Singapore

Singapore is an English-speaking country. In the 1990s, Australian PE professionals who taught in the Singapore teacher-training institute were the first to introduce TGfU, which is now termed *concept-based games*. A core team was subsequently formed to promote TGfU to PE teachers.

With full support from the government, Singapore has been very successful in disseminating TGfU. In the teacher-training institute, TGfU was included in the preservice curriculum for PE teachers. All PE student teachers had to pass the examination on adopting TGfU for teaching games before they could graduate. Eventually, TGfU became a mandatory practice for PE teachers.

In reference to the Ministry of Education of Singapore in 2006, PE curriculum that uses TGfU is categorized into three levels. At the primary level, basic games concepts are introduced through modified games using fundamental skills. At the secondary level, the games skills and concepts are extended through a wide range of sports activities and games. The intention is to provide opportunities for students to enhance their games skills and develop their tactical awareness. At the preuniversity level, the games skills and concepts are refined and acquired through a broader range of activities and games to nurture students' appreciation of games and to improve their game performance.

With full support from the government, Singapore has been very successful in disseminating TGfU. In the teacher-training institute, TGfU was included in the preservice curriculum for PE teachers. All PE student teachers had to pass the examination on adopting TGfU for teaching games before they could graduate. Eventually, TGfU became a mandatory practice for PE teachers.

After a few years of implementation, Rossi, Fry, McNeill, and Tan (2007) conducted a survey and indicated that TGfU was useful to PE teachers. However, the data also reflected that technique-based teaching was still their favorite approach. The PE graduates showed strong support for the adoption of TGfU in their teaching, showing that their students were highly motivated and enjoyed the lessons (Rossi et al., 2007).

In terms of TGfU publications in international journals, Singapore is very active in its contributions. Publications are mostly related to effective teaching, implementing TGfU, and enhancing students' enjoyment during their PE classes (McNeill, Fry, Wright, W. Tan, S. Tan, & Schempp, 2004; Wright, McNeill, Fry, & Wang, 2005; Wright, McNeill, Fry, S. Tan, C. Tan, & Schempp, 2006).

At the teacher-training institute level, academics have built a closer network with the TGfU task force and international scholars. They also have a strong academic link with Australia and New Zealand for conducting joint research projects. Members of the TGfU core team were frequently invited by other Asian countries, such as Taiwan, to conduct workshops or to make presentations (Tan, 2007).

Taiwan

Taiwan is a Chinese-speaking island to the southeast of mainland China that is similarly influenced in the context of PE teaching. Like China, Taiwan emphasizes learning techniques and health-related fitness

In 2000, TGfU was introduced to Taiwan under a different Chinese name than the one used in Hong Kong. The introduction has drawn the attention of PE teachers and has brought a new image of PE teaching.

training (Keh, 2008). In 2000, TGfU was introduced to Taiwan under a different Chinese name than the one used in Hong Kong. The introduction has drawn the attention of PE teachers and has brought a new image of PE teaching. A core group of university lecturers and postgraduate PE students was created by Keh to formulate strategies for disseminating TGfU in Taiwan.

In 2001, education reform was implemented and an innovative teaching approach was required. TGfU was introduced to PE teachers during in-service training courses. It was also taught to master's-degree students during the summer and on weekends to help them design their own games.

Subsequently, a series of TGfU seminars and workshops was organized in 2003, 2004, 2005, 2006, and 2007 (Keh, 2008). Experts from Australia, France, Hong Kong, the United States, and England were invited to share their experiences of implementing TGfU in their countries.

In order to provide evidence and share about implementing TGfU in Taiwan, a group of PE lecturers and PE teachers contributed 19 local publications within 7 years. Most of them emphasized that TGfU has a solid theoretical base; it is in line with the current development of education and meets the needs of education reform (Keh, 2008). Recently, Keh (2008) published a Chinese TGfU book, which covered the theory and practice of teaching different sports activities. Importantly, a three-year TGfU research project was funded by the Taiwan Scientific Committee to study different aspects of TGfU development in Taiwan.

Internally, Taiwan is active in disseminating TGfU to PE teachers in schools and teacher-training institutes. The core group, including Keh, PE lecturers, and postgraduate students, has worked with extra effort toward this goal. To speed up the dissemination, two existing Web sites, for the National Taiwan University PE Research and Development Centre (www.perdc.ntnu.edu.tw) and the Taiwan PE Society (www. Rocnspe.org.tw), were used to upload TGfU information for teachers' reference.

Externally, Taiwan has built a close connection with the TGfU task force as well as with TGfU international experts. Updated TGfU information can be accessed and shared with other countries. At the same time, Taiwan has been very active in organizing delegations to present their TGfU findings and to participate in international conferences, such as those for TGfU, AIESEP conferences, and the International Society for Comparative Physical Education and Sport held in Macau in 2008.

Macau

Macau, a peninsula to the south of mainland China, is a Chinese-majority region where people speak Chinese and Portuguese. In 1999, Portugal handed over Macau's sovereignty to mainland China. Macau has two training institutes for PE teachers: the Macau Polytechnic Institute and Macau University. Owing to their historical background and geographic location, PE teaching in Macau is greatly influenced by mainland China. Their teaching focuses on drilling techniques. The majority of PE teacher training comes from local institutions, mainland China, and Taiwan.

In 2002, I was invited by the Macau Polytechnic Institute to conduct a TGfU workshop for PE teachers in Macau. At the end of the workshop, many questions were raised about the concept and implementation of TGfU, and constructive discussions were exchanged in the sharing session. It was noted that their teaching leaned heavily on techniques and the PE teachers had no idea about TGfU. The following year, I was invited by the Macau University to present a paper to introduce TGfU to undergraduate students and in-service PE teachers.

In 2003, a related TGfU paper was presented at the second international TGfU conference at Melbourne University in Australia. This might be considered the starting point of the dissemination of TGfU in Macau (Ho, 2003). It seemed that no formal and solid plan existed to develop TGfU at the initial stage.

However, Macau has subsequently adopted a proactive attitude for disseminating TGfU. In the following years, two teacher-training institutes invited experts from Hong Kong, Taiwan, and Australia to conduct seminars and TGfU workshops. At the same time, Macau was very active, presenting TGfU papers in international conferences. In 2008, Macau hosted the International Society for Comparative Physical Education and Sport, in which a related keynote address and oral presentation were given on TGfU. Experts from Australia and Taiwan were invited to take part. These examples have demonstrated Macau's positive attitude in bringing TGfU to PE teachers.

Recently, I was invited by the Education and Youth Department of Macau to conduct an inspection of PE schools. In eight secondary and primary schools, I observed little change in games teaching, as the PE teachers still focused on drilling

Macau has subsequently adopted a proactive attitude for disseminating TGfU. Two teacher-training institutes invited experts from Hong Kong, Taiwan, and Australia to conduct seminars and TGfU workshops, and Macau was very active in presenting TGfU papers at international conferences.

techniques. Therefore, Macau needs more effort to promote TGfU and to help PE teachers understand how TGfU works in lessons.

Japan

Japan has its own language. It is quite difficult to access its development of TGfU because most publications are written in Japanese. Some of them might be related to TGfU in Japan.

In 2005, a delegation from the College of Education at Ibaraki University in Japan attended the third international TGfU conference in Hong Kong. Their presentations were related to the relationship between the knowledge of tactical performance in different ball games, and the validation of video-based tests for understanding in different ball games. Their attendance and presentations suggest that TGfU has already landed in Japan, and that it probably started off in teacher-education programs.

It is hoped that more TGfU research findings and publications can be presented and read in the international conference and journals in the future.

Korea

Like Japan, Korea has its own language. It is quite difficult to access the current state of development of TGfU there since many publications and scholarly articles are written in Korean. Some of them might be related to TGfU.

TGfU was launched in Korea in the late 1990s, and came to Korea from the United States.

In 2008, it was encouraging to note that two Korean scholars attended the fourth international TGfU conference in Vancouver, Canada. During discussions and exchanges, I briefly learned that TGfU was launched in Korea in the late 1990s. The route of dissemination was from the United States. Some TGfU research findings were published in local Korean journals. Additionally, Korea is the only country to have translated the TGfU book published by Human Kinetics in 2005.

Recommendations for Future Development

Based on the preceding information, I would like to make some recommendations for the future development of TGfU in these Asian countries and regions:

1. Invite PE teachers and colleagues from other institutions to become members of the core group and to take part in research projects and publications. Their involvement will definitely facilitate a deeper understanding of the TGfU concept. This engagement might help PE teachers become more receptive to this innovative approach (Hong Kong, Singapore, and Taiwan).

2. Set up a core group of academics from different universities to develop strategic plans for the dissemination of TGfU and to initiate academic projects with full sponsorship and support to encourage PE lecturers and teachers to conduct project work for future publications in local and international journals. TGfU scholars should also be invited to conduct workshops for PE teachers and to organize international TGfU conferences, which assemble hundreds of scholars who share their views on the current development of TGfU (Mainland China, Macau, Japan, and Korea).

3. Establish an Asian-Pacific TGfU Council to keep in close contact with the TGfU task force (now renamed as a special-interest group of AIESEP) and to make frequent exchanges with TGfU scholars (Hong Kong, mainland China, Singapore, Taiwan, Macau, Japan, and Korea).

4. Seek the government's support and try to convince the government to incorporate TGfU into school curriculum for PE teachers to implement. Additional government funding is needed to invite experts to conduct a series of TGfU seminars and workshops for PE teachers (Mainland China, Taiwan, Macau, Japan, and Korea).

5. Introduce TGfU to the coaching community to train athletes. In the 1990s, Thorpe was invited by Aussi Sports in Australia to introduce the TGfU concept. As a result, coaches supported and welcomed TGfU. The core team can use this example to help coaching develop in their own country or region (Hong Kong, Singapore, mainland China, and Taiwan).

6. Seek assistance from experts on English in the core team to polish papers for submission to international journals (Hong Kong, mainland China, Taiwan, Macau, Japan, and Korea).

Conclusion

The Asian-Pacific countries have made efforts to disseminate TGfU in their own countries by various means, including incorporating TGfU into PE curriculum, publishing research findings and teaching material, seeking support from respective governments, and inviting experts to conduct TGfU workshops. Each country has done a great job individually. Although they may use different names and implementations for TGfU, the basic idea stays the same. Such differences may be due to culture.

From a global perspective, the Asian-Pacific countries have played an important role in disseminating TGfU, but they have a way to go to match their western counterparts in contributing research and using collaborative effort to disseminate TGfU in the future. With increased research, teaching, and coaching collaborations with our western colleagues, this picture will improve.

Discussion Questions

1. Why do Asian-Pacific countries have less impact than western countries in developing TGfU?
2. What is the most important hindrance for development of TGfU in Asian-Pacific countries?
3. Do recommendations for future development of TGfU in Asian-Pacific countries exist beyond those mentioned in this chapter?
4. After reading this chapter, how will you effectively disseminate TGfU in your country?

References

Bunker, D.J., & Thorpe, R.D. (1983). A model for the teaching of games in secondary school. *Bulletin of Physical Education, 18*(1), 5-8.

Coventry teachers explore teaching for understanding. (1986). Coventry, UK: Health Education Authority.

Curriculum Development Committee. (1974). *A preliminary guide to the curriculum for junior secondary forms.* Hong Kong, China: Hong Kong Government.

Curriculum Development Committee. (1988). *Syllabus for secondary school: Physical education.* Hong Kong, China: Hong Kong Government.

Curriculum Development Institute. (1995). *Syllabus for primary school: Physical education.* Hong Kong, China: Hong Kong Government.

Ho, W.K. (2003, December). *Teaching games for understanding: Model rethink from the integrated perspective.* Paper presented at the second international TGfU conference, Melbourne, Australia.

Kam, K., Li, C., & Cruz, A. (2005, December). *The framework of teaching soccer for secondary school students in Hong Kong – The teaching games for understanding approach.* Paper presented at the third international TGfU conference, Hong Kong, China.

Keh, N.C. (2008). *Teaching games for understanding.* Taiwan, China: National Taiwan University Press.

Li, C., & Cruz, A. (2005, December). *Learning to teach games for understanding: Experiences from four pre-service PE teachers in the Hong Kong Institute of Education.* Paper presented at the third international TGfU conference, Hong Kong, China.

Liu, Y.K. (1994). Innovation of games teaching. *Journal of Primary Education, 4,* 43-48.

Liu, Y.K. (1996). An alternative approach to games teaching in the training of PE teachers. *Physical Education, Recreation & Sports (PERS) Review, 2,* 10-14.

Liu, Y.K., & Thorpe, R. (1997). The introduction of a cognitive approach to games teaching in Hong Kong. *AIESEP Singapore 97 Proceedings,* 125-130.

Liu, Y.K., & Yang, Z.J. (1997). Philosophy of the teaching games for understanding approach. *China School Physical education, 3,* 28-29.

Liu, Y.K. (2002). *Games teaching – Teaching games for understanding.* Hong Kong, China: Hong Kong Institute of Education.

Liu, Y.K., & Cheung, W.Y. (2005, December). *Teachers' responses on the teaching games for understanding: 10 years in Hong Kong.* Paper presented at the third international TGfU conference, Hong Kong, China.

Liu, Y.K., & Cheung, C.Y. (2005, December). *Teaching games for understanding: An alternative approach to teach Tae Kwon Do (free fight).* Paper presented at the third international TGfU conference, Hong Kong, China.

Liu, Y.K., & Yen, H.C. (2006). *Teaching games for understanding.* Beijing, China: Beijing Sport University Press.

Mao, Z.M. (2003). *New PE curriculum and teaching in the 21st century.* Beijing, China: Beijing Normal University Press.

McNeill, M.C., Fry, J.M., Wright, S.C., Tan, W.K.C., Tan, S.K., & Schempp, P.G. (2004). "In the local context": Singaporean challenges to teaching games on practicum. *Sport, Education and Society, 9*(1), 3-32.

Physical Education Section. (1964). *A scheme of PE for Hong Kong primary schools.* Hong Kong, China: Education Department.

Rossi, T., Fry, J.M., McNeill, M., & Tan, W.K.C. (2007). The games concept approach (GCA) as a mandated practice: Views of Singaporean teachers. *Sport, Education and Society, 12*(1), 93-111.

Tan, W.K.C. (2007, July). *Teaching Games for Understanding: Singapore.* Paper presented as keynote address for Teaching Games for Understanding conference at National Taiwan Normal University, Taipei, Taiwan.

Thorpe, R.D., & Bunker, D.J. (1983). Issue that arise when preparing to teach for understanding. *Bulletin of Physical Education, 19*(1), 27-31.

Thorpe, R.D., & Bunker, D.J. (1986). Landmarks on our way to 'teaching for understanding.' In R. Thorpe, D. Bunker, and L. Almond (Eds.), *Rethinking games teaching* (pp. 5-6). Loughborough, UK: Loughborough University Press.

Thorpe, R.D., Bunker, D.J., & Almond, L. (1984). A change in focus for the teaching of games. In M. Pieron and G. Graham (Eds.), *The 1984 Olympic scientific congress proceedings* (p.163-169). Champaign, IL: Human Kinetics.

Wade, A. (1967). *The F.A. guide to training and coaching.* London: Heinemann.

Williamson, T. (1982). A critical look at the games curriculum. *Bulletin of Physical Education, 18*(1), 23-26.

Wright, S., McNeill, M., Fry, J., & Wang, J.(2005). Teaching teachers to play and teach games. *Physical Education and Sport Pedagogy, 10*(1), 61-82.

Wright, S., McNeill, M., Fry, J., Tan, S., Tan, C. & Schempp, P. (2006). Implications of student teachers' implementation of a curricular innovation. *Journal of Teaching in Physical Education, 25*(3), 310-328.

PART

Research:
Reexamination

chapter

2

TGfU: Celebrations and Cautions

Judith Rink, PhD

J osh decided to use a TGfU approach to a new unit on lacrosse. His students have never played lacrosse. He became frustrated at the idea that they knew what they needed to do after a unit in soccer but couldn't do it in lacrosse. He abandoned the idea of doing anything with TGfU and went back to his usual approach, which was to teach all of the skills and then play the game.

Teaching Games for Understanding (TGfU) has a rich history of changing the way we look at developing good games players (Griffin & Patton, 2005). It has made a major contribution to our awareness of the role of tactics in successful game play and the situational nature of the execution of skill. It has brought attention to our failure as a profession to teach tactics and to the importance of teaching skills in the context of games. It has helped us understand how we might transfer responsibility for decision making to the learner in the instructional process.

Basic Assumptions About What Physical Educators Do

As physical educators, we have come to hold some basic assumptions about what we do as truth. These underlie our choices of the content we teach and the methodologies we use to teach that content. Our objective in teaching games is to develop good players who have knowledge of both technique and tactics.

We value games because they are a great form of physical activity at a time when the whole world is looking for ways to increase the activity of youth and adults, and because they have the potential to contribute a great deal to the quality of life of the participants. The current emphasis on the contributions of physical activity to health is driving much of the support for TGfU, as well as Daryl Siedentop's work with sport as play education (2007) and Kretchmar's (2007) ideas about keeping the joy in physical activity. All have made important contributions to our intentions, values, and practices as practitioners.

Tactics involve both knowing what to do in a given game situation and having the ability to execute what you want to do. For many years, the tactics of game play placed a distant second next to techniques. Best practice currently recognizes the significance of both. TGfU has emphasized not only the importance of tactics but also the manner in which tactics are learned. From a pedagogical perspective, we know that students who are engaged at a higher level learn more.

In physical education, we have progressed from the notion of teacher-allocated time, to student-activity time, to academic-learning time, to the approach of engaging students at a high cognitive level. Each qualitative change in the way we describe student participation has refined our notion of student engagement. Students need to pay attention to what they are doing and how they are doing it if they are to learn. Rote-drill practice is not as effective as practice that achieves a high level of engagement. TGfU has the potential to engage students at the level needed for learning to occur.

Methodologies that involve the learner more holistically, both in terms of the domains of learning as well as in terms of content to be learned, have a better chance of producing learning and of contributing to students' development in a broader sense. As educators, we have tried to create rich experiences for learners because we know that learning is not compartmentalized into affective, cognitive, and psychomotor domains, or even into games, skills, and rules. The more we can involve the whole learner, the better the chances that meaningful learning will occur. TGfU has the potential to involve the learner more holistically.

Students' motivation to learn increases when they are engaged in something they perceive to be authentic and personally meaningful.

In the context of games, many adults and adolescents find actual play the most meaningful. However, the attachment to meaning and authenticity is likely to be affected by developmental factors. The 8-year-old dribbling a basketball is likely to perceive the experience as playing basketball. A 13-year-old engaged in the same activity is likely to perceive the experience quite differently, perhaps asking, "When can we play the game?" TGfU has made learning to play games more meaningful to learners by making the experience more authentic. Students can learn both tactics and skill in the context of the game.

None of the preceding statements require that TGfU be used exclusively to teach games, although they do support the pedagogy of TGfU. The problem that we have is that there are many ways to implement these ideas. In fact, some of the best games players learned to be good games players without TGfU. Research on the development of expertise in both sports and other fields specifically identifies the long hours expert players spend in what many of us would identify as practice that is meaningless, out of context, and inauthentic (Starkes & Ericsson, 2003).

So how do we deal with the contradictions? Côté, Baker, and Abernathy (2003) suggest, in their study of the development of experts in sport, that players go through stages in their development. Participants move from a period of play (usually in a variety of activities) and deliberate play—where emphasis is still on the enjoyment of participation, but the participant develops an attitude of wanting to improve at what they are doing—to a period of deliberate practice that is more intense. In deliberate practice participants develop the desire to improve at what they do, and practice takes on an intensity not present in earlier stages. The emphasis in the early stages (through preadolescence) on the importance of play and deliberate play is critical for physical educators. Activities of play and deliberate play are designed to maximize inherent enjoyment while students develop fundamental skills. They

The emphasis in the early stages (through preadolescence) on the importance of play and deliberate play is critical for physical educators.

are also designed to develop internal motivation to participate and to experience the fun and excitement of sport. Although Côté et al. attach age levels to the continuum, it is entirely likely that the stages are more related to the experience the players have with the activity and their interest in playing at a higher level; the difference between a competitive 35-year-old golfer and one who has chosen to remain with a playful approach. For coaches, the suggestions of the authors are important in terms of moving participants through the continuum. For physical-education teachers who work with participants at a stage of play and deliberate play, the suggestions for building internal motivation and skillfulness are critical.

Since 1982, the ideas of Bunker and Thorpe have developed and broadened, finding their way to gymnasiums all over the world relatively quickly, given the time frame of educational change. Advocates of TGfU are passionate about their findings and their successes. For the most part, TGfU has been ideologically based, lacking a theoretical foundation to support the pedagogy. The purpose of the discussion that follows is to continue the dialogue on enriching theory so that the pedagogical practice of TGfU becomes less reliant on ideology. Placing the discussion of TGfU in a theoretical framework allows us to research the issues and to ask good questions.

Assumptions About Teaching and Learning

I make several assumptions about teaching and learning in physical education which are important to share in any discussion of pedagogical practice. These are outlined in the following sections.

Versus Language Is Not Helpful

A lot of the dialogue in the TGfU literature still uses a *versus* model, which compares skills first and games second orientation with TGFU. As the literature has continued to explore the potential of TGfU, the language has become more and more pious, placing the decision to use a TGfU model on a moral plane and judging educators who may choose differently. The literature seems to infer that anyone who uses a technique model buys into a factory ideal of education and mind-body dualism and values performance rather than thinking and making decisions, teacher-directed learning processes, passive learning, and so on. My perspective is that polarizing language and discussion are largely unhelpful because they omit some of the critical points about how and when people learn particular content.

Teaching Models Are Helpful to a Point

As a young professional in physical education at the elementary level, I was a zealot for movement education. I got in at the early stages of the development of this approach to teaching skills, which was predicated on the idea that all we had to do was ask children how many ways can they do a certain task. We believed that the process of exploration alone would increase children's skills, creativity, and critical thinking. Movement education was, for all practical purposes, a model for teaching, as defined by Metzler (2000); meaning that what is learned is tied to how it is learned. What we wanted to teach came with the methodology, "this is the way you do it," including rules for what teachers can do and cannot do if they are true movement educators.

Like TGfU, movement education was an indirect teaching style, paired with the student-centered values that normally accompany such approaches. The biggest rule of all was that if you were going to be true to the model, you couldn't ever tell students how to do anything. With time, movement educators came to understand that they were more effective if they moved in and out of more open tasks, and varied the amount of learner-centered decisions. That is, a process exists in which the content opens up, narrows, and then opens again. Teachers may work on how many different ways students can move from one place to another using their feet then narrow the focus to the action of feet together or feet apart to bring out some different patterns (even working on jumping or hopping better) before opening the focus up again. While apparently narrowing the range of student choices, the teacher was actually expanding the students' responses and, therefore, their learning. The process both expanded the responses and made the students more skillful at the patterns they chose.

TGfU is a model that basically says, "This is the content, these are the objectives, and this is the way it should be taught." When models are used as a recipe for teaching particular content, a danger exists that the roles of teachers and students become rigid, limiting the decisions of the teacher and the learning experiences of the student. From my perspective, the process of teaching is interactive. I like the terms used by our European colleagues that refer to the process as *didactic*—the interaction between the teacher, the content, and the student. As a generic framework for an approach to teaching, particular content models are useful. As recipes that dictate pedagogical decision making, they run the risk of giving us a very false sense of what pedagogy is appropriate (Rink, 2001).

Using Learning Theory as Basis for Selecting a Pedagogical Practice

The third assumption is that learning theory should be the basis for the selection of pedagogical practice. Learning theory attempts to explain how students may come to learn particular content. Teaching is a goal-oriented activity, or at least it should be. The goal of teaching games is to help students become good players, and to do it in a way that inspires lifelong participation. The discussion of how to best achieve this goal should be directly related to learning theory, but should not be prescribed. Some of the literature on TGfU has attempted to move the dialogue to a philosophical discussion of process, rather than of outcomes. For example, TGfU teaches meaning, thinking, and decision making. This approach is contrasted with those who want students to acquire knowledge, skill, and performance.

In reality, I think everyone is on the same page; we all want students to be able to play the game skillfully and we want them to want to continue to play the game. I don't believe it is helpful to place the issue in a philosophical context if we have clear outcomes for what we want students to know and do as a result of our practice as physical education teachers. The appropriate foundation for pedagogical practice is learning theory. The rest of this discussion addresses the issues involved in the selection of learning theories to support TGfU and the implications that those theories have for how we teach games to students.

Selecting Learning Theory

The theory most used to support TGfU is constructivist-learning theory, which aims to describe how knowledge is constructed. We must recognize that TGfU doesn't have a monopoly on constructivism. This theory explains that students construct knowledge based on the interaction of present learning experiences with past ones. That is, students come to us with an understanding of what we are trying to teach, and will hopefully modify or construct new understandings based on the learning experiences we design. The notion is that students actively participate in their own learning. Constructivism is not a model of teaching; rather, it emphasizes how students acquire meaning. From this perspective, the idea is that the *why* of games should come before the *how,* engaging students in inquiry learning.

Constructivism is not a model of teaching; rather, it emphasizes how students acquire meaning.

Choosing constructivism as a learning theory for TGfU also has some liabilities. Constructivist theory asserts that learning experiences that promote inquiry should be based on students' prior knowledge. This idea creates problems for the physical-education teacher. The first issue is that prior knowledge varies from student to student. The second is the assumption that inquiry takes place in the learning experiences that we choose. We may design an experience for discovery and inquiry learning; however, the assumption that all students experience that process may be false.

I am reminded of my very first research study, in which I followed four first grade boys through four weeks of movement-education lessons (Rink, 1969). The lessons were designed primarily for the students to explore teacher-assigned tasks that gave them different amounts of freedom to respond. For instance, the instruction, "Travel in different ways, using two feet," allows a great deal more freedom of response than, "Travel on one foot." I looked at both the number of different responses of students to different kinds of tasks as well as the appropriateness of the response relative to the task. Students were chosen for the study based on their risk-taking characteristics, as identified by the classroom teacher.

The results of the study concluded that for the most part, students who were not risk takers produced few responses, and the responses they chose were largely determined by observing what others were doing and copying what they saw. Students who produced more variety in their responses, meaning that they had multiple responses to a task, also displayed more inappropriate responses. Clearly, the process of engagement was different for these students.

The results of one of our past studies, comparing TGfU with more traditional approaches as well as with a combination of approaches, clearly emphasize the need for teachers to know where a student is situated within the content we are teaching (Rink, 1996). This study used high-school badminton classes as a study group. Students were clearly unskilled in playing badminton, and contact was a problem for many. One of the first experiences we tried with the TGfU class was to present tactical problems related to making your partner move on the court. Even though these students were unskilled in terms of execution, they had clearly learned the basic tactics of net activities at some point. This made our initial experiences inappropriate, since they already had an understanding of what they should be trying to do.

The Role of Skill

Constructivism is a cognitive theory that strongly supports the need for preexisting student knowledge and experience. In learning motor skills and in playing sports and games, the issues related to knowing what to do are surrounded by issues of execution. Students must not only know what to perform, but they must also be able to perform it. The decision of what to do is constrained by the ability to execute that intention. A two-way relationship exists between the decision of what to do and the ability to execute that response. A study done by French, Nevett, Spurgeon, Graham, Rink, & McPherson (1996) with young baseball players illustrates this relationship. Little League players were given different scenarios, such as how many outs, which bases had runners, and where the ball was coming. They were asked what they would do in different positions. In many cases, students knew to repeat the *party line,* that is, what they had been told to do by their coaches. In the end, however, their actual responses were based on their own ability to execute the response. For example, "I know I'm supposed to throw it to first base, but I can't get it there, so I am going to...," or "I know I'm supposed to throw it to first base, but if I do the first baseman can't catch it, so I will throw it to the pitcher to prevent base runners from advancing." At this level of baseball play, base runners can't advance once the pitcher has the ball.

The issues involved in skill and tactics are not questions of which to teach first; rather, skill and tactics develop simultaneously with each other and constrain each other. Placing skill execution at step five or at any step apart from decisions about what to do in reality is just trading one linear model for another. The issue is one of defining the level of skill necessary for the development of particular tactics.

> *T*he issues involved in skill and tactics are not questions of which to teach first; rather, skill and tactics develop simultaneously with each other and constrain each other.

Some of the TGfU literature suggests that if skill is the problem, then we should change the skill. If the sole objective is to develop either an understanding of the game or an understanding of the transfer of tactics from one game to another similar game form, then changing the skill is a viable solution. If, however, we want students to be able to play the game with the skills used in the game (for example, to be able to hit a tennis ball with a racket rather than to throw it over the net), changing the skill that is used so we can teach tactics alone won't result in skillful tennis players. When we go back to the game as played with the original skills (that is, with rackets), the tactics will be constrained by the lack of real-game skills. Students will still choose the response they think they are more capable of executing.

The idea of teaching game types and transferring the tactics to different games of the same type is reasonable. If we can get the tactics to transfer, which I believe we can, we are still back at the point of skill constraining the tactics. It is my sense that some level of control of an object is absolutely essential for putting students in any tactical learning experience. Lacrosse should not look like field hockey because students can't throw and catch the ball in the air, regardless of the tactics. So where does this leave us in making recommendations about skill and tactics? Let's continue our journey to find a learning theory that can guide us.

Potential of Dynamical Systems as a Theory for Teaching Games

In the September issue of the *Review of Educational Research,* Chow and his colleagues made a very good case for what they are calling a *constraints-led theory of learning* as the basis for TGfU (Chow, Davids, Button, Shuttleworth, Renshaw, & Araujo, 2007). The Davis and Broadhead text, *Ecological Task Analysis and Movement* (2007), is also an excellent resource for ecological theory and constraints-led theory and their applications for movement settings. Both have their roots in chaos theory and in dynamical systems theory.

As theorists in all scientific fields began to realize that simplistic and linear models for explaining phenomena could not capture their complex, situational, and sometimes chaotic nature, they turned to a systems explanation. Relative to movement, three constraints function to influence our responses to a particular situation. The first constraint is physical, what Newell in 1986 referred to as *organismic* and later theorists labeled the *constraints of the performer.* Performer constraints include all physical, neuromuscular, and performance characteristics of the individual. The example of Little League is a good one for understanding the effects of performance constraints on student responses.

In one sense, the idea that physical abilities constrain performance is not new. We know that if you give very young children a basketball and put them in front of a basket 10 feet (3 m) from the ground, they will most likely choose to use a two-hand, underhand shot because that is the only way they can get it up there. Chris Everett was the first successful tennis player to use a two-handed backhand. She started playing tennis at an early age, and using two hands was the only way she could generate enough force to get the ball over the net. In the case of the two-handed backhand, the result was positive. In the case of the underhand basketball shot, the choice was appropriate at the time, but the long-term consequences of practicing that technique would not be as desirable.

The second type of constraint is environmental, and includes both the physical constraints of the actual environment as well as the social context in which a response is performed. Again, nothing is really new here. We have always known that physical environment, particularly the perceived social environment, affects what students do. We know that you can get a young child to walk long before they normally would be capable of doing so if you take away the balance problems caused by gravity (Thelen, Ulrich, & Jensen, 1989). We know that some students will not perform well in front of others, and some will vary their performance, both positively or negatively, depending on whom they are with and who is paying attention to what they are doing.

The third type of constraint, *task constraint,* is perhaps the most critical for what we do in physical education and sport, particularly for a TGfU methodology. Task constraints are those related to the context of the task itself, such as the equipment used, the space, the number of players, and what the student perceives as the task. Some examples of how task constraints operate include the following:

- You are teaching an overhand throw pattern and you put students 10 feet (3 m) apart to show you a good example. You wonder why they aren't doing it the way you taught them.

- You want students to dribble with control, but you put them in a competitive situation or in a race for time and wonder where the control went.

When we were doing one of our badminton studies, we had three instructors who were nearly expert badminton players. One was a UK junior champion and two played competitive badminton in the United States. We wanted to film them doing the drop shot and clear. Instead of putting them in a game situation, we fed them the shuttlecock and asked them to perform the skill. In a game situation, each of those players would have disguised their drop shot with a windup. In the filming situation, they resorted to what could be called a chop shot, one with no preparation or backswing. Rather than producing choices, constraints eliminate options for performance. When the constraint of an opponent was removed, these expert players selected a response they could more easily control.

Good teachers have always known that task constraints can elicit a performance without instructions. Three examples illustrate the power of task constraints.

1. *The ball in the sock.* A young tennis coach couldn't figure out how she could get students to keep from stopping their stroke halfway through the windup in the serve. She put a ball in a sock and asked them to serve the sock. If they stopped their movement half way through, the ball would hit them in the back.

2. *The hurdle.* Swimming coaches know that initial attempts at the surface dive always result in swimmers jumping down to the water, instead of up and then in. If you put a low hurdle in front of the swimmer, you can elicit the upward jump that you want.

3. *The swamp.* A study done by Teri Sweeting (Sweeting & Rink, 1999) on the standing long jump with 8-year-olds further illustrates the effectiveness of task constraints. One group used traditional instruction, one used environmental design only (no instruction of how to jump), and a control group received no instruction and didn't practice jumping in their normal physical-education class. We monitored all groups at the pretest and the posttest under two conditions. In the first condition, participants were asked to jump as far as they could on a flat mat. The second condition involved what we called *the swamp*. We put all sorts of pictures of snakes, bugs, and creepy things on the mat and asked them to jump over the swamp. We then taught both groups. The environmental-design group practiced with targets of different colored bands on the mat that they could choose to jump over. All tasks were designed to elicit force production without any instruction on how to produce force. The other group got instruction on how to do the standing

long jump, as well as tasks such as, "Who can get to the other side of the gym in as few jumps as possible?"

The swamp condition in the pretest was more effective in producing jumps that were both longer and more developmentally mature. The flat mat was more effective in the posttest. When we analyzed the process characteristics of the jump, the group that received instruction had a more mature jump, but more notably, the pattern was very different. The leg characteristics of the environmental-design group were more mature, and the arm movements and preparation of the instructional group were more mature.

TGfU does the same thing to elicit tactics through the presentation of movement tasks. So, we now have a theory that can explain why TGfU should be used and how it works, right? Yes and no. We can elicit appropriate tactical responses from learners by using appropriate tasks and changing those tasks. The interaction of the task, performer, and task constraints may in fact produce the desired response. When the student selects the appropriate response at a different level of consciousness, will we finally have a theory of learning that will create good game players? Not quite. If we want to increase the level of performance of the games players, both in terms of the decision and the execution, the level of consciousness is the problem, from a theoretical perspective.

Studies of experts in both sports and other fields have identified the cognitive processes experts use in their fields (Ericsson, Krampe, & Tesch-Römer, 1993). These include the following:

1. Choose correct responses. Experts are both faster at making decisions and more accurate. The underlying cognitive processes allow them to detect key visual cues and to recognize patterns in offensive and defensive play to reach a decision about what to do.

2. Experts use visual search strategies to help them monitor game play (the location of players on the court or field, game context).

3. Experts anticipate and predict game actions from long-term memory (learning or experience). They develop current-event profiles to anticipate what an opponent will do.

4. Experts plan events in advance of play, while novices react.

5. Experts rehearse game plans using active memory (verbal or visual).

6. Experts modify plans based on new information, combining visual search patterns.

These cognitive processes require that learners have a language to think about what they want to do and how to do it. They have verbal labels for both skill and tactics. Constraints theory and ecological approaches to skill development are very useful, and I do not underestimate their value. A problem arises, however, when the pedagogy elicits a response from learners that is subconscious in nature. Learners fail to develop the language for planning and thinking about what they are doing and how they are doing it. They need a language to increase their understanding of the game and to perform at a higher level.

A *problem arises when the pedagogy elicits a response from learners that is subconscious in nature; they fail to develop the language for planning and thinking about what they are doing and how they are doing it. They need a language to increase their understanding of the game and to perform at a higher level.*

The development of a language for skill and tactical growth requires that we gain a greater awareness and understanding of our experiences. Ask questions, such as "What did you do?", "Why did you do it?", "How did you do it?", and "How did it turn out?" The development of skill execution and decision making requires that we assist the learner in this way to refine their performance.

This means that practitioners may need to consider ways to develop the language and understanding of when and how to use these skills. A progression that continues to simply elicit subconscious responses is unlikely to do so, no matter how well we plan.

McPherson and Kernodle (2003) suggest that game players need instruction in order to identify available responses to select from and to develop the diagnostic skills they need for competitive play. Although we can elicit tactical learning through task design, development in tactics depends on our ability to help our students with response selection. This involves ensuring that they have a large number of responses to choose from and that they have the cognitive processes that will help them choose appropriately in different game situations. McPherson and Kernodle (2003) have suggested that beginners, the level most of us will work with, have action plans that are governed by rules. This means that when given a set of observed characteristics of play (where the ball is, what teammates are doing, what opponents are doing), players know exactly what they should do. Action plans are facilitated by instruction that brings the decision-making process to a conscious level.

As the concepts in TGfU have expanded, educators and coaches have selected the ideas that are of use to them. Some versions of TGfU have remained at an eliciting level and some have moved toward the need to bring tactical learning to a conscious level. Some coaches have found environmental design to be an effective way to get players to produce more meaningful responses, just as the hurdle was used to get swimmers to jump up rather than down for the surface dive. Other practitioners of TGfU recognize the importance of skill execution and have taken the time to teach skills to students more directly.

Bunker and Thorpe's original work (1982) was designed to target secondary students in game play. They did not neglect skill, but rather suggested that the teacher needs to recognize when individual students are ready for technique. In one sense, the issue is when to move players from play to deliberate play. The knowledge base and observational skills needed for large classes of students with diverse skill levels may exceed the capacity of teacher-education programs to prepare teachers. Proponents of more indirect teaching methods have always struggled with the idea that this seemingly simple pedagogy is in fact far more difficult than it would appear. Many practitioners, including myself, have struggled with this issue. Is direct instruction actually a better choice than poor indirect instruction? Put another way, if you don't have a class of Van Goghs, will paint-by-number exercises do?

Conclusion

I would like to leave you with a few thoughts. The idea of eliciting tactical responses in the context of game play is a valuable and important pedagogical tool. Tactical learning, which occurs through discovery alone, may not allow the student to grow in their understanding of making game decisions and executing skills.

- Tactical learning needs to be brought to a conscious level in order for students to develop the language they need to plan game play. Either indirect or direct teaching styles can accomplish this goal.

- The relationship between skill and tactics is a reciprocal one; they develop in tandem with each other.

- Some level of control of an object is essential for any tactics to be used, even in the simplest game settings. Changing the skill to a simpler one may help students acquire tactics, but those tactics will be constrained by skill when they are put back in the original game form.

- The notion of task constraints is a helpful theory not only for the development of tactics but also for applications for skill development. Carson, Bulger, and Townsend's (2007) notion of the experimental-progressive approach to skill development is particularly useful here. Manipulating factors, such as equipment, target, distance, and force, in isolation will likely help develop skill in much the same way that the problem setting of TGfU develops tactics. The same precautions apply to tactics development in terms of helping students develop a language for what they are doing and applying it to the development of skill.

- Teachers need the freedom to move from direct to indirect styles of instruction throughout a lesson. Hopper's argument that the skill and tactics approaches can both be effective if delivered with the proper progressions and relevant game context has merit and forces us to think about the real issues in selecting a pedagogy (2002).

Regardless of the pedagogy, the assumption that all students will go through a process simply because we have put them in a response-producing situation can be naïve and dangerous. TGfU has come a long way. We need to celebrate what we now know and to continue to explore how we can improve our practice.

Discussion Questions

1. What is the relationship between skill and tactics in game play?
2. What are the strengths and weaknesses of using teaching models?
3. What is deliberate play and how does it relate to teaching games in physical education?
4. How is TGfU related to the theory of dynamical systems?
5. What is the limitation of dynamical systems as a theoretical base for TGfU?

References

Bunker, D., & Thorpe, R. (1982). A model for the teaching of games in the secondary school. *Bulletin of Physical Education, 18*(1), 5-8.

Carson, L., Bulger, S., & Townsend, S. (2007). Enhancing responsible decision making in physical activity. In W. Davis and G. Broadhead (Eds.), *Ecological task analysis and movement* (pp. 141-159). Champaign, IL: Human Kinetics.

Chow, J., Davids, K., Button, C., Shuttleworth, R., Renshaw, I., & Araujo, D. (2007). The role of nonlinear pedagogy in physical education. *Review of Educational Research, 77*(3), 251-278.

Côté, J., Baker, J., & Abernathy, B. (2003). From play to practice: A developmental framework for the acquisition of expertise in team sports. In J. Starkes and A. Ericsson (Eds.), *Expert performance in sports: Advances in research and sport expertise* (pp. 90-113). Champaign, IL: Human Kinetics.

Davis, W., & Broadhead, G. (Eds.). (2007). *Ecological task analysis and movement.* Champaign, IL: Human Kinetics.

Ericsson, K., Krampe, R., & Tesch-Römer, C. (1993). The role of deliberate practice in the acquisition of expert performance. *Psychological Review, 100,* 363-406.

French, K.E., Nevett, M.E., Spurgeon, J.H., Graham, K.C., Rink, J.E., & McPherson, S.L. (1996). Knowledge representation and problem solution of expert and novice youth baseball players. *Research Quarterly for Exercise and Sport, 67*(4), 386-395.

Griffin, L., & Patton, K. (2005). Two decades of TGfU: Looking at the past, present, and future. In L. Griffin and J. Butler (Eds.), *Teaching games for understanding: Theory, research, and practice* (pp. 1-17). Champaign, IL: Human Kinetics.

Hopper, T. (2002). Teaching games for understanding: The importance of student emphasis over content emphasis. *Journal of Physical Education, Recreation and Dance, 73*(7), 44-48.

Kretchmar, R.S. (2007). What to do with meaning? A research conundrum for the 21st century. *Quest, 59,* 373-383.

McPherson, S., & Kernodle, M. (2003). Tactics, the neglected attribute of expertise: Problem representation and performance skills in tennis. In J. Starkes and K. Ericsson (Eds.), *Expert performance in sports: Advances in research on sport expertise* (pp. 137-168). Champaign, IL: Human Kinetics.

Metzler, M. (2000). *Instructional models in physical education.* Boston: Allyn & Bacon.

Newell, K. (1986). Constraints on the development of coordination. In H. Wade and H. Whiting (Eds.), *Motor development in children: Aspects of coordination and control* (pp. 341-360). Dordrecht, the Netherlands: Martinus Nijhoff Publishers.

Rink, J. (1969). *The movement responses of four first grade boys to teacher stated movement problems.* Unpublished master's thesis. The University of North Carolina, Greensboro.

Rink, J. (Ed.). (1996). Learning and instruction in sport and games. *Journal of Teaching in Physical Education, 15*(4), Summer Monograph.

Rink, J. (2001). Investigating the assumptions of pedagogy. *Journal of Teaching in Physical Education, 20*(2), 112-128.

Siedentop, D. (2007). *Introduction to physical education, fitness, and sport.* Boston: McGraw-Hill.

Starkes, J., & Ericsson, K. (2003). *Expert performance in sports: Advances in research on sport expertise.* Champaign, IL: Human Kinetics.

Sweeting, T., & Rink, J. (1999). Effects of direct instruction and environmentally designed instruction on the process and product characteristics of a fundamental skill. *Journal of Teaching in Physical Education. 18*(2), 216-233.

Thelen, E., Ulrich, B., & Jensen, J. (1989). The developmental origins of locomotion. In M. Woollocott and A. Shumway-Cooke (Eds.), *Development of posture and gait across the lifespan* (pp. 25-47). Columbia, SC: University of South Carolina Press.

chapter

3

Sport and Games Education: Models of Practice

**Connie S. Collier, PhD • Judy Oslin, PhD
Daniel Rodriguez, MA • David Gutierrez, PhD**

> **B**e the change you want to see in the world.
>
> — *Mahatma Gandhi*

In 2001 (Oslin, Collier, & Mitchell), we reported on the development and implementation of two activity courses designed to model innovative curricular approaches, specifically the models of Tactical Games (TG) and Sport Education (SE). The first course, Game Performance (GP) I, is a three-semester, hour-long course with content organized according to three game categories: target games (25 percent), striking and fielding games (25 percent), and invasion games (50 percent). The second course, GP II, is a two-semester, hour-long course that solely focuses on the fourth game category, net games, with an emphasis on volleyball, badminton, tennis, and pickleball. Here, as in 2001, we think it is important to share our vision of how and why it is essential to model pedagogical practices within our physical-education teacher education (PETE) program that are representative of the ways we hope our teaching candidates will instruct sports and games to children in schools.

Comparing TGfU With Tactical Games and Sport Education

Our decision to reorganize these courses, originally titled *team sports* and *individual sports,* stemmed from the philosophical inconsistencies between technical and tactical versions of games education. From a pragmatic (or conceptual) perspective, the reorganization of content to emphasize the tactical similarities among multiple games across each category is more efficient. Teaching Games for Understanding (TGfU) (Bunker & Thorpe, 1982), from which the TG approach evolved, suggests organizing curriculum around the four categories of game play to promote transfer of tactical knowledge between games within the same category. So, the GP courses not only allow us to cover more content, but they also provide a means of demonstrating the transfer of tactical similarities across multiple games within and across categories. This is particularly important given the erosion of activity-based courses to counter increases in general education requirements (Siedentop, 2002), a common problem in PETE programs across the United States.

It is perhaps important to note that the TG approach, although essentially sharing the same conceptual base, is a simplified version of TGfU (Mitchell, 2005). In an attempt to help teachers and undergraduates interpret and implement TGfU, the six-stage model by Bunker and Thorpe (1982) was collapsed to emphasize three primary elements: (a) the game form emphasizing modification-exaggeration, (b) decision making, and (c) skill development (Mitchell, 2005). Within the GP courses, we model the TG approach through a game-practice-game format, in which each lesson begins with a conditioned game with a clearly stated goal. The game is followed by a question-and-answer segment intended to guide students toward one or more solutions to the tactical problem set forth in the initial game (decision making). Students are then given a task in which to practice the solutions (What to do? How to do it?) before returning to game play to apply the solution. In addition to this rather prescriptive lesson plan format, the TG approach utilizes tactical frameworks (Mitchell, Griffin, & Oslin, 1994) to highlight developmentally appropriate levels of performance and game categories (Bunker & Thorpe, 1982) to promote curricular implications of TGfU.

From a philosophical perspective, the TG and SE models are consistent with the PETE faculties' shared philosophies regarding student-centered learning, design and implementation of developmentally appropriate games, development of GP skills in context (opposed to development of technical skills in isolation), and the promotion of lifelong participation. Additionally, these models, particularly SE, contain numerous organizational features that promote sound classroom management practices, such as organizing teams, providing each team with a home court, and assigning students specific roles and responsibilities. According to Metzler (2006), models such as TG and SE contain various elements inherent in best practice, making them ideal for promoting pedagogical content knowledge.

According to Metzler (2006), models such as tactical games and sport education contain various elements inherent in best practice, making them ideal for promoting pedagogical content knowledge.

The GP courses are not just about models of practice; these courses are about modeling best practice. Therefore, the PETE faculty at Kent State University in the United States serve as the primary instructors for these courses. Lunenberg, Korthagen, and Swennen (2007) state that very little research exists about the teacher educator as a role model; therefore, they have examined the act of modeling by teacher educators. Four of the 10 teacher educators in their study did no modeling. During lessons of the six teacher educators who did provide explicit models, modeling appeared to be unplanned and implemented more as "opportunities for learning that suddenly presented themselves during the teaching sessions" (p. 12). Two of the six teacher educators who demonstrated explicit modeling were in physical education. From our experience, this approach is consistent with most PETE programs in the United States. However, most programs continue to emphasize acquisition of content knowledge and, for various reasons, to assign activity courses to coaches or instructors with expertise in a specific content area. Therefore, teaching candidates have a limited vision of what it means to integrate content knowledge with contemporary curricular approaches, as few have witnessed anyone modeling these practices.

By contrast, the PETE program faculty at KSU has been intentional about threading content, curriculum, and pedagogical content knowledge throughout the GP courses as well as through other activity and professional courses. Modeling best practice extends beyond the PETE faculty to clinical faculty who regularly supervise the school-based field experiences. Many of the clinical faculty members, some of whom are KSU alumni, have participated in professional development workshops, and a few have assisted in the presentation of workshops at our university as well as at state and regional conferences. We have invested considerable resources to develop this excellent group of intentional practitioners, enabling our teacher-education program to expand beyond the walls of the university.

It is our belief that contextualized and ecologically rich settings are necessary for learning to teach (Collier, 2009). Therefore, situating our teaching candidates in communities of practice or in field sites where they observe and are mentored by teachers who model and support contemporary curricular approaches is critical to teacher learning. These communities are consistent with situated-learning theory (Lave

It is our belief that contextualized and ecologically rich settings are necessary for learning to teach (Collier, 2009).Therefore, situating our teaching candidates in communities of practice or in field sites where they observe and are mentored by teachers who model and support contemporary curricular approaches is critical to teacher learning.

& Wenger, 1991), in which social interaction and collaboration are essential elements. The concept of legitimate peripheral participation described in the literature on communities of practice (Lave & Wenger, 1991) suggests that teaching candidates learn at the periphery; as their competence grows, they become more intimately involved, moving toward the center of these communities. Learning is viewed as a process of social participation, not necessarily of acquiring knowledge. In addition to observing best practices, teaching candidates consistently engage in critical reflection to deconstruct how their pedagogical approaches best serve their students. As such, we have established a community of practice that embodies specific beliefs and practices, and have developed a sequence of learning activities to encourage teaching candidates to become more engaged in their profession.

Beyond our own TG and SE research (Griffin, Oslin, & Mitchell, 1995; Mitchell & Oslin, 1999; Chouinard, Collier, & Oslin, 2008) and experiences with these models, the rationale for these curricular changes was originally grounded in the research on teacher socialization (Dewar & Lawson, 1984; Doolittle, Placek, & Dodds, 1993; Graber, 1995; Lawson, 1983a, 1983b, and 1986). The socialization literature suggests that in order to offset preservice teachers' subjective warrants, PETE programs need a strong philosophical underpinning shared among faculty. Since the inception of GP I and II, however, the PETE faculty at KSU have considered multiple, yet related, perspectives, such as situated learning, constructivist theories, and ecological perspectives (Mitchell & Oslin, 2007). Viewing the PETE program through these lenses, along with our own research and that of our colleagues, has provided insight as we continue to revise the PETE curriculum. In addition, we are guided by our teaching experiences in GP and in other professional courses, as well as our experiences with clinical faculty.

Methods and Procedures for Tactical Games and Sport Education

The intent of the current project was to investigate the affect of living the curriculum on our preservice teachers, now that many are teachers in their own schools. We selected a design of multiple case studies to describe how they interpret and teach contemporary models of sport and games as experienced teachers. Yin (1994) defines a descriptive case study as "an empirical inquiry that investigates a contemporary phenomenon within its real-life context" (p. 23). For the purpose of this research, four teachers were selected, which allowed for a cross-case analysis of games teaching from a range of experience levels (2 to 10 years), grade levels (grades 3 through 12, ages 8 to 18), and gender (two men and two women). Permission to complete the study was acquired through the Institutional Review Board at Kent State University.

Consistent with Yin's (1994) recommendations, data were collected using a short questionnaire, digital video recordings of lessons, semi-structured interviews, archival documents, and field notes. To ensure consistency in data-gathering techniques, particularly interviewing, the research team engaged in data collection training, which focused on conducting mock interviews using pilot questions, videotaping game play in a similar environment, and reviewing procedures for recording field notes.

Prior to the start of the investigation, teachers completed a questionnaire that elicited biographical information about their teaching, coaching, and personal sporting experiences. Teachers selected the content for their unit of instruction. Two semistructured interviews (before and after teaching), videotaped observations of three lessons, and corresponding field notes served as the primary data sources for this study.

Interview data and field notes were transcribed and uploaded into Atlas. ti, a qualitative-analysis software program, which allowed multiple researchers to code the data and to develop initial concepts. Peer-debriefing sessions permitted researchers to share and agree on a common set of coding protocol. Multiple data sources served to establish credibility through triangulation of evidence (Yin, 1994). Member checks were used to establish trustworthiness, which involved the teachers reviewing and verifying their interview transcripts. In addition, the research team engaged in regular peer-debriefing sessions to discuss issues of potential researcher bias.

Analysis of the sport- and games-teaching elements was done in a deductive fashion by reviewing field notes and video tapes. Both data sources helped researchers determine which elements of the sport and games models each teacher implemented. The field note format included a preapproved list of elements for the TG and SE models, which allowed researchers to compare and contrast the formal intentions of the models with the teachers' interpretations.

Jim's Findings

Jim graduated from KSU in December 2001 and, after a year and a half of substitute teaching, was hired at Harvard Elementary. During this study, he was in his fifth year at Harvard Elementary teaching physical education to fourth and fifth graders (approximately aged 9 to 11). Classes had approximately 20 to 25 students and met once every three days; thus once or twice per week for 35 minutes per class. In addition, Jim coached American football for five years and basketball for four years, and was a varsity-level player in high school.

Jim's physical-education curriculum primarily included invasion games, such as basketball, lacrosse, and flag football. For this study, he used a thematic approach, which included ultimate Frisbee, ultimate football, and soccer. Jim implemented both the TG and SE models during his teaching of this unit. As seen in table 3.1, he consistently demonstrated all of the primary TG elements, starting with a small-sided game, following with a question segment and practice, and then ending with a second game to allow the students to apply what they had learned. He frequently stopped play to highlight specific situations or to emphasize a problem, and posed questions to guide students to the solutions. To promote the transfer of tactics from one game to another, Jim often referenced similar situations in different invasion games. At various points throughout the lesson, Jim had the students switch from Frisbees to footballs or from footballs to soccer balls to highlight the similarities among invasion games and to provide opportunities for students to practice game-specific skills.

As for SE, Jim assisted students by assigning teams and held formal competitions (league and tournament play). Students selected roles, such as captain, equipment manager, athletic trainer, and statistician. "Some jobs [were] more predominant than others . . . in general, some jobs create leadership for different students throughout that particular unit at different times and just kind of create a little bit more ownership for each kid" (Jim's follow-up interview). In addition to providing leadership opportunities for students, assigning roles helped Jim manage students, space, and equipment, and allowed the class to run very efficiently.

Jim integrated some rituals, such as shaking hands after game play, and was a stickler about being a good sport. He chose not to integrate festivities, such as award ceremonies, at the end of a unit or season, stating that he did not want to emphasize winning or star players. "If I do something separate to show off that team or celebrate that team, half the time it turns into gloating for this age group, so I struggle to determine how to achieve recognition of that team without going to the extent that these are the best athletes, because they take it a step too far" (Jim's follow-up interview). Jim did not use longer seasons, but he did teach thematically and scheduled multiple types of invasion games units, one after another. Jim used record keeping, consistently requiring the student statistician to report game scores during closure of each lesson.

The setting at Harvard Elementary was very similar to the contexts modeled in GP. Similar to the invasion game segment of GP II, Jim used

Table 3.1   Elements of Tactical Games and Sport Education Demonstrated by the Teachers

Tactical games (TG)	Jim	Carol	John	Lisa
Game-practice-game approach	√	√	√	√
Question-answer session	√	√	√	√
Used on- and off-ball solutions	√	√	√	√
Applied solutions in game	√	√	√	√-
Used small-sided games	√	√	√	√
Highlighted problem	√	√	√	√-
Aligned with game conditions	√	√	√	√-
Transferred tactics	√	√	√	√
Sport education (SE)	**Jim**	**Carol**	**John**	**Lisa**
Longer season	0	0	√-	√
Team affiliation	√	√	√	√
Roles and responsibilities	√-	√	√	√
Formal competition	√	√	√	√
Culminating event	0	√	√	√
Festivities and rituals	√-	√	√	√
Small-sided games	√	√	√	√
Record keeping	√	√	√	√

√ = fully implemented; √- = partially implemented; 0 = not implemented.

a thematic approach to emphasize the transfer of tactics from one game to the next. A number of routines were nearly identical to those modeled in GP courses. For example, Jim provided verbal instructions and then dismissed students to transition to their assigned courts to begin play. As in Game II, SE roles were used largely to manage the class, with no formal accountability for performance of the roles.

Jim attributed his teaching approach to the experiences he had at KSU. "I attended Kent State and graduated [in] 2001. . . obviously, their

"There was a lot of guidance, from not only the professors [at KSU], but from quality teachers in the field as far as field experience and student-teacher placements. So, I got a really good sense of how to teach tactically within the game within those circumstances, and that kind of carried over to here" (Jim's initial interview).

program is very strong, and when I went through, there was a lot of teaching experience. There was a lot of guidance, from not only the professors there, but from quality teachers in the field as far as field experience and student-teacher placements. So, I got a really good sense of how to teach tactically within the game within those circumstances, and that kind of carried over to here" (Jim's initial interview). Jim also noted the influence of his cooperating teacher: "[For] my secondary student-teaching experience, I had Ms. Robertson at Winsburg High School, and that was a very positive experience for me. I really enjoyed that and she basically taught me. . . she is very knowledgeable about the game. . . and I can remember teaching that unit and having her constantly criticize and correct my teaching because she used her expertise to teach that game within her high-school setting" (Jim's initial interview).

Jim also attributed his use of the skill-based approach to some of his other playing and coaching experiences. He reported that he sometimes used a skill-based approach, depending on the sport and skill level of the students, but overall considered KSU to have a "strong influence" on his teaching. Jim stated that his own K-12 experiences were similar to the KSU approach in middle school, but were very different in elementary and secondary school: "My middle-school experience is probably pretty close to the way that I teach now. . . in certain aspects of it. My elementary and secondary experiences were pretty weak. . . my secondary experience was pretty nonexistent. . . it was more of a babysitting kind of thing" (Jim's initial interview).

Carol's Findings

Carol graduated from KSU in 2004 and had taught for one and a half years at Spring Valley Middle School when she participated in this study. The seventh and eighth grade students (approximately aged 12 to 14) were scheduled for physical education one semester per academic year and met daily for 45 minutes. Carol also coached eighth grade volleyball and was head coach of the girls' varsity basketball team at the high school. She played varsity basketball in high school and college.

Carol's physical-education curriculum included a variety of activities, with about 60 percent focusing on badminton, volleyball, team handball, basketball, softball, and target games. She and her teaching partner taught fitness on Tuesdays and Thursdays and offered games and other activities, such as dance and team building on the other three days. Carol implemented TG and SE models while teaching floor hockey, the unit she chose for this study. She consistently applied all of the elements of the TG model and all but the longer seasons of the SE model. Carol stated that units ran two to three weeks and that she and her teaching partner chose to include a variety of activities throughout the semester. "We don't want to do three net games, back to back to back. . . we try to change it up" (Carol's initial interview). To address the middle-school students' desire to experience a variety of content, Carol and her teaching partner felt it was important to offer a variety of sport and fitness activities.

The setting at Spring Valley Middle School was very similar to the context modeled in GP at KSU. Carol used small-sided, conditioned games during the game-practice-game format and gathered students for questions and a demonstration after the first game. She and her teaching partner set up the teams, but then allowed the students to choose team names, colors, and mascots, as well as to select roles. She used fair play points to reward students who did an exceptional job of performing assigned tasks. Carol also frequently called the coaches (or statisticians) in to explain a task, and then monitored them closely to be sure students completed the task according to her instructions. She also assigned homework according to a particular role. For example, she had the coaches look up a play on the Internet for the next lesson. They typically ended each unit with an awards ceremony, in which she and her teaching partner awarded certificates to the winning teams and "sometimes provided cookies and fruit drinks" (field notes).

Although all of the elements of TG were apparent, Carol's questioning mostly required students to recall information. She then followed with an explanation of the problem and solution, and often needed to adjust game conditions to ensure students did what was needed to perform the solution to the tactical problem. During games and practice segments, Carol monitored students closely, extending and refining tasks (Rink, 2005) as she moved from court to court. She constantly provided feedback and praise throughout each lesson and overall, sustained a well-organized, positive atmosphere.

When asked about experiences that have influenced her teaching, Carol identified the KSU program: "Obviously, Kent State. . . I wouldn't have taught this way; I would have taught like a typical coach. I would have set up a bunch of practice tasks and then let them play. Through Kent State, I learned how to teach through the game" (Carol's initial interview). Her experience at KSU was very different from her "roll-out-the-ball" K-12 experience. Carol also indicated that she often referred to "the books" (Griffin, Mitchell, & Oslin, 1997; Mitchell, Oslin, & Griffin,

2003): "I have my own style. Every teacher has their own style, but the foundation of my lesson. . . and how I teach. . . and how the students learn. . . is from the book" (Carol's initial interview). Carol also identified her teaching partner as being supportive. Although he was from another university and was not familiar with TG or SE, he was "open to learning about these models."

John's Findings

John graduated from KSU in 2000 with majors in health and physical education. Before the study, he had taught at Ridgewood Intermediate School for eight and a half years and had coached baseball, basketball, and football. John teaches 45-minute classes of third, fourth, and fifth graders (approximately aged 9 to 11) with about 20 to 25 students, on a three-day rotation (meeting once or twice per week).

Games made up 70 percent of John's physical-education curriculum. In his first few years, he used games only about 50 percent of the time, but found that by "adding more [games] as I went along, doing more team type activities, my [physical-education] classes were running a lot smoother. When I gave the roles and responsibilities out to the kids while being in the team. . . it actually made for a better physical-education class overall because they knew how to interact with one another, [as] opposed to doing things on their own" (John's initial interview). For this study, John chose to teach a unit of speedball to a class of fifth graders, a game he had taught only once before.

John liked the TG model because "it emphasizes the little things that take place in a game, and when you come back to a whole game, you're actually building [developing] a student. . . for example, attacking the basket or playing defense, when they come back to the whole game, it actually makes them a better all-around player" (John's initial interview).

As seen in table 3.1, John implemented all of the primary elements of TG and SE. Following warm-ups, John explained the conditions of the first game, questioned and demonstrated the practice, then concluded with a game. During game play and practice, John carefully monitored play. If he did not see what he wanted, he adjusted game conditions or practice tasks to match the various levels of his students and achieve the goals of the lesson. John stated that he liked the TG model because "it emphasizes the little things that take place in a game, and when you come back to a whole game, you're actually building [developing] a student. . . for example, attacking the basket or playing defense, when they come back to the whole game, it actually makes them a better all-around player" (John's initial interview).

John enthusiastically embraced SE. He stated that it helped keep things running smoothly, and felt that it was important that students were "part of the team," and that "they know the role and what they need to do" (John's initial interview). He also stated that being on teams and having roles and responsibilities allowed the students to "interact with a team and [learn] how to become socially responsible" (John's initial interview).

John identified the GP courses as having a strong influence on his teaching: "College had a lot to do with that. . . . as far as how I teach it, I teach it tactically. We're kind of instilled at Kent State. There are other ways of doing it, but I believe that the best way of teaching is tactically because you're breaking it down to the simplest form for every single student" (John's initial interview). John also credited his student-teaching experience with influencing his teaching, stating that while the cooperating teacher (CT) generally used large-sided games, she allowed him to use TG and SE. The CT's approach was more similar to the way John reported being taught during his own K-12 experience. "There were times when the ball was rolled out and we would play. There were a lot of lines" (John's initial interview).

Lisa's Findings

Following graduation in 2004, Lisa taught for two years at a private girl's school before taking a job at Winsburg High School. She was at the end of her second year at Winsburg during this study. Her teaching assignment included physical education for grades 9 through 12 (students aged 14 to 18). Students were required to take one semester of physical education, which most did during ninth grade. Students in 10th through 12th grade could choose to take a variety of fitness, dance, and games courses through an elective physical-education program. Lisa also coached varsity soccer and played varsity soccer in high school and college.

For this study, Lisa chose to teach lacrosse to students in a required physical-education course. She had taught lacrosse at her previous school, but had not taught it at the high school. The class met five days per week, 90 minutes per day, throughout the semester. Lisa taught games on Monday, Wednesday, and Friday and fitness on Tuesday and Thursday. She implemented both TG and SE models and, as shown in table 3.1, demonstrated all elements of each model.

Lisa started each lesson with a conditioned game; however, the game often broke down because the students were not able to adequately cradle or send and receive with the lacrosse sticks. Recognizing this, she implemented a series of drills to help students work on their stick-handling skills. She had learned these drills from a colleague who was also a lacrosse coach. When asked why she diverted from her lesson, Lisa said, "It was new to them. A lacrosse coach, whom I actually got a lot of information from, helped me out with teaching it; she said to do the shuttle drills and lines because they do that at varsity practices" (Lisa's follow-up interview).

It was apparent from student responses that they knew what to do and it was obvious from game-play observation that they knew where to move to provide support and to advance the ball up the field, but they struggled to keep possession. Because the students could not do what Lisa had planned and she needed to change the focus midlesson, a misalignment existed between the problem set in the first game and the practice and follow-up game. She did question students after the initial game, but these were often recall questions. Rather than telling students how to perform a skill, Lisa would ask them to show her what they did and, in this way, would guide students to solutions. Lisa referred to this as using the *discovery method;* for example, "Show me how to hold the stick when cradling the ball" (Lisa's lesson transcript). She would then pinpoint hand position and stick position relative to the body. Since most of the content focused on skill development, there was little emphasis on tactics. When opportunities arose, Lisa prompted students to get open, provide support, and to advance the ball toward the goal.

Lisa implemented all of the primary elements of SE. Students were placed in teams, with assigned courts, roles, and responsibilities. She was diligent about holding students accountable and assigned fair play points when students did what was required. Seasons were long and ran for four weeks, 90 minutes per day. In addition, invasion-game seasons often ran back to back, allowing for emphasis on the tactical similarities between games. The 90-minute classes and length of season afforded Lisa time to implement, multiple elements of SE, such as organizing a championship game and holding an awards ceremony.

The setting at Winsburg High School had many similarities to the GP contexts. The SE elements were presented in more depth than the GP elements. Lisa's teaching partner, who was also her cooperating teacher during student teaching, used a similar approach. As with GP methods, Lisa gathered coaches and provided instructions for the first game. She also set up a demonstration prior to gathering students for question-answer segments, which is very similar to the GP context. The overall organization of Lisa's class was also comparable to that used in GP: students entered and went to their assigned courts, the athletic trainer led the team through the warm-up, coaches were gathered and given instructions for the first game, and the game-practice-game format was utilized.

Lisa attributed her teaching approach to KSU and her recent experience in a D-License soccer clinic, which contained a game-sense approach: "I think GP was huge. I think that being in a class and being a student going through the class, you learned a lot more than if you were lectured. Actually, we were in teams during GP, we did GPAIs and other stuff that was extremely helpful." She also stated that her knowledge of soccer helped her with other games. "I used my knowledge of soccer and what I learned at Kent (sport education and tactical courses), so I just applied it to other games" (Lisa's initial interview). Lisa also referred to the influence of the content and methods courses at KSU on her teaching, saying that she found that "being able to go apply and teach it" was particularly helpful (Lisa's initial interview).

> **"I** think GP was huge. I think that being in a class and being a student going through the class, you learned a lot more than if you were lectured."

Cross-Case Analysis

Research on teacher socialization suggests that most teachers instruct based on the way they were taught in their own educational environments during grades K through 12 (Lawson, 1983a; 1983b; 1986). Constructing PETE programs that transform the traditional teacher-centered approach into the multiactivity-curricular model has challenged teacher educators for some time (McCaughtry, Sofo, Rovegno, & Curtner-Smith, 2004). The findings of the cross-case analysis of these teachers contradict these traditional notions. The cross-case comparison resulted in two primary assertions: teachers identified the PETE curriculum as significantly influencing how they taught sport and games, and they taught sport and games similarly to the way they were modeled in PETE curriculum.

PETE Program as a Significant Influence

All four teachers acknowledge the affect of the instructional approaches associated with the SE and TG models as valuable aspects of their university experience and the distinct difference from the way that they were taught as K-12 students. Teachers recognize the relevance of the various learning experiences within the PETE curriculum, which gave them multiple opportunities to learn the SE and TG approaches. All of the teachers identified the GP courses as influential in their process of learning to teach sport and games. For example, during her initial interview, Lisa commented that the PETE faculty at KSU "impacted everything. My physical-education experience was totally different from what I learned at Kent State" (Lisa's initial interview).

The authenticity of the games courses, particularly the instructional approaches that reflected a realistic physical-education environment, enabled the teaching students to see the models in action before taking on the role of instructor. As John stated, "As far as teaching it the tactical

The authenticity of the games courses, particularly the instructional approaches that reflected a realistic physical-education environment, enabled the teaching students to see the models in action before taking on the role of instructor.

way, [KSU professors] helped us through as far as teaching. . . it kind of clicked in my head that this is what they're trying to emphasize here [in GP]. . . actually putting us through it" (John's initial interview).

Other influential experiences included opportunities in which the teachers applied what they learned by teaching the models in school settings with the support of a mentor who were either experts on the models or were supportive of implementing approaches. These findings lend support for legitimate peripheral participation within a learning community and for the value of scaffolding the learning experiences with similar but different levels of sophistication and responsibility (Lave & Wenger, 1991).

Teaching Similarly to the Models From the KSU Program

Although the four versions of SE and TG portrayed by the teachers were very similar to each other, with a few exceptions, these models of practice also reflected similar representation from within the PETE curriculum. As illustrated by John's statement, all of the teachers explicitly identified the GP as an influential factor for their teaching.

"It was instilled from the very beginning in our first couple of courses— [GP I and GP II]—they were actually showing us and putting us through all this and they were actually teaching us how to do it. When we're actually going through it, we had [real] practice time to do it; we actually understood, as far as teaching it the tactical way" (John's initial interview).

Differences represent the teachers' interpretations of the models and reflect how they adjusted the models for their teaching context and for students' developmental levels. The two male teachers who had the most experience and who taught at the elementary level adapted the models to meet their students' affective, psychomotor, and cognitive demands. For instance, John stated, "It took me probably two or three years to get everything up and running. Whether it was tweaking my lesson a little bit as far as making it simpler for the elementary kid, as opposed to teaching tactically for eighth graders and high-school students. . . how am I going to incorporate and separate both teaching tactically with the sport and also incorporating the sport ed. model? That was kind of my main consideration when I started teaching each sport" (John's initial interview).

Jim also explained how he downplayed the culminating event to counter the younger children's tendency to demonstrate inappropriate elitist attitudes associated with winning championships:

"I love the tournament play aspect of [SE], but I go back and forth [about] if a celebration or festivity is necessary at this particular level. I think they internally have the celebration during the tournament play, but if I do something separate to show off that team or celebrate that team, half the time it turns into gloating for this age group. So, I struggle to determine how to achieve recognition of that team without going to the extent that these are the best athletes or best football team, because they take it a step too far" (Jim's follow-up interview).

The secondary teachers, both of whom had less experience, taught versions of the models that were nearly identical to SE and TG. Their interpretations related most closely to the way the sport units were scheduled in the curriculum. Both secondary teachers taught fitness lessons on alternate days amid the sport seasons. The secondary teachers also emphasized aspects of the model that highlighted their students' developmental capacities. For example, Lisa and Carol used duty teams to help run tournament events. "I found that with my classes, five [teams] is a good number; one team does refereeing, keeps score. . . if we're doing stats or something like that" (Lisa's follow-up interview). The secondary teachers often asked students to contribute assignments outside of class, such as a sport report, logo creation, or strategic play.

In summary, although each teacher made minor adaptations that reflected their teaching context, most of the features of the models aligned with how they were taught within the university curriculum. The pedagogical approaches of the SE and TG models within GP courses represented a consistent frame of reference for the teachers as they shaped their own curriculum. These findings reinforce calls for PETE programs to develop shared philosophical positions and to construct learning experiences that align with these positions (Locke, 1992; Randall, 2008; Siedentop, 2002).

Implications of Tactical Games and Sport Education

These teachers' interpretation of TG and SE approaches suggests that modeling of sport and games curriculum by faculty and mentors associated with the university program significantly influenced their practices. In addition, the modeling promoted a limited scope of how to structure and implement sport and games instruction across all grade levels, forcing instructors to figure out how the contextual demands of their teaching sites required them to make slight but unique adjustments. These factors suggest that future considerations for instruction within the PETE program and for professional development workshops should emphasize and model how grade level and curricular context may influence how to implement SE and TG.

Conclusion

The need to adapt and adjust to a variety of contextual demands high-lights the importance of reflection as a part of learning student-centered approaches to sport and games. Teachers in this study cited the value of reflection and the desire for more professional development. Because many teachers have limited access to formal professional development, we need to develop support networks or communities of practice. These communities could serve teachers by providing access to practical knowledge about how to modify the essential elements of these models to meet varying contextual demands. If teacher networks include video examples, modeling of best practices would likely be more powerful. Studying the notion of modeling best practice as a means of professional development suggests that teacher educators must represent sound pedagogical content knowledge in their own PETE programs if they hope to see change in school programs for grades K through 12.

Discussion Questions

1. What is the value of modeling pedagogical practices in PETE curriculum?
2. How does models-based instruction, particularly SE and TG, promote best practice?
3. What aspects of the KSU PETE program did the teaching candidates find most applicable to their real-world teaching experiences?
4. How is the role of communities of practice relative to promoting models-based instruction?
5. What are the implications of this study's findings to your PETE program and practices?

References

Bunker, D., & Thorpe, R. (1982). A model for the teaching of games in secondary schools. *Bulletin of Physical Education, 18*(1), 5-8.

Chouinard, A., Collier, C., & Oslin, J. (2008). Student sport experiences within models-based instruction. *Research Quarterly for Exercise and Sport, 79,* A-40.

Collier, C. (2009). Teacher learning within an inquiry model of PETE. In L. Housner, M. Metzler, P. Schemp, and T. Templin (Eds.), *Historic traditions and future directions of research on teaching and teacher education in physical education* (pp. 355-362). Pittsburgh: FITT.

Dewar, A.M., & Lawson, H.A. (1984). The subjective warrant and recruitment into physical education. *Quest, 36,* 15-25.

Doolittle, S.A., Placek, J.H., & Dodds, P. (1993). Persistence of beliefs about teaching during formal training of preservice teachers. *Journal of Teaching in Physical Education, 12,* 355-365.

Graber, K.C. (1995). The influence of teacher education programs on the beliefs of student teachers: General pedagogical knowledge, pedagogical content knowledge, and teacher education of course work. *Journal of Teaching in Physical Education, 14,* 157-178.

Griffin, L.L., Mitchell, S.A., & Oslin, J.L. (1997). *Teaching sport concepts and skills: A tactical games approach.* Champaign, IL. Human Kinetics.

Griffin, L.L., Oslin, J.L., & Mitchell, S.A. (1995). An analysis of two instructional approaches to teaching net games. *Research Quarterly for Exercise and Sport, 66*-supplement (1), A-64.

Lave, J., & Wenger, E. (1991). *Situated learning: Legitimate peripheral participation.* New York: Cambridge University Press.

Lawson, H.A. (1983a). Toward a model of teacher socialization in physical education: The subjective warrant, recruitment, and teacher education. *Journal of Teaching in Physical Education, 2,* 3-16.

Lawson, H. A. (1983b). Toward a model of teacher socialization in physical education: Entry into schools, teachers' role, orientations, and longevity in teaching (Part 2). *Journal of Teaching in Physical Education, 3 (1),* 3-11.

Lawson, H.A. (1986). Occupational socialization and the design of teacher education programs. *Journal of Teaching in Physical Education, 5*(2), 107-116.

Locke, L. (1992). Changing secondary school physical education. *Quest, 44,* 361-372.

Lunenberg, M., Korthagen, F., & Swennen, A. (2007). The teacher educator as a role model. *Teaching and Teacher Education, 23,* 586-601.

McCaughtry, N., Sofo, S., Rovegno, I., & Curtner-Smith, M. (2004). Learning to teach sport education: Misunderstandings, pedagogical difficulties, and resistance. *European Physical Education Review, 10,* 135-155.

Metzler M. (2006). *Instructional models for physical education* (2nd ed.). Champaign, IL: Human Kinetics.

Mitchell, S.A. (2005). Different paths up the same mountain: Global perspectives on TGfU. Keynote presentation at the third international TGfU conference, Hong Kong, China.

Mitchell, S.A., Griffin, L.L., & Oslin, J.L. (1994). Tactical awareness as developmentally appropriate for the teaching of games in elementary and secondary physical education. *The Physical Educator, 51(1),* 21-28.

Mitchell, S.A., & Oslin, J.L. (1999). An investigation of tactical understanding in net games. *European Journal of Physical Education, 4,* 162-172.

Mitchell, S., & Oslin, J. (2007). Ecological task analysis in games teaching: The tactical games model. In W. Davis and G. Broadhead (Eds.), *An ecological approach to human movement: Linking theory, research and practice* (pp. 161-178). Champaign, IL: Human Kinetics.

Mitchell, S.A., Oslin, J.L., & Griffin, L.L. (2003). *Sport foundations for elementary physical education: A tactical games approach.* Champaign, IL: Human Kinetics.

Oslin, J., Collier C., & Mitchell S. (2001). Living the curriculum. *Journal of Physical Education, Recreation and Dance, 72,* 47-51.

Randall, L. (2008). Implementing TGfU in the field. *Physical and Health Education Journal, 72,* 16-20.

Rink, J.E. (2005). *Teaching physical education for learning* (5th ed.). New York: McGraw-Hill.

Siedentop, D. (2002). Content knowledge for physical education. *Journal of Teaching in Physical Education, 21,* 368-377.

Yin, R. (1994). *Case study research: Design and methods* (2nd ed.). Thousand Oaks, CA: Sage Publishing.

Theory: Understanding, Learning, and Complexity Thinking

4

Teaching Games for an Understanding of What? TGfU's Role in the Development of Physical Literacy

James Mandigo, PhD • John Corlett, PhD

> **"I**f a round ball and enthusiastic feet on a patch of bare land can evolve into the spectacle of the World Cup, then surely, we believe, that same round ball and those same enthusiastic feet on that same patch of bare land can become the spectacle of active, healthy nations."
>
> — *Kofi Annan (former Secretary-General of the United Nations)*

In 2005, the United Nations challenged the global community through the International Year of Sport and Physical Education (IYSPE) to consider ways in which sport and physical education could serve as a catalyst for addressing some of the world's most pressing issues, such as peace, sustainable development, education for all, equality for girls and women, and the prevention of disease. By the end of 2005, at the culminating conference for IYSPE, the international community ratified the Magglingen Call to Action, which stated the following:

"We resolve to use sport, with due attention to cultural and traditional dimensions, to promote education, health, development and peace. In doing so, we respect the principles of human rights—especially youth and child rights—human diversity, gender equity, social inclusion and environmental sustainability."

In essence, the global community was challenging sport and physical education to consider ways in which we can make a difference in the

Sport and physical education are ideal tools to also teach life skills such as respect, inclusion, cooperation, and teamwork, and metacognitive skills, such as problem solving, critical thinking, and goal setting. These skills will result not only in better movers within sport and PE, but also in a healthier and more successful society.

lives of all people. This international call to action recognized that, through sport and physical education, individuals can develop the skills, knowledge, and attitudes needed to make healthy choices for themselves in consideration of others and their environment.

The traditional objectives of developing fundamental movement and sport skills still exist. However, there is an ever-pressing need to ensure that skills across a number of activities are developed in order to help children and youths develop a repertoire of skills in order to become physically literate. Simply teaching them physical skills is not enough. Children and youths also need to be able to move in a way that is respectful of others and that fosters the development of important cognitive skills. As a result, sport and physical education are ideal tools to also teach life skills such as respect, inclusion, cooperation, and teamwork, and metacognitive skills, such as problem solving, critical thinking, and goal setting. These skills will result not only in better movers within sport and PE, but also in a healthier and more successful society.

The purpose of this chapter is to present a case for the role that TGfU can play in helping to fulfill the mandate set out by the international community. Specifically, we will argue that when games are taught using TGfU, a learner-centered approach, children and youths will potentially develop the physical-literacy skills necessary to make healthy choices to benefit both themselves and others around them and in their community. Based on the extant literature, the evidence presented in this chapter suggests that the development of physical literacy through a TGfU approach to games can not only benefit the development of technical and tactical skills within and among games, but can also foster the development of life skills (interpersonal, communication, critical-thinking, and problem-solving skills) outside of the game; this area is relatively unexplored in the TGfU literature but is at the root of the original curriculum model first presented by Bunker and Thorpe (1986).

What is Physical Literacy?

Individuals who are physically literate enjoy moving with competence across a wide variety of physical activities. They possess the motivation and abilities to understand, communicate, apply knowledge, and critically analyze movement in ways that confidently, competently, and creatively demonstrate versatility of movement. These abilities enable individuals to make healthy, active choices that are respectful of themselves, others, and the environment throughout their lives (Mandigo, Lodewyk, Francis, & Lopez, 2009). Margaret Whitehead (2007) has been credited as one of the leading experts in physical literacy. She defines a physically literate person as one who has "the motivation, confidence, physical competence, understanding, and knowledge to maintain physical activity at an individually appropriate level, throughout life."

Her definition of physical literacy was supported in a recent international study by Hayden-Davies (2008) who asked 12 experts from around the world, "What is physical literacy?" The core principle of physical literacy that emerges was "the ability to capitalize on the interaction between physical competence and affective characteristics" (p. 19). This ability is characterized by the application of this interaction across a wide variety of situations which embrace both lifelong participation and the development of life skills. Hayden-Davies (2008) goes on to suggest that these characteristics are "developed through an interaction and interplay between an individual, environments, and others," and that "any expression of physical literacy will be linked to the individual's unique capacities and the individual's culture" (p. 19). Penney and Chandler (2000) have also recognized that competent movers do not operate in isolation from their social environment. Hence, individuals who are physically literate have the knowledge, skills, and attitudes to lead healthy lifestyles, and also to assist others in acquiring these skills.

As a result of this evidence, Hayden-Davies (2008) concludes that Whitehead's (2007) definition of physical literacy is likely the one that resonates best with educators due to the interplay between the individual, their peers, and their community. It recognizes not only the importance of developing the skills, knowledge, and attitudes to lead healthy, active lives, but also the importance of the processes that students go through in the development of these skills.

This applied and holistic notion of physical literacy is consistent with current global viewpoints of literacy. According to the United Nations Educational, Scientific, and Cultural Organization (UNESCO; 2003), literacy is more than just reading and writing. It is about communication in society, social practices, and relationships about knowledge, language, and culture. Literacy can be viewed as falling somewhere on a continuum that ranges from a set of skills to a basis for rational and ethical action (Bailey, Hunsberger, & Hayden, 1998). Literacy, therefore, is more than just the acquisition of knowledge and the understanding of content. It includes both a personal and social responsibility to use the attained knowledge in ethical and just ways. As a result, being literate includes using critical

Margaret Whitehead (2007) defines a physically literate person as one who has "the motivation, confidence, physical competence, understanding, and knowledge to maintain physical activity at an individually appropriate level, throughout life."

and creative thinking skills and processes, conveying information through various forms of communication, and applying knowledge and skills to make connections within and among various contexts.

Based upon the holistic nature of physical literacy, Mandigo and Holt (2004) introduced the notion of games literacy to indicate the merits and skills that students will acquire from experiencing high quality games instruction. They proposed that the aim of teaching games is to produce players who are games literate. Students are games literate if they (a) have knowledge and understanding that enables them to anticipate patterns of play, (b) possess technical and tactical skills to deploy appropriate and imaginative responses, and (c) can experience positive motivational states while helping facilitate motivation among others involved in the game. Rather than being literate in a single game, children with games literacy will be able to engage with poise, confidence, enthusiasm, and responsibility in a wide range of games. Mandigo and Holt (2004) suggested that the most effective way to facilitate the development of physical literacy is through TGfU.

The Role of TGfU to Foster Physical Literacy Within Games

Can games help foster this holistic notion of physical literacy? Given the large amount of time (typically over 50 percent) devoted to games within physical-education programs around the world (Mandigo, Spence, Thompson, Melnychuk, Schwartz, Marshall, & Causgrove Dunn, 2004; Hardman & Marshall, 2000), games are uniquely positioned to have a significant effect on the development of physical literacy. However, the key to games being the vehicle for such changes lies in the pedagogy, or the way, in which they are delivered.

In Bunker and Thorpe's (1986) seminal chapter on the TGfU curriculum model, they made the following observations about highly structured games lessons in which traditional authoritarian approaches were used:

- A large percentage of children achieved little success due to the emphasis on performance, or "doing."

Salvadoran teachers attending a TGfU workshop at Pedagogica University use their creativity to modify a target game.

- The majority of school leaders knew very little about games.
- Supposedly skillful players in fact possessed inflexible techniques and poor ability to make decisions.
- Performers were dependent on teachers and coaches.
- The approach failed to develop "thinking" spectators and "knowing" administrators at a time when games (and sport) were an important form of entertainment in the leisure industry.

In response to these concerns, the TGfU curriculum model emerged, which provided an alternative approach, steeped in humanistic approaches to physical education. Humanistic approaches to games involve "a concern for man above all else behaviourally and [a] concern for man's social and emotional well-being" (Hellison, 1973, p. 3). The goals of a games program which adopts a humanistic approach include the development of self-esteem, self-actualization, self-understanding, and positive interpersonal relations with others. In turn, these goals help students make their own body-world connection, provide a sense of community, and facilitate a playful spirit (Jewett & Bain, 1985). The original TGfU model with the learner in the center encouraged the development of physical literacy through games designed to enhance students' performance, cognitive responses (decision-making processes), and skill development across a wide variety of activities in a highly motivational setting (Oslin & Mitchell, 2006). The following section supports the effect that a humanistic approach such as TGfU can have on the development of games literacy as defined by Mandigo and Holt (2004).

The goals of a games program which adopts a humanistic approach include the development of self-esteem, self-actualization, self-understanding, and positive interpersonal relations with others. In turn, these goals help students to make their own body-world connection, provide a sense of community, and facilitate a playful spirit (Jewett & Bain 1985).

Knowledge and Understanding

One of the central characteristics of physical literacy is the development of knowledge and understanding that enables individuals to read the game and to apply their knowledge across a wide variety of games (Mandigo & Holt, 2004). TGfU provides an ideal mechanism for developing knowledge and understanding in ways that are consistent with physical literacy. Kirk and MacPhail (2002) argue that TGfU enables the learner to be actively engaged within the learning environment, resulting in an increased ability to make sense of new knowledge, which in turn fosters the development of intelligent game players (Kirk, 1983). Research has provided consistent evidence to support the effect of TGfU approaches on enhancing game knowledge and understanding in ways that foster the development of physical literacy.

For example, TGfU has been linked to the development of enhanced tactical knowledge. Turner and Martinek (1999) reported that students in a TGfU group scored higher on measures of declarative and procedural knowledge in field hockey than a control group that was taught with a more technique-oriented approach. Similarly, Allison and Thorpe (1997) reported that students who were taught invasion games with a TGfU approach showed improvements in knowledge and understanding of when to pass, shoot, or dribble, and how to make effective decisions to provide support off the ball. Grade six students in two separate studies reported higher levels of tactical knowledge in invasion (Mitchell, Griffin, & Oslin, 1995) and net/wall games (Griffin, Oslin, & Mitchell, 1995). Combined, this research supports the positive influence that TGfU can have on the development of tactical knowledge and understanding across many different types of games.

Given the active engagement of the learner, TGfU is an ideal vehicle to help foster the development of higher-order cognitive processes

(Oslin & Mitchell, 2006). McBride and Xiang (2004) have suggested that TGfU supports thoughtful decision making, which in turn facilitates metacognitive processes, such as decision making, critical thinking, and problem solving. When a TGfU approach is used, the learner develops an appreciation for a game, which serves as a foundation for

> **G**iven the active engagement of the learner, TGfU is an ideal vehicle to help foster the development of higher-order cognitive processes (Oslin & Mitchell, 2006).

making good decisions (Oslin & Mitchell, 2006). For example, playing a simple game of keep away, in which the player in possession of the ball cannot move and the team must make five successful passes in a row to score a point, creates a scenario that forces learners to make good decisions about how to best maintain possession to score a point. Players soon realize that if they do not get into an open position to support their teammate with the ball, the success of their team to score points is drastically undermined. Hence, the structure of the game forces players to problem solve (most effectively together) around ways in which they can best maintain possession of the ball as a team to score points (short passes, communication, move into open space, and so on).

The development of knowledge and understanding from one game also has the potential to be transferred to a variety of games. Due to the emphasis on sampling commonly used as a pedagogical principle within TGfU, tactical solutions learned in one sport may be transferred to solve tactical problems in another sport within the same games category. In a study conducted by Mitchell and Oslin (1999), 21 students in grade 9 were assessed on their decision-making abilities following five badminton lessons and five pickleball lessons that used a TGfU approach. The results demonstrated both that the students' decision-making abilities improved after the five initial TGfU badminton lessons, and that their tactical decision-making skills in a new net/wall game of pickleball were maintained, thus demonstrating that students were able to transfer their decision-making skills from one net/wall game to another.

As a pedagogical vehicle to deliver game programs, the evidence presented in this section supports the role that a TGfU approach to games can have in developing skills needed to enhance learners' knowledge and understanding. This approach has the potential to help foster not only

> **D**ue to the emphasis on sampling commonly used as a pedagogical principle within TGfU, tactical solutions learned in one sport may be transferred to solve tactical problems in another sport within the same games category.

the development of better game players across a number of different types of games, but also the knowledge and understanding of good decision-making and problem-solving skills. These skills in turn have the potential to be transferred outside of the games environment. This ability to apply knowledge and understanding across a number of different domains (both within and outside the games environment) is an indicator of the power of TGfU to foster the development of physical literacy.

Technical and Tactical Skills

The ability to move with poise and competence across a wide variety of activities is another key characteristic of physical literacy. A literate games player can perform a broad range of skills in ways that are both technically and tactically effective. For example, knowing and being able to perform the technical aspects of a drop shot in badminton are not enough. Physically literate players will know that their opponents first have to be in a position that creates space at the front of the court before they can perform a drop shot. A TGfU approach has demonstrated development of both technical and tactical skills during game performance. Studies have shown that this approach effectively enhances the development of not only technical skills (MacPhail, Kirk, & Griffin, 2008), but also overall game performance and ability.

Salvadoran teachers attending a TGfU session at a national congress at the National University participate in a target game called 21.

For example, Mitchell and Oslin (1999) reported significant improvements in overall net/wall performance for a group of ninth grade students who were taught using a TGfU approach, as compared to traditional behaviorist approaches to games. Turner and Martinek (1999) also reported that sixth and seventh grade students who were taught field hockey using a TGfU approach scored significantly higher on overall ratings of game ability than those taught using a traditional method. Keh and Yu (2007) reported higher levels of skill and overall game performance after 10 lessons of

Korfball instruction that adopted a TGfU approach. Similarly, French, Werner, Taylor, Hussey, and Jones (1996) reported that students who were taught badminton using either a skills approach or a tactical approach performed better on game-play measures (forceful shots, cooperative shots, game decisions, and serve decisions) than students taught using a combination of both approaches.

By learning skills through games as opposed to strictly for games, learners gain a deeper understanding of how to apply their skills within game situations. This ability to communicate and apply knowledge across a number of different situations is one of the central tenets of physical literacy. Much like Bunker and Thorpe's (1986) original concerns about students lacking the understanding of how to apply their skills within the game, despite having proficient technical skills outside of the game, the ability to apply knowledge within and across specific situations is central to physical literacy. The evidence would seem to suggest that when learners develop technical and tactical skills through a TGfU environment, they are much better prepared to apply their knowledge across a wide range of activities.

Salvadoran teachers attending a TGfU session at a national congress at the National University use available equipment to participate in a target game that fosters critical thinking and problem solving skills.

Individuals who are physically literate are motivated to be active and are also cognizant of their role in helping others around them enjoy movement.

Positive Motivational States for Self and Others

A third major tenet of physical literacy is the focus on the joy of movement. Individuals who are physically literate are motivated to be active and are also cognizant of their role in helping others around them enjoy movement. As a learner-centered humanistic approach to teaching games, TGfU often results in a positive motivational state for the learner. Turner (1996) reported antidotes from sixth and seventh grade students who said they enjoyed the TGfU approach more than traditional approaches to learning games. Strean and Holt (2000) have also reported that participants in their study preferred to learn games by playing games rather than by using drills that focused on developing technical skills. As a result, they suggested that TGfU is an effective approach to increasing fun in sport. Mitchell et al. (1995) also suggested that, although sixth grade students in their study reported higher levels of enjoyment when taught using a TGfU approach as opposed to a technical approach, the difference was not significant.

In some cases, motivation in a TGfU environment is affected by dispositional characteristics of the learner. Allison and Thorpe (1997) have suggested that game ability may influence student motivation. In their study, students with low technical abilities in invasion games reported more positive enjoyment and competence scores than higher-ability students. Similarly, Light (2002, 2003) reported that preservice teachers who initially had negative attitudes toward PE reported more enjoyment using a TGfU approach because they believed it was more inclusive and supportive, and focused less on developing technical skills.

TGfU can empower individuals to create positive environments for others as well. Hastie and Curtner-Smith (2006) reported that students were more enthusiastic in a class that combined TGfU with sport education, and as a result, demonstrated teamwork, cooperation, play with friends, inclusion, fair play, and creativity while deemphasizing the importance of winning. Mandigo, Holt, Anderson, and Sheppard (2008) have also reported that elementary students who took part in a TGfU lesson not only reported high levels of enjoyment, but also commented through open-ended questions that because they had so much fun, they wanted other children to also take part in the activities so they could have fun as well. Butler (2005) and Hastie and Curtner-Smith (2006) have also advocated for the use of TGfU to instill aspects of sport citizenship, such as democracy, negotiation, inclusion, and creativity. Combined, this evidence supports the intrinsic values that a humanistic approach to games, such as TGfU, can instill. The enjoyment of movement that is fostered through TGfU environments enable learners to understand and appreciate the benefits of being active through games. Evidence also exists to support the idea that adopting a TGfU approach can create a positive games environment that fosters other critical social skills, such as social responsibility, fair play, and democracy. These types of positive and supportive environments are central for developing movers who are respectful of themselves, others, and the environment; a central characteristic of physical literacy.

The preceding results and those from summaries conducted by others (Holt, Strean, & Benogoechea, 2002; Oslin & Mitchell, 2006) consistently suggest that when using TGfU as a model to deliver game programs, learners demonstrate improvements that are consistent with being physically literate. Specifically, the evidence presented suggests that when utilizing a TGfU approach, individuals commonly report enhanced knowledge and understanding, technical and tactical skills, and positive motivational states for themselves and others within the games environment. These characteristics of games literacy in turn serve as a foundation for the development of physical literacy, which fosters motivation, competence, and versatility of movement.

The Potential of TGfU to Foster Understanding Through Games

The previous research demonstrates the benefits of TGfU to foster the development of physical literacy within the game environment. Specifically, the evidence suggests that applying the TGfU model, in which learning takes place through games, results in the development of games literacy. But what about outside of the games environment? Can TGfU help foster the development of important skills that can be used by learners when they are not playing games? Can the development of physical literacy through games help children and youth make healthy choices related to important personal and social issues, such as being more active, making good nutritional choices, solving conflict peacefully, or fostering respect for one's self and others in order to prevent the spread of diseases such as AIDS/HIV? Whatever the major public health issue, the IYSPE raises awareness around the world of the potential that games have to create healthy nations when delivered in pedagogically sound ways.

The IYSPE raises awareness around the world of the potential that games have to create healthy nations when delivered in pedagogically sound ways.

As indicated previously, literacy is not simply the acquisition of knowledge.

Rather, it includes the application of knowledge and skills in order to make connections both within and among various contexts. Previous researchers have suggested that children and youths can learn important life skills through appropriately structured sport and games, which can lead to prosocial behaviors, such as conflict resolution, social inclusion, and character building (Kidd & Donnelly, 2007). Life skills have been defined as "a large group of psycho-social and interpersonal skills which can help people make informed decisions, *communicate* effectively, and develop coping and self-management skills that may help them lead a healthy and productive life. Life skills may be directed toward personal actions and actions toward others, as well as actions to change the surrounding environment to make it conducive to health" (UNICEF, nd). Life skills are often grouped into three categories: (1) communication and interpersonal skills, such as negotiation and refusal skills, empathy, cooperation, teamwork, and advocacy; (2) decision-making and critical-thinking skills; and (3) coping and self-management skills, such as those that increase internal locus of control, and help manage feelings and stress.

However, simply telling children to use their skills in their daily lives is not enough to ensure that they will do so. Learning by doing and experiencing is one of the most effective methods. As a result, games provide an ideal and safe setting not only to foster an understanding of the importance of key life skills, but also to provide learners with an opportunity to actively engage in activities that help them practice and gain life skills. When properly instructed, these life skills can be transferred both within and outside of the games environment, which in turn benefits the individual and the community as a whole. Given the humanistic pedagogy that the learner-centered TGfU model affords, such environments are much more conducive to fostering healthy development through games and to achieving requisite life skills that many claim sport and games can help build. Through carefully constructed and administered games environments, learners receive opportunities to develop life skills which form the backbone of healthy behaviors.

> **G**ames provide an ideal and safe setting not only to foster an understanding of the importance of key life skills, but also to provide learners with an opportunity to actively engage in activities that help them practice and gain life skills.

For example, by utilizing principles that are intertwined with the process of delivering a TGfU lesson (democracy, negotiation, inclusion, and creativity), learners can also develop skills related to problem solving, critical thinking, communication, and teamwork (Butler, 2005). This transfer of knowledge, skills, and attitudes learned through games to everyday life represents the true demonstration of literacy. Although the evidence to date is scarce, awareness is increasing of the potential of games for developing life skills when taught in humanistic practices, such as TGfU.

Since the United Nation's IYSPE in 2005, the global community has steadily identified more and more ways in which sports and games can be used to address major social issues, such as providing primary education, ensuring equality for women, preventing diseases, and resolving conflict peacefully. A report by the Sport for Development and Peace International Working Group (2007) identified more than 30 programs around the world that foster healthy development through various sports and games. Although not all of these programs specifically utilize TGfU as their pedagogical approach to games, the following examples illustrate an increasingly common use of games to address major social issues:

- In Bam, Iran, after a devastating earthquake that killed approximately 30,000 people and left 75,000 more homeless, the Swiss Academy for Development used games and sport to support the psycho-social rehabilitation of children and youth, helping them channel frustration and fear, lay the foundation for peaceful and social integration and interaction, and provide leisure activities to facilitate the return to normal existence. For more information, visit the Web site (www.sportanddev.org/newsnviews/search.cfm?uNewsID=37).

Salvadoran teachers attending a TGfU workshop at Pedagogica University participate in a modified net/wall game, Sepak Takraw.

• In Zambia, citizens have the fourth lowest life expectancy in the world (38 years) and children and youth are particularly at risk, due to a high prevalence of HIV, acute food shortages, and poverty. The Sport in Action program is using games to teach critical health skills. For more information, visit the Web site (www.sportinaction.org.zm). Through games, children and youth in rural and urban settings are developing prevention strategies that demonstrate the realities, risks, and challenges of preventing AIDS/HIV. The program also uses traditional games from Zambia which carry important cultural messages, stressing the importance of education and the value of cooperation.

• In the refugee camps surrounding Afghanistan, groups such as Right to Play are implementing their SportWorks program as a way to use games and sports to support the inclusion and equality of girls and women. For more information, visit the Web site (www.righttoplay.com).

• In Israel and the West Bank, PeacePlayers International have used basketball as a tool to bring together Palestinian, Arab-Israeli, and Jewish-Israeli boys and girls in order to help impart values for peaceful coexistence, sportsmanship, and leadership. For more information, visit the Web site (www.peaceplayersintl.org). The program also attempts to demonstrate what children and youth have in common and, in turn, raise awareness of cultural similarities as opposed to cultural differences.

> *"[P*hysical education] is more than throwing a ball, playing soccer. It goes beyond that. It involves a series of elements such as mental health, physical health, the development of self-esteem. . . and being able to practice other aspects, such as values. These values and principles will be transmitted into the homes and communities."*

• In El Salvador, the Salud Escolar Integral program has adopted TGfU as the core of its educational-reform program (Mandigo, Corlett, & Anderson, 2008). For more information, visit the Web site (www.fahs.brocku.ca/chdspa). Specifically, local stakeholders, such as teachers, university faculty, local coaches, and preservice students receive workshops and courses on using games and sport as a tool to create life skills that help prevent youth violence. El Salvador has one of the highest youth homicide rates in the world (World Health Organization, 2002) and it costs the country 4.3 percent of its total gross-domestic product to treat the causes of violence across the country (World Health Organization, 2004). In contrast to more authoritarian approaches to sport and PE, which in many cases only perpetuate the cycle of violence (Salas, 1997), the humanistic nature of TGfU has been an effective tool for providing prac-

Salvadoran teachers attending the first National Physical Education Congress in over 25 years in Santa Ana participate in a TGfU session using net/wall games to demonstrate life skills such as cooperation and team work.

tical examples of critical life skills, such as communication, inclusion, respect, problem solving, critical thinking, and negotiation. The quote on the previous page by one of the key stakeholders demonstrates the depth to which teachers and coaches are beginning to view the power of sports and games to foster the healthy development of a postconflict nation, such as El Salvador:

Combined, these international examples demonstrate an increased need for game programs which foster understanding of major social and health issues through games. Due to its learner-centered and humanistic nature, TGfU is an ideal venue for delivering games to meet these humanitarian goals.The preceding examples demonstrate a global movement to foster children's understanding of key life skills through sports and games. Specifically, they provide examples of how to apply knowledge generated through games into real-life settings. This application of knowledge, gained through a TGfU approach to games, demonstrates the true essence of physical literacy. Although few published examples exist of subsequent research for development programs and projects with TGfU as a central model, the increased exposure of TGfU on the international stage (Griffin & Butler, 2005) and the need for effective evidence-based programs *(Magglingen Call to Action,* 2005) situates TGfU as a promising model for current and future sport-for-development projects.

Conclusion

This chapter suggests that based on the evidence to date, TGfU has the potential to foster not only understanding of games but also understanding of a number of other life skills through games, an area relatively unexplored to date but gaining increased awareness. Although the research to date suggests that TGfU effectively develops physical literacy (more specifically, games literacy) and an increase in international support for the role of sports and games in fostering healthy community development, few global examples of research and development projects exist which bridge the gap between theory and practice. TGfU has the potential to help children and youths become better game players. Through the humanistic philosophy and constructivist pedagogy embedded in the TGfU model, it also has the potential to help children and youths develop the skills, knowledge, and attitudes to make healthy choices and become better people. Despite the prevalence of TGfU for nearly three decades (Bunker, Thorpe, & Almond, 1986), the concept of fostering understanding outside of games is relatively new. Given the increased global pressure to consider ways in which games and sports can be an effective vehicle for developing healthy children, healthy communities, and healthy nations, the evidence suggests that TGfU provides the educational grounding to support the role that games can play in fostering the development of physically literate individuals around the world.

> *TGfU has the potential to help children and youths become better game players. Through the humanistic philosophy and constructivist pedagogy embedded in the TGfU model, it also has the potential to help children and youths develop the skills, knowledge, and attitudes to make healthy choices and become better people.*

Discussion Questions

1. Despite their benefits, games are not always inherently good. There are numerous examples of games provoking anti-social behavior, such as violence or cheating. How can games taught using a TGfU approach be an effective way to promote healthy development through games?

2. Why are games an effective way to foster the development of physical literacy? What is the evidence to support that TGfU is an effective way to facilitate physical literacy?

3. Numerous examples from around the world of teaching life skills *through* games were provided in this chapter. Identify other examples within your own community of how games are being used to facilitate the development of life skills. What is it about these games that facilitate the development of life skills? What is it about TGfU that helps to facilitate the development of life skills? Why is the development of life skills important when playing games? Why is the development of life skills through games important outside of the games environment?

References

Allison, S., & Thorpe, R. (1997). A comparison of the effectiveness of two approaches to teaching games within physical education. A skills approach versus a games for understanding approach. *British Journal of Physical Education, 28*(3), 9-13.

Bailey, P., Hunsberger, M., & Hayden, K.A. (1998). The diverse faces of critical literacy: Only knowledge or also social action? *Alberta Journal of Educational Research, 44,* 120.

Bunker, D., & Thorpe, R. (1986). The curriculum model. In R. Thorpe, D. Bunker, and L. Almond (Eds.), *Rethinking games teaching* (pp. 7-10). Irthingborough, UK: Nene Litho.

Bunker, D., Thorpe, R., & Almond, L. (1986). *Rethinking games teaching.* Irthingborough, UK: Nene Litho.

Butler, J. (2005). TGfU Petagogy: Old dogs, new tricks and puppy school. *Physical Education and Sport Pedagogy, 10,* 225-240.

French, K.E., Werner, P.H., Taylor, K., Hussey, K., & Jones, J. (1996). The effects of a six-week unit of tactical, skill, or combined tactical and skill instruction of badminton performance of ninth grade students. *Journal of Teaching in Physical Education, 15,* 339-463.

Griffin, L.L., & Butler, J. (2005). *Teaching games for understanding: Theory, research, and practice.* Champaign, IL: Human Kinetics.

Griffin, L.L., Oslin, J.L., & Mitchell, S.A. (1995, March). *Two instructional approaches to teaching net games.* Poster session presented at the American Alliance for Health, Physical Education, Recreation, and Dance National Convention, Portland, OR.

Hardman, K., & Marshall, J. (2000). The state and status of physical education in schools in international context. *European Physical Education Review, 3,* 203-229.

Hastie, P.A., & Curtner-Smith, M.D. (2006). Influence of a hybrid sport education and teaching games for understanding unit on one teacher and his students. *Physical Education and Sport Pedagogy, 11*(1), 1-27.

Hayden-Davies, D. (2008, September). *So what is physical literacy (and what use is it)?* Paper presented at British Educational Research Association annual conference, University of Edinburgh, UK.

Hellison, D.R. (1973). *Humanistic physical education,* Englewood Cliffs, NJ: Prentice-Hall.

Holt, N.L., Strean, W.B., & Benogoechea, E.G. (2002). Expanding the teaching games for understanding model: New avenues for future research and practice. *Journal of Teaching in Physical Education, 21,* 162-176.

Jewett, A.E., & Bain, L. (1985). *The curriculum process in physical education.* Dubuque, IA: Win. C Brown Pub.

Keh, N.C., & Yu, S. (2007). Effectiveness of teaching games for understanding approach on Korfball learning. *Research Quarterly for Exercise and Sport, 78*(1), A63-A63.

Kidd, B., & Donnelly, P. (2007). *Literature reviews on sport for development and peace.* Toronto, ON: Sport for Development International Working Group [Online]. Available: http://iwg. sportanddev.org/data/htmleditor/file/Lit.%20Reviews/literature%20review%20SDP.pdf.

Kirk, D. (1983). Theoretical guidelines for "teaching for understanding." *Bulletin of Physical Education 19*(1), 41-45.

Kirk, D., & MacPhail, A. (2002). Teaching games for understanding and situated learning: Rethinking the Bunker-Thorpe model. *Journal of Teaching in Physical Education, 21,* 177-192.

Light, R. (2002). The social nature of games: Australian pre-service primary teachers' first experiences of teaching games for understanding. *European Physical Education Review, 8,* 286-304.

Light, R. (2003). The joy of learning: Emotion and learning in games through TGfU. *Journal of Physical Education in New Zealand, 36*(1), 93-108.

MacPhail, A., Kirk, D., & Griffin, L. (2008). Throwing and catching as relational skills in game play: Situated learning in a modified game unit. *Journal of Teaching Physical Education, 27,* 100-115.

Magglingen Call to Action. (2005, December). Presented at second Magglingen conference on Sport for Development, Magglingen, Switzerland [Online]. Available: http://www.magglingen2005.org/downloads/Magglingen%20Call%20To%20Action_6%20Dec%202005.pdf.

Mandigo, J.L., & Holt, N.L. (2004). Reading the game. Introducing the notion of games literacy. *Physical and Health Education Journal, 70*(3), 4-10.

Mandigo, J.L., Holt, N.L., Anderson, A., & Sheppard, J. (2008). Children's motivational experiences following autonomy-supportive games lessons. *European Physical Education Review, 14*(3), 407-425.

Mandigo, J.L., Spence, J.C., Thompson, L.P., Melnychuk, N., Schwartz, M., Marshall, D., & Causgrove Dunn, J. (2004). What's going on in physical education classes? An Alberta example. *Avante, 10*(1), 1-15.

Mandigo, J.L., Corlett, J., & Anderson, A. (2008). Using quality physical education to promote positive youth development in a developing nation: Striving for peace education. Chapter in N. Holt and R. Bailey (Eds.), *Positive youth development* (pp. 109-120). New York: Taylor and Francis.

Mandigo, J. L., Lodewyk, K., Francis, N., & Lopez, R. (2009). Physical literacy for educators. *Physical and Health Education Journal, 75*(3), 27-30.

McBride, R.E., & Xiang, P. (2004). Thoughtful decision making in physical education: A modest proposal. *Quest, 56,* 337-354.

Mitchell, S.A., & Oslin, J.L. (1999). An investigation of tactical transfer in net games. *European Journal of Physical Education, 4,* 162-172.

Mitchell, S.A., Griffin, L.L., & Oslin, J.L. (1995, March). *A comparison of two instructional approaches to teaching invasion games.* Poster session presented at the American Alliance for Health, Physical Education, Recreation, and Dance national convention, Portland, OR.

Oslin, J., & Mitchell, S. (2006). Game-centred approaches to teaching physical education. In D. Kirk, D. MacDonald, and M. O'Sullivan (Eds.), *Handbook of teaching physical education* (pp. 627-651). London: Sage.

Penney, D., & Chandler, T. (2000). Physical education: What future(s)? *Sport, Education and Society, 5,* 71-87.

Salas, L.M. (1997). Violence and aggression in the schools of Colombia, El Salvador, Guatemala, Nicaragua and Peru. In T. Ohsako (Ed.), *Violence at schools: Global issues and interventions* (pp. 110-127). Paris: United Nations Educational, Scientific and Cultural Organization.

Sport for Development and Peace International Working Group. (2007). *From the field: Sport for development and peace in action.* Toronto, ON: Right to Play.

Strean, W.B., & Holt, N.L. (2000). Coaches', athletes', and parents' perceptions of fun in youth sports: Assumptions about learning and implications for practice. *Avante, 6*(3), 83-98.

Turner, A. (1996). Teaching for understanding: Myth or reality? *Journal of Physical Education, Recreation, and Dance, 67*(4), 46-51.

Turner, A.P., & Martinek, T.J. (1999). An investigation into teaching games for understanding: Effects on skill, knowledge and game play. *Research Quarterly for Exercise and Sport, 70,* 286-296.

United Nations Educational, Scientific and Cultural Organization. (2003). *Literacy, a UNESCO perspective* [Online]. Available: http://unesdoc.unesco.org/images/0013/001318/131817eo. pdf.

UNICEF. *Which skills are life skills?* Retrieved May 13, 2008, from www.unicef.org/lifeskills/index_whichskills.html.

Whitehead, M. (2007, February). *Physical literacy and its importance to every individual.* Paper presented at the National Disability Association Ireland, Dublin, Ireland [Online]. Available: http://www.physical-literacy.org.uk/dublin2007.php.

World Health Organization. (2002). *The world health report 2002.* Geneva, Switzerland: World Health Organization.

World Health Organization. (2004). *The world health report 2004: Changing history.* Geneva, Switzerland: World Health Organization.

chapter 5

Feeling Flow Motion in Games and Sports

Rebecca J. Lloyd, PhD • Stephen Smith, PhD

"**H**i, Mom! I'm home."
"Hello, Pat. How's it going? How was volleyball?"
"Good."
"How good?"
"Oh c'mon, Mom . . . it was pretty good; we won."
"Were there any highlights? Moments where you felt . . ."
"Mom, what's with all the questions? It was a good game, okay?
I really enjoyed it. What's for dinner?"

Is the experience of joy at the heart of our lesson planning and our peda-gogical interactions in physical education? Positive feelings for physical activity are implicit to the approach of Teaching Games for Understanding (TGfU). After all, it is the enjoyment of playing games that provides the motivation for learning the tactics and skills involved. Traditional sports-based programs in physical education, by comparison, create frustrations in the seemingly meaningless repetition of isolated skill-based drills. Students say, "We did this last year! Can't we just play the game?" (Butler & McCahan, 2005, p. 33). Such enjoyment, as motivation for learning that comprises game performance, is the affectivity we want to explore in this chapter. Our premise for advocating TGfU is that this approach holds great promise for cultivating an explicit sense of joy within the detailed and nuanced experiences of both playing and learning.

The enjoyment of playing games need not actually foster the tactical and skill learning that the TGfU approach advocates. Games just for fun and learning can take place beyond the reflective comportment associated with understanding. So, let us then be a little more discriminating in what we mean by positive feelings and actions associated with learning how to play games. Rather than an all-encompassing yet nondiscriminating notion of enjoyment associated with the playing of a game, as exemplified in the opening dialogue between a mother and daughter, let us consider the dynamic feeling of joy in the actual movements that comprise a game. Let us take a present-moment focus which positions the learner within the joyful flow of movement. Accordingly, we can discern joy in the smile, the banter, and the expressions of playful delight in a game that is played particularly well. We can attend even more particularly to motions within a game—the well-played shots, passing patterns, rallies, volleys, and game sequences that lift the spirits of the players—to better understand this nuanced affective realm of TGfU.

Returning to our opening example, perhaps Pat's mother would find out, if pressed further, that her daughter experienced many such moments. She may well find that Pat felt connected to the ball from the moment it was served. Rather than feeling as if she were fighting to reach the ball (her usual tendency in learning the defensive Libero position), Pat had learned to soften her low stance as she felt the ball's trajectory and to propel herself forward just enough by a delicate push from her metatarsals to position herself right under the ball. In this particular moment, she felt as if she had all the time in the world to receive the ball and pass it effortlessly to her teammate, Rita, who then set the ball for a perfectly orchestrated attack.

Joy is a feature of these moment-to-moment highlights within a game that merge to form the collective feeling of general enjoyment one associates with playing a game. Just imagine if players like Pat were able to relive such highlights and recall them somatically in conversation. Would these moments happen more often? Would the experience of playing a game be more joyful?

This discrimination between enjoyment of game playing and joy in specific movements provides a point of departure; consider further the positive feelings of physical activity that can be cultivated through the TGfU approach. We propose that this TGfU approach can engender feelings of *flow motion* (Lloyd & Smith, 2006a; 2006b), or the durational feelings of joy and delight in the physical actions, sequences, and patterns of game play. These feelings can wax and wane, crescendo in bursts and rushes of excitement, and diminish in plays that come slowly or abruptly to a halt. We'd like to emphasize the potential for sustaining flow motion in the TGfU model of teaching and structuring games and sports.

Sustainability of Flow

Joy is not necessarily the first emotion that students associate with learning how to play a new game. Anxiety and frustration may arise if they are placed in a situation of complex challenge. Students may experience joy within the TGfU framework because individualized rules may be implemented to accommodate learners of varying abilities (Brown

We propose that this TGfU approach can engender feelings of flow motion (Lloyd & Smith, 2006a; 2006b), or the durational feelings of joy and delight in the physical actions, sequences, and patterns of game play.

& Hopper, 2006). Modifications include, but are not limited to, changing rules to accommodate varying levels of proficiency, changing boundaries, changing the size and softness of manipulatives, and changing the number of players on each team. Such modifications help students learn how to connect with the joy of the well-played game.

The TGfU approach, which matches players' skill level with the challenge of playing a game, creates certain delights—moments of synergy in which participants create and captivate relational space as they dance in and out of patterns of skillful action. Yet such moments are fleeting, somewhat akin to "a fickle guest [who] is liable to leave without giving a moment's notice" (Kretchmar, 2005, p. 204). More sustained are the passages of flow – durations of game immersion in which a balance exists between challenge and skill and a sensation of action merges with awareness. During flow, players receive a set of clear goals and immediate feedback to their actions. They lose feelings of distraction at being excluded and worries of failure and enter a state where they lose any self-consciousness and have a distorted sense of time (Csikszentmihalyi, 1996, 1997, 2000). Yet flowing passages of play are too often regarded as exceptional or difficult to achieve (Newberg, Kimiecik, Durand-Bush, & Doell, 2002, p. 258). We tend to forget that flow can be experienced on a continuum from "repetitive, almost automatic acts (like doodling or chewing gum), to complex activities," like games and sports (Csikszentmihalyi, 2000, p. 54).

Delight and flow bring some theoretical insight to the joy that can be experienced in games and sports. These concepts, described by Kretchmar and Csikszentmihalyi, begin to characterize the affective backdrop of the TGfU approach. In this chapter, we offer a more detailed consideration of the dynamic ebb and flow of feelings that both accompany learning how to play games and sports and are intrinsic to the process. Emotions, such as joy and delight, are embedded in the motions of games and sports. They provide moments and passages of flow motion. Thus, we offer an affect-oriented TGfU approach for those interested in enlivening the learning experience of physical education through joyful, delightful, flow motions.

We develop this affective TGfU approach through reference to the original Bunker and Thorpe (1986) curriculum model. Shifting the emphasis from the cognitive register (making appropriate decisions), we encourage sensing vitality affects, feeling appropriate moments, enacting movement pairings, patterns, and sequences, and thus discerning the expressions and the purposes of games and sports. This affective-temporal emphasis allows us to extend the categories of game appreciation, tactical awareness, skill execution, and performance (as summarized in figure 5.1). In so doing, we highlight feelings and flow motions of vitality that provide reference points in teaching for enhanced understanding, appreciation, and love of games and sports.

- *Game appreciation to game affect.* Students are encouraged to feel the wide range of emotions, or vitality affects, in game play, preparation, and reflection afterward.

- *Tactical awareness to present moment awareness.* Students are encouraged to get in touch with the present moment; for example, they should know not only how to create and defend space strategically, but also how to emphasize the bodily sensation of connecting with others through space and time.

- *Skill execution to movement pairings, patterns, and sequences.* Students are taught to become aware of the organic pairing and progressive approach to maturing movement rooted in inhalation and exhalation that develops into the felt sense of balance within the contractions, extensions, movement patterns, and sequences that constitute game play.

- *Performance to expressive and purposive flow motion.* Students become aware of the experience of flow motion in the rhythms of expressive and purposive game play.

The following elaborations offer guidance on how the vitality of flow motion can be felt as game and sport understanding is enhanced through the TGfU approach.

Game Affect

Students need an appreciation of "the rules of the game to be played" (Bunker & Thorpe, 1986, p. 3) that accommodates the modifications required for different levels of ability. They need, in other words, to understand and appreciate the basic organization and specifications of the game. Yet, when the game begins, students have the opportunity to get a feel for it and for the motions that constitute it. They can become proficient within the progressions of game play (however simplified), and thus enhance their chances of experiencing joy or delight.

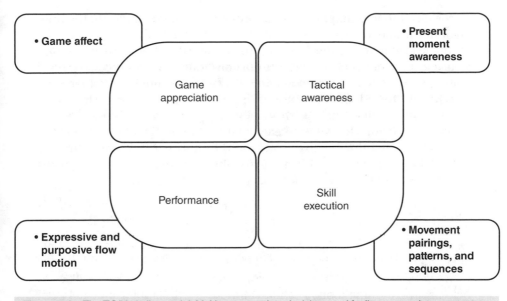

Figure 5.1 The TGfU vitality model: Making appropriate decisions and feeling appropriate moments.

But when are students most likely able to get in touch with such emotions? At the end of a game when they have the time to distinguish the highlights from the lowlights as they develop a reflective approach to game appreciation? Or do affective states occur during the game but are experienced in the motions themselves? Surprisingly, Mihaly Csikszentmihalyi's thoughts on happiness in relation to the experience of flow suggest the former.

> It is the full involvement in flow, rather than happiness, that makes for excellence in life. When we are in flow, we are not happy because to experience happiness we must focus on our inner states, and that would take away attention from the task at hand. . . Only after the task is completed do we have the leisure to look back on what has happened, and then we are flooded with gratitude for the excellence of that experience—in retrospect, we are happy. (Csikszentmihalyi, 1997, p. 32)

Since the theory of flow is based on intrinsically motivated (autotelic) activity, which Csikszentmihalyi describes as "activities that people [do] for the sake of doing the activity, without experiencing any external rewards" (2000, p. xv), it follows that a true intrinsic experience has pleasure built into it. The preceding quotation, however, describes happiness as an end product or an interruption of the flow experience, as if emotion cannot happen while one is in the moment of flow. If you were to realize you were happy, it would be a reflective thought rather than an active process.

The temporal separations of motional awareness, emotional realization, and game appreciation are really a consequence of different orders of somatic engagement. Prior to playing the game, students may experience anxiety and trepidation, in spite of the modifications made. Afterward, having played vigorously with evident joy and delight, they can feel happily satisfied. This general experiential profile does not mean that motions and emotions are separate; on the contrary, it requires that we consider a more-nuanced affective profiling of game play that recognizes the emotions in the flow of motion. "E-motions themselves are a kind of motion, hence we say we are 'moved' when we experience deep emotion" (Mazis, 2002, p. 160). Conversely, all motions of a volitional nature carry emotion. Our task is to recognize these emotions, not simply as summary feelings of joy and happiness, but as moment-to-moment feelings of positive affect that add up to the joyfulness of the game.

We introduce the term *vitality affect,* as defined by Daniel Stern (2004), to help us recognize the motion within emotion. Stern distinguishes between categories of feeling, like delight and joy, and vitality affects that are the moment-to-moment feelings which may aggregate as delight, joy, or even sadness, grief, and shame. The former are said to be moods or feeling states that may have some duration, while the latter are akin to Rudolf Laban's "effort shapes" (Laban & Lawrence, 1974) and characterize the emotional contours of bodily activation from one moment to the next.

A vitality affect, which emerges as a moment unfolds, can be characterized by words such as pulsing, surging, fleeting, exploding, crescendoing, accelerating, fading, rushing, climaxing, and bursting (Stern, 2004, p.36; pp. 62-64).

*T*he term vitality affect, as defined by Daniel Stern (2004), helps us recognize the motion within emotion. A vitality affect, which emerges as a moment unfolds, can be characterized by words such as pulsing, surging, fleeting, exploding, crescendoing, accelerating, fading, rushing, climaxing, and bursting (Stern, 2004, p.36; pp. 62-64).

Vitality affects can be experienced as rushes of excitement, energy, and movement; bursts of speed and activity; surges of enthusiasm, energy, and inspiration; and swells of emotion and motion, as well as risings, undulations, waves, and flows that characterize the vitality dynamics of particular movements. More specifically, we can experience these surges and swells as forceful bodily expansions and extensions that differ from bursts and rushes in terms of their energetic cadences and generative motions. Rising, which is characterized by springing, leaping, and jumping, differs from waves and undulations, since the latter also includes landing, holding, contracting, and pausing before the next upswing or leadoff motion. Flows are even more sustained, characterizing motion that is fluid, floating, and connecting.

Vitality affects, such as these rushes, bursts, surges, swells, risings, undulations, waves, and flows are more than the affective components of movement; they are indicative of key bodily motions of vitality. It is certainly the case that a person can be described as being lively and animated without specification of the motions that indicate liveliness and animation. The dynamic that is indicated may be evident in a range of rushing, bursting, surging, swelling, rising, undulating, waving, and flowing movements that have similar affective connotations. Conversely, certain vitality affects can be discerned in a range of motions that have quite dissimilar affective meanings. We can experience a rush of gladness or sadness, a burst of laughter or anger, a surge of confidence or fear, swellings of pride or hurt, and waves of many feelings. But these attributions are progressively abstract; the further removed they are from the specific motions indicative of a state, a style, and manner of being healthy and physically active, the less descriptive they are of what it actually means to be alive and animated (Smith & Lloyd, 2006, p. 257).

What is particularly exciting about Stern's work is that he has taken the construct of emotion that is classically understood in the Darwinian sense (happiness, interest, surprise, anger, and so on), and researched it with temporal, spatial, and relational sensitivities. In doing so, he has also indicated that vitality affects can register not only for the participant or player but also for the observer or teacher who attunes to them. Stern (1993) writes:

> There is a third register of feelings that can operate in parallel with the categorical and vitality affects. These concern the feelings of being loved, esteemed, thought wonderful, special, or hated, and the feelings of being secure, safe, attached, alone, isolated, or separated. These feelings are obvious to all of us in our personal lives and occupy a significant place in clinical discourse and in research on motivation. . . They clearly cannot be reduced to the categorical and vitality affects, but constitute a third type [which I call] "relational affects" because they are largely about the current feeling status of a relationship (p. 207).

These relational affects characterize the interpersonal dynamics of teaching and learning. The implications of Stern's (1993, 2002, 2004) research are very fitting for those interested in educating students in a manner that cultivates joy in movement in that we can shift the concept of emotion from personally experienced feelings, or after-the-fact emotional attribution, to a dynamic, engaged, and interactive process. When a teacher observes a smile on the face of a student, for example, much more than the categorical affect of happiness is projected. A "smile can 'explode' or 'dawn' or 'fade'" (Stern, 1993, p. 206); the "difference between them lies, in part, in their characteristic temporal contours" (Stern, 2004, p. 63); and these subtleties can influence the way an affect-oriented teacher moves in response to students' motion experiences.

Although Stern's research on interpersonal attunements was directed initially at the vitality affects of infant-mother relationships, physical educators may draw clues for connecting with the affective contours of movement from these examples:

> A ten-month old girl accomplishes an amusing routine with mother and then looks at her. The girl opens up her face (her mouth opens, her eyes widen, her eyebrows rise) and then closes it back, in a series of changes whose contour can be represented by a smooth arch. Mother responds by intoning "Yeah," with a pitch line that rises and falls as the volume crescendos and decrescendos (Stern, 1985, as cited in Stern, 1993, p. 140).

Stern draws attention to how the mother's voice picks up the duration and quality of the baby's mouth and eyes as they open and close. The words themselves aren't just soft and sweet with that all-too-familiar tone we use with babies, but are paced in a way that matches the rhythm of the observed movement. Physical educators interested in teaching games and their component movements in ways that unite both affect and intellect might thus pick up on the contours found within all spoken words.[1] More specifically, if they stop a game to assess understanding by asking students questions related to the tactics of game play (Hubball, Lambert, & Hayes, 2007) and by encouraging what Richard and Wallian describe as a "debate of ideas" (2005, p. 22), they can also attend to the vitality affects of the words themselves (not only what they say, but also how they say it).

Spectators engrossed in the movements of the game can certainly pick up kinetic contours and express them as whoops and thunderous cheers when, for example, a goal is scored. Pedagogical contours, however, take on more subtle amplitudes. In fact, what separates teachers from spectators is the degree to which the former contribute to movement understanding. Rather than simply assuming the role of a cheerleader, whose enthusiasm overshadows or amplifies the joy naturally present in movement, the vocal vitality affects of instruction can carry the emotions and feelings associated with the movements themselves. A teacher may emphasize the *swoosh* in a serve, the *swish* of a basketball going through a net, or the *bong* in a bounce, by verbalizing a sound that resonates with the felt motion. The contours of movement are amplified through such vocalizations, which can both make a difference in movement quality and inform the orchestrated or choreographed feel of the game.

Rather than simply assuming the role of a cheerleader, whose enthusiasm overshadows or amplifies the joy naturally present in movement, the vocal vitality affects of instruction can carry the emotions and feelings associated with the movements themselves.

Rebecca, the first author of this chapter, only became aware of how much she relied upon onomatopoeia in her pedagogical interactions with elite figure skaters, whom she trained off the ice with ballet-infused exercises, when her students decided to jokily repeat the sounds back to her. Rather than perform the desired movement which she described with a series of sound effects (*shoop ba, shoop ba*) and demonstrative hand gestures, they sang the sounds of the movement back to her in farcical manner. After the shared laughter died down, she realized how much she uses vitality contours to emphasize movement quality.

Present-Moment Awareness

In addition to these verbal reinforcements, we also need to move demonstrably in response to the unfolding, living moments of game play (Lloyd & Smith, 2006a). David Levin (1985) asserts that "we are beings who need to give thought to being in the thoughtfulness of our posture, our stance, our gait and comportment, and in the thoughtful gestures of our hands" (p. 92). We need, as teachers, "to pay closer attention to the way of standing and responding gesturally in [student/teacher] interactions with the intention of critically reflecting on and questioning the interactive nuances of the motions used to teach" (Lloyd & Smith, 2006b, p. 237). These somatic details of how we move matter since, as Maxine Sheets-Johnstone (1999) confirms, "[a]ny time one moves, a vitality affect is present" (p. 257).

Moving in response to students' game experiences requires us to enter the unfurling nature of the present moment, making the teachable moment tangible and palpable. When lesson plans are organized around predetermined goals to meet curriculum requirements, teachers can easily get caught up in preconceived expectations of what should happen when, and can interrupt students' game activity unnecessarily. Elsewhere (see Lloyd & Smith, 2005), we likened the physical-education teacher entering the time and space of student experience to the attentive motions of a double-dutch skipper swaying back and forth, feeling the rhythmic cadence of the turning ropes before becoming a central

The ability to attune oneself to the present moment is more easily said than done, since attentiveness extends beyond the cognitive confines of making a decision; students must feel the motions that comprise that moment.

part of the movement and jumping in the game. Such attentiveness can act as a point of entry for evaluating the effectiveness of game lessons[2] and the degree to which we promote student understanding through affect and intellect. We must ask ourselves, "Are we teaching games in a way that projects and refines the desired emotions and motions that are true to the nature of the game?"

In the original curriculum model proposed by Bunker and Thorpe (1986), the category of tactical awareness emphasizes "creating space and denying space" as well as observing "opposition weakness, e.g. a poor backhand" to "overcome the opposition" (p. 3). In order for students to perceive a connection to space as well as to their opposition, therefore, they must be able to enter the present moment of game play. This means that worries within the contexts of the game, physical-education class, peer interactions, school, or home life are temporarily suspended; only an awareness of the present moment of the game exists. Of course, the ability to attune to the present moment is more easily said than done, since attentiveness extends beyond the cognitive confines of making a decision; students must feel the motions that comprise that moment. Simply stated, they can become more aware of a movement, such as a passing play in a game, by reflecting on how they experience it in their bodies. Examples include the sense and placement of particular body parts and the refinement of key movements (such as the fingertip release), the perceived tempo of the play, the ability to sense one's connection to space (such as the playing field), and relational position in respect to teammates and the opposition. Kinesthetic sensitivity is cultivated in paying such close attention to the micro movements we typically overlook in daily life and to the "small momentary events that make up our worlds of experience" (Stern, 2004, p. xi).

Movement Pairings, Patterns, and Sequences

Within the original model by Bunker and Thorpe (1986), the evaluation of a skillful movement is always "seen in the contexts of the learner and the game" (p. 5). It may include "some qualitative aspect of both the mechanical efficiency of the movement and its relevance to the particular game situation" (p. 4) as students explore and refine authentic patterns, reactions, and movements required in game play. The problem that Bunker and Thorpe noted, however, is that even if students know what they are supposed to do (for example, perform a "defensive clear in badminton"), they may lack the "strength" or "technical development" (p. 4) to complete the motion.

Although we recognize the value in rewarding appropriate decisions and having the skill base to execute such decisions, we also think that ways of developing game proficiency exist that are attuned to movement maturation. In fact, movements performed well that enhance a very positive feeling for the game in question are not simply skillful and appropriate, they are movements that carry the feelings of inhalation and exhalation (through the kinetic pairings of contraction and expansion, throwing and catching, striking and receiving, and so on) into patterns and sequences of exhilarating game play. When a game is played particularly well it is, so to speak, breathtaking.

In fact, movements performed well that enhance a very positive feeling for the game in question are not simply skillful and appropriate, they are movements that carry the feelings of inhalation and exhalation (through the kinetic pairings of contraction and expansion, throwing and catching, striking and receiving, and so on) into patterns and sequences of exhilarating game play.

Physical-education textbooks and curricular frameworks list all the possible permutations of movements the body can perform within the realms of locomotor, nonlocomotor, and manipulative skills. Yet a specific focus on the kinds of movement patterns and skill progressions that optimize a bodily vitality is missing. For instance, basic locomotion, as in "walking, running, hopping, jumping, leaping, rolling, skipping, galloping, climbing, sliding, and propulsion through water" is vitally about running and stopping, leaping and landing, propulsion and resistance. Likewise, the manipulations of "receiving: e.g. catching, collecting; retaining: e.g. dribbling, carrying, bouncing, trapping; sending: e.g. throwing, kicking, striking" and the stability patterns of "turning, twisting, swinging, balancing, bending, landing, stretching, curling, hanging" (Alberta Learning, 2000) can be paired in terms of pushing and pulling, giving and receiving, grasping and yielding, venturing and withdrawing, extending and contracting, and expanding and condensing. As Cohen (1993) has pointed out, such action pairings are features of human development that can be traced to the "original kinetic bodily pairings – of inhalation and exhalation, for example, of opening and closing (eyes, mouths, or fist), of walking on one foot then the other, and so on" (Sheets-Johnstone, 1999, p. 157). Therefore, objective lists of motions derived from bodily movements are conceived as organic life forms or, in other words, as life-giving, vital motions (Lloyd & Smith, 2005, p. 122).

Building on the TGfU emphasis on game units, we depart from the mechanical learning of motor skills to focus on opportunities to experience dynamic patterns in games. Provided that they are not done repetitively and lifelessly, drills can serve us well as patterns of play that give students a feel for the movement pairings, patterns, and sequences that comprise the game.

Flow Motion as Expressive and Purposive

The TGfU model uses performance criteria that compares players and rates learners' appropriately skillful motion against "criteria that are independent of the learner" (Bunker & Thorpe, 1986, p. 4). Although external indicators of performance must be used when ranking a player or a team, significant moments within the games themselves should also be highlighted. Game highlights reported on sport television programs, for example, provide more than tables of statistics. Significant moments from both winning and losing teams draw attention to greatest catches, plays of the week, or the top 10 goals. Video footage shows the breathtaking moments. The mass appeal of these moments has us wondering if such a focus might at least complement the objective criteria of scores, distances, and times that are traditionally used to assess performances in physical education.

If encouraging the joyful and delightful feelings of flow motion in addition to praising efficient skills is key to game affect, then perhaps we need to pay more attention to the especially expressive moments of game play: those moments when pairings, patterns, and sequences of movement carry deep satisfaction. Games and sports are surely sustained by the enjoyment they provide. In this regard, games and sports differ little from other movement disciplines. The key difference is that games and sports are seen as purposive rather than as expressive activities. We suggest that this difference is significant; however, it also prevents us from fully appreciating the expressive qualities of games and sports. In particular, we tend to lose sight of the expressions of feeling that are inherent to games and sports and those that occur moment to moment and are evident in the vitality of the game and in the vital engagements of the players.

Conclusion

The TGfU approach provides a valuable framework for maximizing the enjoyment of playing games and sports. It is a significant curriculum initiative that motivates children and youths to engage in healthy and active living. Our desire is that this initiative be continued with increasing stress on the affective register of game play. We maintain that joy and delight are manifestations of the vitality affects that occur moment to moment when playing a game. We enhance the joys and delights of a game when we become more mindful of these vitality affects and start paying closer attention to the movement pairings, patterns, and sequences that comprise the flow motions of the well-played game.

Joy and delight are manifestations of the vitality affects that occur moment to moment when playing a game. We enhance the joys and delights of a game when we become more mindful of these vitality affects and start paying closer attention to the movement pairings, patterns, and sequences that comprise the flow motions of the well-played game.

Such attentiveness requires much training for teaching games and sports. We advocate a perceptual shift from the visual and cognitive sense of how actions are performed to the kinesthetic and affective sense of how actions are experienced. We also recommend that teachers shift their attention from the overall appearance of the game to its telling moments. We require that teachers develop a movement consciousness that enables them to discern the teachable moments. We shall have to leave these important considerations for another time. For the moment, it shall have to suffice that the TGfU approach provides the most promising curricular framework for this type of teacher training. Flow motion in games and sports gives learners and teachers, the children whom we want to pursue active, healthy lives and those of us who teach them, the means to this moment-to-moment, daily, and lifelong goal.

Discussion Questions

1. *Vitality affects.* Imagine that you are playing your favorite game and it is going well. Using a series of action-oriented verbs, describe the range of emotions connected to your game-play experience. How are these various emotions communicated to others (your teammates, teachers, coaches, the spectators, and so on)?

2. *Relational affects.* Imagine that you are using the TGfU approach in your physical education game-based lesson and the lesson is

becoming emotionally flat. What are some possible reasons for the lack of enthusiasm? What authentic pedagogical actions could cultivate a burst or rush of excitement so that students are enticed to get back in the game?

3. *Present-moment awareness.* Have you ever experienced a teachable moment? Describe your moment in as much detail as you can. Consider the extent to which focusing on the present moment was necessary. Analyze your reflection and identify which factors help you stay present so that you may experience teachable moments more often.

4. *Movement pairing.* Think of a typical skill that is taught in isolation (for example, kicking a ball with the inside of the foot). Situate the development of that skill with its natural pairing action (for example, trapping or receiving a ball). Design an activity that promotes the learning of this skill in a way that is both authentic and joyful. What measures could you use to assess the variable presence of joy? (Hint: Revisit question 1).

5. *Expressive and purposive flow motion.* Consider the expressive actions of both a figure skater and a hockey player. Compare and contrast a movement sequence within a program or game that could be considered breathtaking. To what extent is each athlete in tune with his or her cadence of breath, balance, timing, and overall feeling of the experienced movement? Describe the benefits of getting in touch with movements and moments that are deeply satisfying.

Endnotes

[1] "Without contours, words would sound as if they were spoken by a robot" (Stern, 2004, pp. 63-64).

[2] For an example of a reflection on how relational gesture, posture, and position inform an effective pedagogical interaction, see the article, *Interactive Flow in Exercise Pedagogy*, by Lloyd & Smith (2006b).

References

Alberta Learning. (2000). *Physical education guide to implementation.* Alberta, Canada. Accessed June 2006 from http://education.alberta.ca.

Brown, S., & Hopper, T. (2006). Can all students in physical education get an 'A'? Game performance assessment by peers as a critical component of student learning. *The Physical and Health Education Journal, 72*(1), 14-21.

Bunker, D., & Thorpe, R. (1986). The curriculum model. In R. Thorpe, D. Bunker, and L. Almond (Eds.), *Rethinking games teaching* (pp. 7-10). Loughborough, UK: University of Technology.

Butler, J., & McCahan, B.J. (2005). Teaching games for understanding as a curriculum model. In Griffin, L. & Butler, J. (Eds.), *Teaching games for understanding: Theory, research, and practice* (pp. 33-54). Champaign, IL: Human Kinetics.

Cohen, B.B. (1993). *Sensing, feeling, and action: The experiential anatomy of body-mind centering.* Northhampton, MA: Contact Editions.

Csikszentmihalyi, M. (1996). *Creativity: Flow and the psychology of discovery and invention.* New York: Harper Collins.

Csikszentmihalyi, M. (1997). *Finding flow: The psychology of engagement with everyday life.* New York: Basic Books.

Csikszentmihalyi, M. (2000). *Beyond boredom and anxiety: Experiencing flow in work and play.* San Francisco: Jossey-Bass Publishers.

Hubball, H., Lambert, J., & Hayes, S. (2007). Theory to practice: Using the games for understanding approach in the teaching of invasion games. *The Physical and Health Education Journal, 73*(3), 14-20.

Kretchmar, R.S. (2005). Teaching games for understanding and the delights of human activity. In L. Griffin and J. Butler (Eds.), *Teaching games for understanding: Theory, research, and practice* (pp. 199-212). Champaign, IL: Human Kinetics.

Laban, R., & Lawrence, F.C. (1974). *Effort.* Plymouth, UK: Macdonald and Evans.

Levin, D.M. (1985). *The body's recollection of being.* London: Routledge.

Lloyd, R.J., & Smith, S.J. (2005). A 'vitality' approach to the design, implementation and evaluation of health-related, physical education programs. *AVANTE, 11*(2) 120-136.

Lloyd, R.J., & Smith, S.J. (2006a). Motion-sensitive phenomenology. In K. Tobin and J. Kincheloe (Eds.), *Doing educational research: A handbook* (pp. 289-309). Boston: Sense Publishers.

Lloyd, R.J., & Smith, S.J. (2006b). Interactive flow in exercise pedagogy. *Quest, 58,* 222-241.

Mazis, G.A. (2002). *Earthbodies: Rediscovering our planetary senses.* Albany, NY: State University of New York Press.

Newberg, D., Kimiecik, J., Durand-Bush, N., & Doell, K. (2002). The role of resonance in performance excellence and life engagement. *Journal of Applied Sport Psychology, 14*(4), 249- 267.

Richard, J.-F., & Wallian, N. (2005). Emphasizing student engagement in the construction of game performance. In L. Griffin and J. Butler (Eds.), *Teaching games for understanding: Theory, research, and practice* (pp. 19-32). Champaign, IL: Human Kinetics.

Sheets-Johnstone, M. (1999). *The primacy of movement.* Philadelphia: John Benjamins.

Smith, S.J., & Lloyd, R.J. (2006). Promoting vitality in health and physical education. *Qualitative Health Research: An International, Interdisciplinary Journal, 16*(2), 245-267.

Stern, D.N. (1993). The role of feelings for an interpersonal self. In U. Neisser (Ed.), *The perceived self: Ecological and interpersonal sources of self knowledge* (pp. 205-215). Cambridge, UK: Cambridge University Press.

Stern, D.N. (2002). *The first relationship: Infant and mother.* Cambridge, MA: Harvard University Press.

Stern, D.N. (2004). *The present moment in psychotherapy and everyday life.* New York: W.W. Norton & Company.

chapter 6

Enabling Constraints: Using Complexity Research to Structure Collective Learning

Brent Davis, PhD • Dennis Sumara, PhD

> **"N**on-polarized groups can consistently make better deci-
> sions and come up with better answers than most of their
> members and ... often the group outperforms the best member."
>
> — *Suroweicki, 2004, pp. 189-190.*

This chapter is focused on what might be called "the conditions of complex emergence," a phrase that refers to a set of elements that complexity researchers have studied over the past few decades in their efforts to prompt the emergence of healthy, creative, and robust systems. Our main focus is on *enabling constraints,* that is, the tasks and structures that support both individual and collective learning. Specifically, we explore the importance of establishing and maintaining harmonies among seemingly opposed aspects, such as self-interest and collective good, and the simultaneous need for rules and flexibility.

To the surprise (and very much to the chagrin) of many Canadians, in the early rounds of men's hockey at the 2006 winter Olympics, the Canadian team lost to Switzerland. Grasping for explanations, the headline in one national newspaper the next morning read, "Canadians play like all-stars; Swiss play like a team" (*National Post*).

Defining moments of national identity aside, the result was a powerful reminder of the simultaneous importance of individual abilities and collective cohesion—and the fact that the latter can sometimes more than compensate for the former. Clearly, wholes can exceed the sums of their parts when it comes to team play.

Another emerging literature that can be used to address some of the relevant issues in this type of situation is complexity research. In this chapter, we draw on that domain, focusing in particular on the nature of collective action and how an educator or leader might intervene to prompt such action. To these ends, we organize the chapter into four parts. We start with a discussion on the nature of complex systems: how they are recognized, how they behave, and why they defy linear-causal logic of classical science. In the second section, we present what is currently known about the conditions necessary to trigger the emergence of complex collective action. We then elaborate on those conditions in the third section as we consider specific and unique properties of collective *human* action. In the final part, we offer a detailed illustrative example as we move toward the pragmatic implications for educators who are interested in the emergence of games and other collective phenomena.

Recognizing Complexity: Some Qualities of Complex Phenomena

One of the frustrating aspects of complexity research is that no unified definition of a complex phenomenon exists. Rather, definitions of complexity tend to be expressed in terms of the speaker's particular interests. For example, a biologist would likely offer a definition in terms of living systems, a physicist in terms of nonlinear dynamics, and a sociologist in terms of self-maintaining but ever-evolving cultural identities.

As educators, we lean toward the notion that a complex system is one that learns. Brains, social collectives, bodies of knowledge, and so on can all become broader, more nuanced, capable of more diverse possibilities as, simultaneously, individual agents adapt to one another and the system they comprise adapts to its grander circumstances. This interpretation has prompted us, for example, to think of classroom groupings as collective learners rather than merely as collections of learners—a shift with pragmatic implications that we explore later in this chapter.

Because no unified definition of complexity exists, complex phenomena tend to be described in terms of common qualities. For example, complex systems are *emergent* or *self-organizing*, meaning that each arises in the interactions of many subcomponents or agents without the need of a centralized controller. The critical quality that distinguishes emergent collectives (complex phenomena) from simple collections is that the former exhibit properties and behaviors that are not present in any of the agents or subsystems. Economies arise in but cannot be reduced to the self-interested activities of individual people; the best hockey teams are not necessarily made up of the best players, and consciousness relies on, but cannot be equated with, the networked interactions of regions of the brain. By contrast, simpler, more mechanical systems (such as computers) can be reduced to the predictable sums of their parts.

A second important quality of complex unities is that they are *self-transforming* or *self-determining*. That is, the way that a complex system

The critical quality that distinguishes emergent collectives (complex phenomena) from simple collections is that the former exhibit properties and behaviors that are not present in any of the agents or subsystems.

responds to a situation is determined by the system itself, not by the situation. To draw a comparison with a mechanical system, one could use fairly simple principles of physics to make a confident prediction of what will happen when a ball is kicked. However, one would never be able to predict with confidence what would happen if a person were kicked. Moreover, one could not rely on experiments to predict future responses because, unlike a kicked ball, a kicked person is prone to self-transformation. The same is true of economies, teams, cities, anthills, and ecosystems. The range of possible responses in each case is clearly limited, but the precise response can never be prespecified—a point that any experienced teacher or coach knows well.

The unpredictability of specific responses is tightly linked to another quality of all complex systems: *disequilibriation*. Complex phenomena exist far from equilibrium. Indeed, in terms of complex activity, equilibrium is equivalent to death. In terms of learning, it is not simply the case that complex systems can learn; it is that they must learn. Internally, agents must constantly adapt to one another; externally, the system must adapt to its dynamic context. Archetypical images of complex dynamics include climate fluctuations, stock market fluctuations, brain activity, and team sports—which, although massively different, have very similar profiles when considered on appropriate time scales.

Phrased differently, complex unities are *dynamically self-similar*. Even though ecosystems do not learn at the same pace as human culture, and human collectives (such as teams) do not learn at the pace of individual people (such as athletes), all obey similar internal dynamics—even as they often participate in the emergence of more complex phenomena.

This reiterative quality of systems giving rise to systems is what lies behind the common observation that complex unities tend to be *nested* in one another. We have attempted to represent this nestedness in figure 6.1 by identifying some of the systems that are of particular interest to educators (see Davis & Sumara, 2006, for a fuller account of

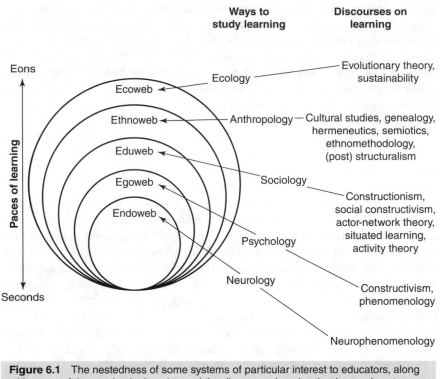

Ways to
study learning

Discourses on
learning

Eons

Ecology — Evolutionary theory,
sustainability

Ecoweb

Ethnoweb — Anthropology — Cultural studies, genealogy,
hermeneutics, semiotics,
ethnomethodology,
(post) structuralism

Eduweb

Egoweb — Sociology

Endoweb — Constructionism,
social constructivism,
actor-network theory,
situated learning,
activity theory

Paces of learning

Psychology

Neurology — Constructivism,
phenomenology

Seconds

Neurophenomenology

Figure 6.1   The nestedness of some systems of particular interest to educators, along with some of the academic domains and the discourse domains that have arisen to account for such levels.

these phenomena). A vital point here is that, to understand and affect complex unities, one must *level jump* – that is, simultaneously examine the phenomenon in its own right (for its particular coherence and its specific rules of behavior) and pay attention to the conditions of its emergence (the agents that come together, the contexts of their coactivity, and so on).

This list can be extended to include other qualities, such as recursively elaborative, decentrally networked, permeably bounded, and organizationally closed. However, the preceding list (complex phenomena are self-organizing, self-transforming, disequilibriated, dynamically self-similar, and nested) suffices for our current purposes.

Prompting Complexity: Some Conditions of Complex Emergence

For most of its history, the emphasis in complexity research has been on descriptive study of diverse phenomena, such as anthills, brains, social groups, and immune systems. Starting roughly in the 1950s, researchers began to notice some commonalities across domains, prompting the emergence of systems theory, cybernetics, and other transdisciplinary movements. But it was not until the early 1980s that the notion of *complexity* arose as a means to pull these strands into a grander conversation, which in turn prompted research to move beyond the identification of common qualities (such as those discussed previously) toward discussions of how one might affect a system. That is, a current emphasis in complexity research is how to trigger, occasion, and otherwise affect complex phenomena. To our thinking, this shift places complexity research in harmony with educational action. In particular, it renders complexity research of use to those who are interested in the collective phenomena, including games.

Of course, in the same way that complex activity does not lend itself to simplistic descriptions, it does not lend itself to ready-to-use prescriptions either. Rather, the advice for working with complex phenomena tends to arrive in terms of *conditions* that must be present to allow for the emergence of complexity. Unfortunately, lists of these conditions are often quite long and unruly. We will focus on six conditions here: namely, redundancy, diversity, independence, interdependence, rules, and flexibility.

Before developing these conditions in detail, it is important to highlight that these conditions are not factors which can be isolated. Nor is it the case that seeming opposites (such as redundancy and diversity) exist in tension. Even more paradoxically, they do not even exist in balance. Such notions, factors, tension, and balance, are firmly rooted in a mechanistic, classical scientific mindset. The word *balance*, for instance, is derived from the Latin *bi-lanx*, or two pans, in reference to the balance scale. A classic icon of fate and justice, the balance figures prominently in western mind-sets. As the thinking tends to go, "Your loss is my gain." An implicit zero-sum logic exist in which, whenever two opposing qualities come together, if one goes up, the other must go down.

Critiques of this sensibility are at the core of complexity thinking, and they are coming to be broadly represented in the popular literature. Bill Clinton's (2000) comments are illustrative:

> "The more complex societies get and the more complex the networks of interdependence within and beyond community and national borders get, the more people are forced in their own interests to find non-zero-sum solutions. That is, win–win solutions instead of win–lose solutions.... Because we find as our interdependence increases that, on the whole, we do better when other people do better as well—so we have to find ways that we can all win, we have to accommodate each other" (Breslau & Heron, 2000).

All of this raises the question, if redundancy doesn't balance diversity, independence isn't the opposite of interdependence, and rules and flexibility aren't in tension, how exactly are they related?

Our response to this question comes from an insight expressed by Chinese colleagues during a presentation we offered on complexity in Beijing. At the time, we used the word *balance*. A response shared by several audience members, invoking Confucian and Taoist principles, is that we should be framing the relationships among the conditions of complex emergence in terms of *harmonies*. Derived from the Greek *harmonia*, which means agreement or concord of sounds, harmony has to do with fitting, joining, and flowing together. In brief then, as we pry apart a few conditions of complex emergence, we endeavor to remember that they can never operate in balance, but they must exist in harmony.

Internal Redundancy and Internal Diversity

The word *redundancy* is popularly used to refer to unnecessary duplications and excesses in a system. Within complexity research, the qualifier *unnecessary* is deleted. To illustrate the point using the example of a hockey team, obvious redundancies include abilities such as skating and handling a stick, as well as knowledge of the rules. More subtly, redundancy also extends into areas of specialization. For example, although in principle those playing forward and defense have some distinct skills, some level of redundancy across these specialized roles is clearly important to a strong team.

In brief, internal redundancy in a system is what enables agents to work together and to substitute for one another. It is thus the source of a system's robustness. This is especially obvious within human systems, such as hockey teams. If the game revolved around extreme specialization, whenever a player was penalized or injured, the team would be at an extreme disadvantage.

> **A** *need exists for a harmony of internal redundancy and internal diversity.*

At the same time, however, a hockey team without some level of specialization among its members is disadvantaged, which points to the need for a harmony of *internal redundancy* and *internal diversity*— the latter of which refers to range of responses that a system can draw on in new situations. It might be described as the source of a system's intelligence and creativity; it is what a system draws from when facing a situation it hasn't previously encountered.

Using the team as the unit of analysis, the harmonious relationship of internal redundancy and internal diversity can be recognized in, for example, a common set of physical skills complemented by specialized roles. Both are necessary to move from a group of players to a team—from a collection to a collective. Vital diversities include positions (in terms of the game) and dispositions (in terms of personalities). More subtly, redundancies and diversities infuse the collaborative skills needed to coconstruct the game and to operate sometimes as teammates and sometimes as opponents.

Independence and Interdependence

One of the most important insights into complex systems is that their agents always have a certain level of autonomy, whether discussing the cells in an organic system, players in a game, or the species in an ecosystem. Agents must be allowed to act in self-interest if this system is going to be viable. In other words, independence and interdependence of agents are inextricably intertwined in complex unities. Far from existing in tension, very often the action of enhancing one can also enhance the other. This concept might be illustrated in the contrasts between democratic and totalitarian states, team sports and aerobics classes, or the Canadian and Swiss Olympic-hockey teams.

In the context of human systems, *independence* refers to the individual's opportunities to define their own roles and rights. It is about opportunities and choices, which can only be articulated in relation to *interdependence*—one's obligations to and responsibilities for the group. In other words, in situation of complex coactivity, individual, self-defined roles exist within shared, collectively defined projects.

Rule-Bound and Flexible

Perhaps the most provocative difference between systems that are causal, mechanical, and reducible and those that are learning, living, and complex concerns the nature of the rules that define the actions and interactions within the system. For causal systems, such rules are *imposed* and *prescriptive*; for complex phenomena, rules are *emergent* and *proscriptive*.

To elaborate, as already developed, the laws of Newtonian physics are sufficient to characterize mechanical systems. Complex systems must also abide by Newton's laws, of course, but new rules of acting and interacting also emerge. For example, for human societies to cohere, codes of conduct must be articulated and enforced.

Perhaps more interesting is the nature of these emergent laws.

> *F*or causal systems, such rules are imposed and prescriptive; for complex phenomena, rules are emergent and proscriptive.

Whereas the rules governing mechanical systems are *prescriptive* (that is, they dictate what must happen under specific circumstances), emergent laws within complex systems tend to be *proscriptive* (that is, they dictate what cannot happen). The Ten Commandments, a collective of "Thou shalt not ..." statements, is a good illustration, one whose structure is reflected in most modern legal systems. The same proscriptive quality is found in the rule books that govern most sports, mainly expressed in terms of prohibitions with regard to boundaries, contact, time, and so on.

A system defined only by prescriptive rules (what must happen) will be rigid and predictable. In contrast, proscriptive rules (what must not happen) can open spaces to diverse and flexible possibility. Put differently, in a proscriptive situation, what is not forbidden is allowed—a point that is almost certainly better made through a few specific examples. Capitalism and team sports are two excellent illustrations of systems governed by proscriptive rule systems. Regarding the former, the introduction of capitalist economics almost always coincides with explosions of invention and innovation. With regard to the latter, every hockey game is a new invention, unrepeatable and pregnant with novel possibility.

To recap, among the many conditions that have been identified as necessary to permit the emergence of complex coactivity (see Davis & Sumara, 2006 for a more complete list), we find the three harmonious pairings presented previously to be particularly useful and productive, with regard to our responsibilities as educators.

Human Collectivity:
Some Emergent Considerations

There is an implicit danger in what we have just done—namely, lump all complex phenomena into the same category. As noted in an earlier section, new laws and new rules of action arise with each level of complexity, and so it is important to consider the more-or-less universal conditions just mentioned alongside conditions that are specific to human coactivity.

For example, the human capacities to formalize and represent are unique among complex phenomena. Most importantly, perhaps, they enable us to consider the consequences of our actions before actually committing to those actions. In the process, they present the possibility—even the need—for a mode of teaching that, to our knowledge, is unique to humans, one that is organized around highly refined abilities to highlight features and orient attentions.

Elsewhere (Davis, Sumara, & Luce-Kapler, 2008) we have drawn on contemporary-consciousness research to draw an analogy between individual human consciousness and the role of the teacher or leader in a human collective. This analogy is organized around the realization that individual consciousness is neither locatable nor controlling. Rather, on the first point, it is a distributed phenomenon that relies as much on cultural context as it does an extraordinarily complex and differentiated brain structure (Donald, 2001). On the second point, and more significant to the current discussion, individual consciousness does not control, it orients. Individual consciousness supports a feeling of control by steering attentions toward and emphasizing particular aspects of experience. (In fact, only a tiny portion of one's sensory experiences—in the order of one out of every million events that impinge on the senses—ever bubbles to the surface of consciousness.) It is thus the case that what we perceive, know, and do is utterly dependent on consciousness. However, we must guard against the temptation to assume that these are determined by consciousness. Again, individual consciousness does not control, it orients.

Extending these points to the phenomenon of human coactivity, and specifically those occasions with an explicit pedagogical component, we are prompted to argue that teaching and leading are principally about orienting attentions, through processes of noticing, emphasizing, and reflecting aspects back to the collective. Teaching and leading, that is, are not about controlling, but about serving as the consciousness of the collective. Teachers and leaders are not principally responsible for directing or guiding, but for being expansively aware of systemic possibilities within particular situations. In offering their expanded awareness to the collective – by, for example, highlighting opportunities or deficiencies—they help to define the space of possibility for the system.

Coupled with the harmonies of redundancy and diversity, rule-bound and flexible, and independence and interdependence that are present in all complex unities, the addition of a sophisticated consciousness to human collectivity gives rise to some extraordinary possibilities. We illustrate this point in the next section with the development of the notion of enabling constraints. Our suggestion through this example is that the complex dynamics of writing poetry are not far removed from the complex dynamics of inventing games.

Enabling Constraints: Toward a Pragmatics of Transformation

How might one go about a lesson on writing a poem? Clearly the opportunity (or perhaps the imperative) to write a poem is inadequate. As we elaborate in this section, a likely reason for its ineffectiveness, in complexity terms, is that it is too open. It does not place sufficient constraints on choice. However, simply imposing a tighter constraint, such as "Write a haiku about tying your shoes," would likely be disabling, for almost the opposite reason. This instruction is too closed. How, then, might one define constraints that enable complex coactivity?

We return to this situation once again in the closing paragraphs of the chapter, after presenting a more fully developed example. Since we're not experts in physical education, we draw here on our experience in teacher education—oriented by the conviction that, while the specifics of the enabling constraints presented in the example are particular to the situation, their general structure applies to most domains of human interactivity. (The voice in the example is Dennis's.)

Writing Poems

It is a bitterly cold day and I am giving a poetry writing workshop to 32 preservice teachers who are enrolled in a teacher-education methods class. To begin, I ask them about their previous experiences with poetry writing. They tell me familiar stories:

> "We were told to just write what we felt."

> "We were told to write a sonnet for our Shakespeare unit."

> "I remember writing free-verse poems."

From what the students tell me, it seems that poems were seen as artifacts that could either be plucked from the air or extracted from deep inside one's inner being by those few students who had some gift or talent for poetic expression. I tell them to forget everything that they think they know about writing poetry. Then we begin.

Following some of the practices for teaching poetry developed by Luce-Kapler (2004), I begin by spreading a collection of buttons taken from many different articles of clothing on a large table in the middle of the classroom and then invite students to choose one that is interesting to them. Once they are seated, I ask the students to examine the button and decide what sort of article of clothing was previously attached to it, and to write down their decision. Next, I ask them to imagine the person who is wearing this article of clothing and, with a partner, to share what was imagined and then to create a situation where these two people meet. As they are making these decisions, I move around the room passing out envelopes that contain photographs I have gathered from different collections. I ask the pairs of students to examine the photographs and answer the questions, "What happened just before this photograph was taken?" I then ask them to incorporate this event into the situation that they just invented for their two characters.

Next, I ask students to work together to write a couple of paragraphs that represent the plot they have just invented. Finally, I ask each pair to show the class the buttons and photographs they have worked with and to read the paragraphs aloud that they have written. Even though they have only been working on this activity for about 30 minutes, students always produce complex, interesting plots—the beginnings of interesting fictional narratives.

Next I present students with examples of several contemporary poems. I ask them to read these to one another in their groups, paying attention to how the authors of the poems have created poetic effects. For homework, I ask the students to collaborate with their partners to choose one of these poems that they find appealing and to use it as a model for a new poem that they will create together, using the plot developed from the button-and-photograph activities. I remind them that they must collaborate with one another throughout the process of creating the new poem.

The next day, I ask students to read aloud the small poems they have created. One poem, written by Margaret and Dwayne, follows:

> *First Date*
> A sweater with puff sleeves.
> A hockey game.

Although well aware this poem is neither finished nor an intellectual *tour de force*, we liked it because it used a very simple form and very few words to vividly depict a situation ripe with interpretive possibilities.

Margaret told the class about her experience of creating the poem with Dwayne:

> I began with a small pink button that reminded me of a sweater my older sister used to wear. Dwayne had a button that he said reminded him of a winter coat he used to wear when he was in high school. We decided that these two characters could meet on the downtown bus. They would see each other for weeks and not know that one was noticing the other—and then one day they would end up sitting next to one another.
>
> The photograph that we were given showed a simple church in the background and a snow-covered parking lot in front. It reminded me of going to church when I was a kid—but when Dwayne looked at it he was reminded of going to hockey practice on cold winter mornings. We eventually decided that our two characters would get into a conversation on the bus about a hockey game that had happened the night before, which would lead to each revealing how much they like hockey and then to a decision to go to a game together.
>
> Writing the two paragraphs was easy—the plot and the characters were so clear to us. Dwayne and I worked on the poem online last night, sending ideas back and forth. We tried to copy the style of Lorna Crozier (1992), who uses very simple

structures with short phrases and everyday images. The poem that we started with was more of a narrative poem. It was a lot longer, telling the story of how these two characters met and so on. We kept editing out more and more until we ended up with what we thought was the poetic essence—a poem that announced a lot of possibilities, but one that also had concrete details. It's interesting how our final poem developed. I don't think that either of us could say who wrote what.

So, in brief, not only did participants learn about poetic form and English language-arts pedagogy, they also created novel poems—and, we would argue, they learned something about the structures of engaging learners in productive interaction through the process.

Looking more critically at the structure of the activity, we would argue that the set of tasks constituted an enabling constraint for the group of preservice teacher educators who participated. We'll develop this point by revisiting the three harmonies and the notion of the consciousness of the collective, presented in the previous sections. At the same time, we highlight how and why we emphasize these points when working with prospective teachers.

Rule-Bound and Flexible

Each of the many steps in the poetry-writing task can be understood as a constraint on choice—in effect, each served to proscribe action. The task of imagining a garment based on an actual button is vastly more constrained than, for example, the instruction, "Imagine a piece of clothing."

At the same time, this particular proscription was clearly enabling, in large part by virtue of the way it delimited possible imaginings. Each of the subsequent steps can be interpreted in very much the same way, as surges in creativity sponsored by a tightly constrained imaginative space. The rules (instructions) were rigid and limiting, but in a proscriptive manner that invited flexibility.

> *The major issue here is not that rules or instructions exist, but that these are stated in ways that open up possibilities, rather than shut them down.*

When working with teachers, then, we flag the harmony of *rule-bound* and *flexible* to foreground the simultaneous importance of task specificity and response variability. The major issue here is not that rules or instructions exist, but that these are stated in ways that open up possibilities, rather than shut them down. Pruning will eventually be necessary, but it's often better to allow it to be an organic and emergent (rather than a mechanical and immediate) process.

Independence and Interdependence

Another aspect of the success of the activity was that the tasks compelled participants to move between independent and interdependent actions. They were able to exercise autonomy in the development of characters and situations while simultaneously bringing those characters and situations into conversation with others.

In terms of their responsibilities as teachers or leaders, then, a critical point is to consider the coemergence of personal choice and collective possibility when structuring an engagement. In our experience, it is important to be explicit about these details, as there seems a tendency to ignore or downplay one category or the other if both aren't made explicit and simultaneous issues for consideration.

> **A** critical point is to consider the coemergence of personal choice and collective possibility when structuring an engagement.

Internal Redundancy and Internal Diversity

Of course, none of this would work without the diverse experiences of the participants. The teacher could rely on the fact that different imaginings and associations would be triggered. However, although it is tempting to suggest that variety among participants was the critical element, none of it would have happened without the transparent backdrop of profound similarities in ability, interest, language, social class, and expectation. The system was vastly more redundant than diverse. In fact, the many aspects of the activity were aimed at developing further redundancy (focusing on the structures of one poet's opus).

As might be expected, given the longstanding emphasis on redundancy within formal education (such as common curricula, standardized tests, and age-appropriate routines), teachers tend to be adept at identifying important redundancies in their teaching. By contrast, they are often less fluent with creating tasks and engagements that present opportunities to express and extend the sorts of diversities that are inevitably present in collectives (such as personal interests and skills). Nevertheless, when they are compelled to attend to redundancies and diversities at the same time, we've witnessed some remarkable educational events.

The Teacher as the Consciousness of the Collective

While the preceding conditions were all necessary for the explosion of creative possibility within the poetry writing class, that emergent result was clearly dependent on—but, importantly, was not determined by—the teaching.

Enabling constraints are guidelines for emergent engagement in collective spaces. In developing them, the teacher is attuned to what might happen, rather than what must happen.

That is, the teacher's role was more than merely pivotal in this complex human collective. In emphasizing and reflecting aspects back to the group from the myriads of possibilities that were presented, Dennis was acting as a sort of consciousness to the collective body—not a controller or director, but an orienter. To reemphasize, then, enabling constraints are guidelines for emergent engagement in collective spaces. In developing them, the teacher is attuned to what might happen, rather than what must happen. In this sense, enabling constraints might be characterized as a sort of thought experiment.

Conclusion

We leave it to the reader to think about how the principles and harmonies presented here might translate into a games setting. By way of preliminary thought, it strikes us that, in most sports, rules have little regard for individual players or coaches; what matters is the game. What we can say with confidence is that paying deliberate attention to some of the necessary harmonies in complex emergence has proven an effective and powerful strategy for many teachers in structuring their classrooms.

And so, how might we think about inventing games? How might the notion of enabling constraints be applied?

We actually can say very little here, given that (as developed in the first part of the chapter), we don't know much about sports beyond our own immediate participation. We're also keenly aware that the best-laid plans often fail—given that, in events of complexity, it is the system that determines the response to an intervention. As such, what works brilliantly in one situation may be disastrous in another very similar context. We thus preface our remarks with the general rule that one must be attentive to local and immediate circumstances. Who is involved? What tools are available to them? What is known about the social dynamic, and who might be fulfilling (or be capable of fulfilling) the role of the consciousness of the collective?

The list, of course, goes on. These primary considerations aside, the notion of enabling constraints and the three underpinning harmonies of complex emergence do provide some direct advice on where to focus, specifically around aspects that allow (or disallow) choice. For instance, what is the physical space like? What sorts of options does it permit? Are they too varied? Too limited? How can they be manipulated? What sorts of invitations for action and interaction can be presented that both offer autonomy to the individual and compel some level of coactivity? Should the space be altered by adding or removing particular details?

And perhaps most importantly, what do the participants bring? What do they have in common? How do they differ? What sorts of redundancies might need to be introduced and practiced? What sorts of diversities might the collective draw on to tailor activities to those present?

With this knowledge, the teacher or leader—taking on the responsibility of the collective consciousness—should be able to help define playful and productive possibilities, not by specifying rules but by presenting choices, inviting suggestions, and most critically, selecting, amplifying, and reflecting back those options that seem to offer greater promise.

That last phrase seems an apt place to end, as it points to a domain of expertise that we, with disciplinary interests that are much removed from physical education, simply do not have. Nevertheless, important correlates exist in our own areas, where teachers' disciplinary knowledge is a topic of immense current interest. What does a teacher, leader, or representative of the consciousness of the collective need to know about games in order to enable collectives to construct their own productive possibilities?

Discussion Questions

1. The principle of *emergence* suggests that a team should be capable of more than the combined abilities of its players. In what ways is this true?

2. Effective teachers, coaches, and other leaders tend to be fluid *level-jumpers*. What does this mean? Discuss a few examples.

3. Distinguish between *zero-sum logic* and *win-win logic*. How might this distinction figure into thinking about inventing games?

4. Choose a game, sport, or other complex human activity and identify some of the necessary redundancies and diversities among participants.

5. Describe the difference between *prescriptive rules* and *proscriptive rules*. Give examples of activities that are defined by one or the other (or both).

References

Breslau, K., & Heron, K. (2000). The debriefing: Bill Clinton. *Wired* [Online], *8*(12). Available: www.wired.com/wired/archive/8.12/clinton.html.

Canadians play like all-stars; Swiss play like a team. (2008 February 19). *National Post*, p. A1.

Davis, B., & Sumara, D. (2006). *Complexity and education: Inquiries into learning, teaching, and research*. Mahwah, NJ: Erlbaum.

Davis, B., Sumara, D., & Luce-Kapler, R. (2008). *Engaging minds: Changing teaching in complex times*. New York: Routledge.

Donald, M. (2001). *A mind so rare: The evolution of human consciousness*. New York: W.W. Norton.

Luce-Kapler, R. (2004). *Writing with, through, and beyond the text: An ecology of language*. Mahwah, NJ: Erlbaum.

Suroweicki, J. (2004). *The wisdom of crowds*. New York: Doubleday.

7

Occasioning Moments in the Game-as-Teacher Concept: Complexity Thinking Applied to TGfU and Video Gaming

Tim Hopper, PhD • Kath Sanford, EdD

In games lessons, we too often have "a technique section which is seen as essential by the teacher but not by the pupils, and a game which is inappropriate to the ability of many of the children. . . Of course, there are teachers who have realized that for many children the techniques are of little value and have let the children get on with the game only to realize that they seem to enjoy themselves more with less interference from the teacher. If this is so, what then does the teacher teach?" (Bunker & Thorpe, 1986, p. 11).

Through the idea of game as teacher, video games largely address and solve "the paradox involving skills: people do not like practicing skills out of context over and over again, since they find such skill practice meaningless, but, without a lot of skill practice, they cannot really get any good at what they are trying to learn. . . People learn and practice skills best when they see a set of related skills as a strategy to accomplish goals they want to accomplish" (Gee, 2007, p. 40).

Through game modification by exaggeration or representation (Thorpe and Bunker, 1997), the model of Teaching Games for Understanding (TGfU) creates conditions for students to learn a more effective coordination of movement patterns through which they can unlock their capacity to really play the game. This paper will explore this idea of conditions for learning, drawing on complexity theory as informed by a constraints-led approach to learning skills in relation to the tactical awareness of playing a game (Davids, Button, & Bennett, 2008). As such, the game offers the conditions for learning, and if designed with consideration of what the learner needs to advance in game play, creates the idea of the game as teacher. By way of illustration, we draw on two specific examples: playing a modified net/wall game and playing a video game.

Complexity thinking focuses on adaptive, self-organizing systems in which learning emerges from experiences that trigger transformation in learners (Davis & Sumara, 2006). In complexity thinking, learners are considered agents of a self-organizing system that they cocreate through their actions and their commitment to a common intent or to related goals. The notion of self-organization creates an overarching metaphor for understanding learning that, coupled with constraints placed on the learner by tasks and environment, offers new ways of understanding motor development and perceptual-action coupling (Davids et al., 2008; Davis & Broadhead, 2007). From this perspective, Davis, Sumara, and Luce-Kapler (2008) help us to understand that "teaching is not based on 'accountability' and 'evidence-based practices'—notions that are rooted in empiricist science. . . not about replication." Rather, they suggest, teaching is "about creating something new through moments of connecting and reconnecting with one another, with the past, and with the environment. . . in terms of the possibilities that arise when personal and cultural diversities are brought into conversation" (pp. 12-13).

*O*ccasioning is "presenting opportunities for things to 'fall together' in ways that cannot be fully anticipated" (Davis et al., 2008, p. 222).

This implies that learning is dependent on, but not determined by, teaching. Teachers can plan for learning, create the conditions for the expected and unexpected to emerge, but essentially, they react to the system of learners in that they can read each student's learning as multidomain, personal, and interconnected. In complexity thinking, this is referred to as *occasioning,* or "presenting opportunities for things to 'fall together' in ways that cannot be fully anticipated" (Davis et al., 2008, p. 222). In this paper, we apply the idea of occasioning to game-play in TGfU teaching and video gaming.

We understand a game as an activity structured by rules and a commonly understood conclusion or outcome, with players who invest effort in order to achieve that outcome. Game play in this paper refers to the inherent complexity in playing a game, where the outcome is indeterminate and dependent on how the players engage in the game. A game that is designed to initiate game play refers to an action space. Such a space is developed by the player's actions in a game, enabled by the aim of the game and the rules set by the teacher or computer programmer; that is, designed for engaged play to happen. It is a place of uncertainty located within the structure of a game. Gee (2007) refers to this action space in video games and describes it as space where problems are designed to help the learner traverse the trajectory of learning challenges within an area.

Similarly, through a TGfU approach, Thorpe and Bunker's (1997) modification of games by exaggeration or representation creates conditions for students, in game play, to learn more effective coordination of movement patterns, including perception and related actions, and to play a certain game, followed by more complex games that lead to the adult version of a game. These conditions create the "occasioning" of learning, the teachable moments to which the teacher draws students' attention or the programmer guides the user to recognize patterns of responses in the game from repeated correction experiences of trial and error. These occasions bring learners' perception and actions together, creating a perception-action coupling (Davis & Broadhead, 2007; Chow, Davids, Button, Shuttleworth, Renshaw, & Araujo, 2007).

As discussed by Hopper, Sanford, and Clarke (2009), despite the public concerns about video games, these types of games have been identified as sites for powerful learning. Gee (2003) suggests that game "designers face and largely solve an intriguing educational dilemma, one also faced by schools and workplaces: how to get people, often young people, to learn and master something that is long and challenging—and enjoy it, to boot" (p. 1). In video games, the game itself is the primary teacher; problems are ordered to teach the player skills and understandings that lead to more complex challenges. In video gaming, the concept of game as teacher refers to learning to play the game through progressions of subgames known as sandboxes (Gee, 2007). In other words, a video-game programmer creates the conditions for players to learn from within the game through trial and error, transferring knowledge from one experience to another through conversations with others and just-in-time and as-needed prompts within the game programming that enable game play (Gee, 2005).

> *In video games, the game itself is the primary teacher; problems are ordered to teach the player skills and understandings that lead to more complex challenges.*

Game play implies that the game is the critical site of learning; in a sense, the game becomes the direct teacher. Therefore, games designed for physical-education lessons, just like video games, must be modified for the developmental needs of the learner and constructed in a way that allows for tactical awareness (problems) and skill needs (solutions) to emerge from the context of game play (Mitchell, Griffin, & Olsen, 2006; Thorpe and Bunker, 1997). A key challenge in the TGfU approach is for the teacher to respond to and allow different responses to unfold based on the needs of diverse learners. Based on a constructivist understanding of learning, we know that students do not learn skills in the same way and at the same time; rather, they learn in relation to game play and to adaptations for the task.

Occasions for Learning in TGfU

To try to create this idea of an occasion for learning, the following account of a teachable moment from a TGfU lesson (Hopper, 1997) has been purposely structured in a poetic form to evoke an emotional and connected feeling for the reader (Hopper, Madill, Bratsch, Cameron, Coble, & Nimmon, 2008). Poetic representation is a way of analyzing social worlds and communicating their findings to others by the "use of spaces, word emphasis, positioning on the page, line breaks, metaphor, and imagery" (p. 226). This is done to create a structure that engages the reader in the felt experience, captured in the text, as they read and make sense of the text based on their own related experiences (Sparkes, Nilges, Swan, & Dowling, 2003). The following account creates the poetic form for the reader to connect to the lived experience of realizing a teachable moment in a TGfU lesson.

Context for Emily's teachable moment: The students are in the middle of learning to play a modified net/wall game. We join the fifth grade lesson where the teacher is working with the students on consistency with keeping the ball going after a bounce and where to position themselves after striking the ball. Following the exploration of catching the ball after one bounce and experimenting with different weighted and bouncy balls tossed above their heads, the teacher worked with the children on bending their knees to catch a falling ball, then tossing to a spot marker on the ground to catch again. Two tasks had been set: "How many in a row can you do?" and "Where should you go after tossing the ball?" Through trial and error, the students had come to realize that they should go on the other side of their spot as quickly as possible in order to receive the ball to send again. The students were moving in this way, mostly catching the ball after locating where it would bounce. The teacher then got the students working in pairs, tossing the ball back and forth, locating themselves across from where their partners would aim the ball. He then added a small bat to the activity. As we join the lesson, we notice Emily, a small, slight, very shy student who tends to withdraw from most physical-education activities.

Emily never smiled. She did as asked but showed no emotion. She never made an effort to get a partner. Emily always needed a partner assigned.

The children were in their own space with plastic bats, target, and ball, eager to start. The teacher set the task to alternate in pairs striking a chosen ball after one bounce,

"Try hitting to head height. Where do you go after a hit to keep the ball going?"

"Like before, opposite your partner," a child responds.

"Good." Teacher nods.

Students went to try, but were excited by the bats. It had become whack-a-ball! Teacher circulating sensed the need for focus. A ball hit the roof, ricocheting off two pupils.

"Try not to swing aimlessly—get beneath the ball and anticipate where it will go. Good Jason. Bend your knees, Emily...nice. Where do you go after you have hit the ball?" he reinforced.

In an improvised moment, the teacher stopped the class.

"Now, most of you are having a tendency to hit the ball too hard." He paused. "The idea is how many hits [you can get] in a row with your partner."

Then in a natural progression, he continued:

"Now watch Emily and me." There was a surprised shock. Giggles and muted whispers prophesied imminent disaster. "Hit the ball up, Emily."

His eyes communicated confidence; as if hypnotized, Emily responded. The ball bounced and the teacher responded, cueing Emily. An impressive rally of 11 hits; teacher caught 12th. . . more possible.

"Now see if you can match that," the teacher challenged the class.

Emily had kept the ball going; she had moved to where the ball was being sent.

"Move to the bounce, control your hits, and bend your knees like Emily," the teacher reinforced.

The class rushed to try. The teacher turned to Emily. "Thank you, Emily." He sensed a hint of a smile on her face.

The lesson developed from this point to the students creating a scoring system, adding another target and changing their bats and balls as they thought was appropriate. In every game, the students moved in anticipation of where the ball would land, bent their knees, and tried to hit the ball to the target. The coherence around playing a keep-up activity allowed them to develop their own tennislike games.

In the lesson, the students' actions initially seemed chaotic, almost out of control, but the prompts from the teacher and Emily's demonstration created what is known in dynamic-systems theory as an attractor that "provide[s] a stable base of support for actions" (Davids et al., 2008, p. 95). Emily's demonstration, after the chaotic experimentation, focused the students on the actions to address the task and also inspired them all to try. Emily's unexpected success caught the attention of the rest of the students, creating a common goal-directed activity (*How many hits with your partner?*), an occasion for the students, as part of a system, to learn.

Game Play and Complexity Learning in a TGfU Lesson

In complexity thinking, we understand learning as an emergent process, an ongoing negotiation of the perceived boundary between personal knowing and collective knowledge. As such, learners in a game observe and act in the game world through a self-organizing process in relation to the rules of the game and what is observed and experienced. A game, if structured in a way that engages the learners in play, will create the conditions, with teacher prompts, for the players to adapt their perceptions and actions to the constraints of the game (Davids et al., 2008; Davis & Broadhead, 2007). Enabling the shift from teacher-directed activity to game as teacher, with the players engaged in the game, is critical to learning.

However, in order for this to happen, the learners must self-organize according to the constraints of the game. As agents of a system formed by their class, learners have to be connected to each other to learn from interactions with each other. Initially the teacher, also an agent within the system, has to prompt the students to connect, to draw from actions that cohere to the tasks. As students move to the anticipated flight of the ball and prepare to strike the ball, they engage in game play. The concept of game as teacher is then realized.

Initially, in Emily's lesson, the students were engaged in an activity, but not in game play. They were randomly whacking the ball, which seemed counterproductive to the aim of the lesson. By trying to play, the students were learning about the environment. The diversity of their responses was evident, but most did not address the task; they were not able to create a shared game-play experience. The teacher tried to focus students' attention on key points to bring some coherence to the task, stating, "Try not to swing aimlessly—get beneath the ball," and encouraging players to learn from each other (neighbor interactions) by focusing on successful agents in the system, "Good Jason. Bend your knees, Emily. . . nice." With teacher guidance, particularly in Emily's demonstration, this chaotic situation soon became dynamic and flowing as the students "rushed to try" to keep the ball going. Students, as agents of the collective system learning to play tennis, were initially unstable in their actions, but as they learned to play within the constraints of the tasks (ball, bat, space, the movements of others, the spot), they discovered increased possibilities, a to-and-fro process, and coherence with the actions of the other players.

Framed by a constructivist epistemology, learners are understood as complex systems with diverse prior experiences that interact and adapt differently in the learning situations created by the teacher (Light, 2008). The keep-up game based on the idea of consistency and ball placement represents a nested version of typical games, such as tennis, squash, and volleyball, within a net/wall-games category (Hopper & Bell, 2001). This nested quality means that the game being played has similar qualities to the key components of net/wall games. For example, the components in the keep-up game relate to tennis with two players hitting the ball alternately, aiming at a target, moving to cover where the ball is sent, and striking a ball in front of the body (see Hopper, 2003 for a more extensive analysis).

In the lesson, the teacher selected Emily to demonstrate, not because she was necessarily the best performer, but because her demonstration would teach more than the skill of striking the ball. Her successful demonstration enabled her to reframe her social status and to gain confidence in her ability to play, "sensing a hint of smile." In this way, learning is understood in terms of experiences that trigger transformations in the learner that are both physical and behavioral. These triggers are based on the interactions of the individuals' perceived (affective and social) and actual (cognitive and psychomotor) abilities (developed from previous interactions with game-play constraints) and tasks set by the teacher in relation to the fixed environment associated with the game (Davids et al., 2008).

In complexity thinking, learning occurs in a system that is self-organizing, self-maintaining, and adaptive. Complexity thinking allows learning to be described in terms of living and social systems, which create a more dynamic interpretative process for understanding learning as emerging from experiences that transform learners (Richardson & Cilliers, 2001). With complexity thinking, we are concerned with a complex reality that is indeterminable but can be influenced by human action. In the lesson, each student is considered an agent of the system, a complex structure that will adapt to an environment that the student cocreates, in part through engagements with other students. As described in the poem, the students created the environment of the lesson through their actions. Initially, the lesson was open to possibilities as the students

Complexity thinking allows learning to be described in terms of living and social systems, which create a more dynamic interpretative process for understanding learning as emerging from experiences that transform learners (Richardson & Cilliers, 2001).

experimented but the lesson had become too open, almost random, since "It had become whack-a-ball!"

As "a ball hit the roof ricocheting off two pupils," the teacher realized the need for a major intervention to stabilize the system. Rather than demonstrating by himself, the teacher chose Emily after he spotted her success, "Bend your knees, Emily... nice." She had just demonstrated the desired behaviors, and she had also moved in anticipation of where the ball would land next. This intervention, although risky if Emily had been unable to respond, represented a bottom-up learning process, since the teacher used an agent from within the system, an agent seen as lacking ability by her peers, ("Giggles and muted whispers prophesied imminent disaster") to focus the students on the task. As Emily performed—"11 hits; teacher caught 12th... more possible"—the class became focused. If Emily could do it, surely they could; actions and ideas had come together in an occasion for learning. The teacher could stand back, taking himself out of the center of the lesson, allowing the students to engage in the game.

Learners engaged in an experience change structurally, conditioned by the experience according to their "complex biological-and-experiential structure" (Davis and Sumara, 2006, p. 13). In the poem, Emily changed; from then on in that unit, she became a keen participant in the lessons. Her smile indicated a change. The teacher had read the "teachable moment," the occasioning moment (Davis et al., 2008), that would trigger effective learning for Emily and game-play learning for the whole class as they engaged in the constraints of game. The teacher planned the lesson and created the game, but for the game to function as teacher, the instructor had to get an agent within the system (Emily), to inspire the students to create a self-organizing system (Davis and Sumara, 2006) in which they could play a "tennislike" activity.

Occasions for Learning in Video Gaming

Video games, such as role-play games, simulation games (race-car driving, flying), sports games (football, soccer), or shorter puzzle games (Tetris, Bejewelled) create occasioning moments that teach players how to play the game. As noted by Gee (2007), the teacher is the game itself, created by a behind-the-scenes programmer who has attempted to create an environment, through many trials and revisions, that actively engages the player in meaningful experiences related to the game. The game, however, must allow the players to connect to its purpose and interface, and to achieve the game outcomes, to understand the conditions set out, and to enjoy the engagement (Gee, 2005). The rules established by the programmers are recognized, attended to, and then navigated in the game-play space between the game and player as the player gains and adapts skills to the conditions set by the game. The delight of challenging and manipulating the game rules in order to achieve a successful outcome (attaining a high score, beating the opponent) is implicit throughout the game.

> *Video-game programmers are increasingly drawing on what education sciences have discovered about optimal human learning in relation to situated-learning and systems theory (Gee, 2007).*

Successful video games model this idea of the game as teacher through occasioning moments where, through trial and error and with hints from the programmer, the player develops perception-action couplings, finding ways to solve problems presented in the game play (Davids et al., 2008; Gee, 2007). In this way, video-game programmers increasingly draw on what education sciences have discovered about optimal human learning in relation to situated-learning and systems theory (Gee, 2007). These findings are being connected to the growing body of literature on complexity science and non-linear dynamic systems (Chow et al., 2007; Davis & Sumara, 2006). The game is programmed to scaffold learning at a rate that the player (whether novice or expert) can manage. Each constraint placed on the player develops skills that create an in-depth understanding of the game rules, enabling more advanced play later in the game. The player determines how long to engage, when to play, when to stop, and how to learn more strategies and skills.

Insights of Adolescent Boys Playing Halo 3

To identify how occasions for learning occur within a video game, we have taken a short narrative extract from Sanford and Madill's (2008) research on video-game play and learning. As noted by Clandinin (2007), narrative is used as an insight on social reality; it provides a third-person view of social structure formed around a certain phenomenon. The following passage describes a gathering of four young men, aged 13 to 16, all playing one of 2007's most popular video games, Halo 3. They have come together because of their common interest in the game, but are not friends in other aspects of their lives.

Gathered around a large screen are the four players, connected by their common interest in Halo 3 play. The screen is divided into four quadrants; the play for each player lies in one of the four quadrants. Although the implicit rules of the game dictate that they focus only on their own quadrant, it is possible for them to look at the other three areas. And while the players are of different ability levels in relation to playing Halo 3, they are all experienced videogame players and know their way around the controllers and this particular virtual world play-space.

The game begins and they are immediately focused. For minutes at a time, their eyes never leave their part of the screen, as they engage their avatar in the action. Soon, brief disjointed comments are heard, "Awwww!", "No way!", and laughter, as the avatars are successful (gaining a position, "killing" an opponent) or are not successful (failing the mission, losing "health"). Comments showing appreciation for an opponent's skill are heard ("Nice one!"), and questions asked of each other ("How did you get over there?", "How do you get that weapon?"). As process questions are asked, they are responded to with instructions about how to go about improving their progress ("Use this key to jump..."); responses are brief but friendly and there is no hesitancy about sharing information in order to make the action of the game continue. For example, when one player in Halo 3 starts to get frustrated, the enemy in a certain area always killed him; another player easily shows how a change in light indicates a teleport that can whisk you from harm's way. Immediately, this action was used on the next turn and the players exchange a smile and a nod of approval. Sometimes, as in this occasion, players divert their eyes from the screen to share information and moves with each other, but they quickly shift back to screen focus. Intermittently, they reach for a drink, or a handful of chips, but these distractions do not interrupt the flow of the game.

As the game proceeds, there are comments of appreciation about each other's play as points are scored, vehicles and weapons are captured, and progress is made. The storyline, while not complex, keeps the game flowing as it interweaves with the more complex strategies and controller skills of play. And while the implicit rules of the game demand focus only on the player's particular quadrant, it is acceptable to shift focus to other quadrants in response to questions or request for assistance, or to keep the game going if the action stalls because of another player's difficulty. The attention paid to another player's quadrant usually results in a suggestion for better positioning, action, or a new strategy. The rules about "cheats" and "cheating" are themselves highly complex and need to be negotiated by the players of each game. So while "cheats" that enable game play to continue (found on the Internet, through conversation with a friend, in a magazine), "cheating" to increase the player's own individual chances of winning (spying on each other, stealing knowledge) is not acceptable.

As the game proceeds and players get accustomed to each other's style and skill level, the edge of competition increases. Players begin to engage in "trash talk" about each other's characters and play choices. All in good fun, but this banter increases the level of engagement, challenge, and competition. Most comments result in retorts or laughs by the other players, common in-jokes, appreciation of each other's skills, and enjoyment of the game. Players can opt in or out of the game as they wish, if they have had enough of the play, if their performance isn't keeping up to that of the other players, or if they have to leave. This doesn't interrupt the flow of the game.

It is a complex game that draws on its two earlier versions, building on previous knowledge of the game play and backstory. Players codesign and customize the game for themselves, as individual players or as members of a team, feeling as if they are actively involved in the game and can shape how the game evolves. The game changes as the player gains skills, changes playing partners, or tries out new riskier strategies. As players progress through a game with partners or opponents, they will adapt their game play if they are familiar or unfamiliar, determining the level of risk they are willing to take in front of others.

Players have the opportunity to try out a range of avatar characteristics, changing physical appearance, personality traits, even gender. They can shape their character's actions and reactions to reflect their own personality, or to try out a different personality, in a relatively risk-free environment. They can "become" someone else as they engage in a fantasy world with fantasy challenges, trying out a range of responses to the problems posed by the game and other players. These responses help players understand and make sense of their virtual worlds.

Game Play and Complexity Learning in a Video-Gaming Session

As with the TGfU lesson, the Halo game is an activity structured by rules and a commonly understood conclusion or outcome, with players invested in the outcome. Action develops when the player chooses to interact with certain structures created by the computer programmer that enable a play space, a place of uncertainty. Players' actions are structurally self-organized, determined in a virtual context that is proscriptive (limits based on what cannot be done), but inviting multiple adaptive behaviors from the players to overcome challenges.

As discussed earlier, learning in video games is an emergent process, an ongoing renegotiation of the perceived boundary between personal knowing and collective knowledge. These boundaries arise as a person observes and acts in the world through a self-organizing process in relation to what is observed and experienced from interactions with others: "Comments showing appreciation for an opponent's skill are heard ('Nice one!'), and questions asked of each other ('How did you get over there?')." Unlike Emily's lesson, the video-game session initially did not look unstable. For nongame players, a situation in which a "screen is divided into four quadrants; the play for each player lies in one of the four quadrants," looks incredibly chaotic, almost out of control. The players, through hours of engaging in the tasks of the video game, have developed perceptual-action couplings that allow dynamic and flowing game play.

> **L**earning in video games is an emergent process, an ongoing renegotiation of the perceived boundary between personal knowing and collective knowledge. These boundaries arise as a person observes and acts in the world through a self-organizing process in relation to what is observed and experienced from interactions with others.

Players are now agents of a collective system in playing Halo 3; however, when they first played the game, they were erratic and unstable in their game play. As they learned to play within the constraints of the tasks, they were liberated to discover infinite possibilities, a to-and-fro process, with limits providing coherence as their actions complement and enable the actions of other players. In the story, similar to Emily's demonstration, a frustrated player who was always killed by "the enemy in a certain area" received just-in-time and as-needed guidance from "another player [who]...shows how a change in light indicates a teleport that can whisk you from harm's way." The player then reenters the game and immediately is successfully engaged in game play, receiving "a smile and a nod of approval." This neighborly interaction, made possible by the game, creates a learning system that forms between players. In addition, the computer programmer often builds in this type of feedback information "on demand and just in time" (Gee, 2007, p. 37) through characters or from tips programmed into the game. This neighbor interaction needs sufficient density to allow the occasion for the emergence of rich interpretative moments (Davis and Sumara, 2006). In video games, this density is often achieved through online communities, "'cheats' that enable game play to continue (found on the Internet, through conversation with a friend, in a magazine)."

Learning in video games is understood in terms of experiences that trigger transformations in the learner. The virtual environment of the videogame interacts with the task at hand (mission) and the capacity of the player to coordinate their avatar. Just as in the poem, these triggers are based on the interaction of the constraints of players' perceived and actual abilities, task conditions or goals, and the environment (Davids et al., 2008). Gee (2005) notes that after every mission, the player's avatar gains new skills and new insights on the game that can be saved and used in later missions. The avatar has changed, and the player who controls the avatar has changed as well. As noted in the narrative, players experience "success (gaining a position, 'killing' an opponent) or [lack of] success (failing the mission, losing 'health')." These interactions for the players are ongoing and rapid, leading to small adaptive changes as they develop their capacity to play the game and self-organize their actions around attractors of success that stabilize as skills. Learning emerges as the players experience success and take the skill or strategy to the next level or mission.

In complexity thinking, each player is considered an agent of the video-game system. In the multiplayer example of Halo 3, the players become a system, a complex structure that will adapt to an environment, which each player in part cocreates by engaging with other players and with the game structure. Successful video games like Halo 3 build on the capacity for players to customize the game: "Players co-design and customize the game for themselves. . . try out a range of avatar characteristics, changing physical appearance [and] personality. . . in a relatively risk-free environment." As players become accustomed to the game controls, they are able to access more options and explore a variety of characters with different skill sets in environments where they can regulate the level of difficulty.

In the physical-education lessons, as students become engaged in a game initiated by the teacher, they are offered opportunities to customize options for game play, such as the space they play in, the bat they use, or a ball selected from a variety of different balls that can bounce and fly at different speeds. For both video gaming and TGfU games, giving players ownership allows them to reinvent game play and adapt the game to either their own abilities or those of their coplayers.

The Game as Teacher and the Conditions for the Emergence of Complexity

In both examples of video games and physical education, many features of complexity thinking are present. Using these examples, we have noted self-similarity, neighbor interactions, enabling constraints, bottom-up learning, decentralized control, emergent process, knowledge distributed across players, body (real and virtual) and tools, and adaptation qualities of complex-learning systems. In this last section, we will focus on the notion of game as teacher and will summarize how complexity thinking guides the design of conditions in order for complex learning to emerge.

In the notion of game as teacher, the game is set as the condition for the emergence of complex learning. This means that rather than breaking a game into parts (such as skills, rules, strategies, and tactics) the game is seen as a system of interacting and adapting subsystems that must be learned as a self-similar whole. This whole creates the conditions for the complexity of a game to emerge from exploration of the task and environment. As Rovegno and Kirk (1995) note, teaching games then becomes "concerned with learners' explorations and attention while performing appropriate tasks within an appropriate environment, an environment that is matched to the characteristics and capabilities of the individual" (p. 461). In relation to video games, Gee (2005) notes that "learning is based on situated practices. . . lowered consequences for failure and taking risks. . . learning is a form of extended engagement of self as an extension of an identity to which the player is committed" (p. 112). All these features reframe learning as an interactive process in which humans take pleasure, a process they own as they adapt to the game.

For both video gaming and TGfU games, giving players ownership allows them to reinvent game play and adapt the game to either their own abilities or those of their coplayers.

In agreement with other theorists (Clarke & Collins, 2007; Clarke, Erickson, Collins, & Phelan, 2005; Davis, 2008), Davis and Sumara (2006, p. 136) suggest the following conditions must exist for complex learning to emerge:

1. tension between diversity and redundancy,
2. neighbor interactions enabled through decentralized control, and
3. enabling constraints that balance randomness and coherence.

Tension Between Diversity and Redundancy

Internal diversity is critical in a complex system to allow a source of possible responses to emergent circumstances. In both examples in this paper, players learn by trial and error through stages of exploration, experimentation, and selection, and are guided by the on-demand and just-in-time information provided by the teacher or computer programmer. This information encourages diversity to surface as players learn to modify their actions for the game environment. Diversity among the learners provides generative possibilities that systems need in order to adapt and learn, such as other players experimenting with the racquet in the physical-education lesson or getting killed in the video game, learning and then trying again and again as they interact with peers.

However, redundancy as the complement of diversity means that a complex system also needs a lot of shared features between agents, such as common language, similar experiences, common skills, and related responsibilities. These redundancies are the backdrop of social action that allow coherence to be maintained, enabling interactions among agents and allowing agents to compensate for the weaknesses of others. The common experience of playing together, adapting to the same game rules creates the redundancy that allows diverse responses to the game play to flourish. Too much diversity would lead to chaotic actions and disconnect (for example, players "whack-a-ball" or "start to get frustrated"), with each agent specializing and disconnecting from the other agents. Too much redundancy could lead to sameness, the inability to adapt, and the loss of creativity.

Enabling Neighbor Interactions Through Decentralized Control

Complexity thinking offers some insight into how individual interests and collective interests can be mutually supportive. A key idea is that agents within a complex system must be able to affect another's activities. As Davis and Sumara (2006) stress, it is critically important for a complex system to activate "these potentials in the hope that they might trigger others and, in the process, be blended into more sophisticated possibilities" (p. 142). One way to understand this is through conversation as agents engage and exchange ideas around a common intent. Within the TGfU example, the teacher continuously comments on the students' actions during the activity, relaying these insights back to the other students. Students may not communicate as the teacher does, but their actions in the context communicate ideas, since students learn by doing and by seeing others act. In video games, players show and tell each other as they do new moves and discover new skills. Players in both the TGfU lesson and the video-game example see each other's ideas develop as they play and practice together. This process creates a self-organizing effect on the class, as actions created by each student inform and add to actions created by another.

In both examples, the players create a knowledge-producing system that increasingly relies less on the feedback, tips, and hints from the teacher or computer programmer to direct their learning, instead relying more on the interactions of the agents in the game to produce the game play. In this way, the authority for the game shifts from the teacher or computer programmer to the players as they create the game play, refine it, practice it, and ultimately play and replay as others join their game.

Enabling Constraints: Balancing Randomness and Coherence

Enabling constraints may seem like an oxymoron; however, it is a critical condition for the emergence of complex learning. Constraints enable the structural conditions that determine the balance between sources of coherence, which allow the collective to maintain a focus of purpose, and sources of difference and randomness, which compel the collective to adjust and adapt. Both examples show rule-bound complex systems with a progression of tasks that enable game play. As Davis and Sumara (2006) note, for complexity to emerge you must have "sufficient coherence based on sufficiently constrained domain, and an openness to randomness in order to allow for the emergence of unanticipated possibilities" (p. 149). This flexibility is a characteristic of being part of a complex emergent unity.

Given that learning depends on many changing factors, teaching always needs to be responsive to the location of the learner at the moment of play; the situation is always influenced by many diverse individual and environmental factors. Teaching in TGfU, then, requires ongoing adaptation as the teacher attempts to create conditions conducive to learners' ongoing development and improvement. Davis and Sumara (2006) note that "complexity thinking helps us actually take on the work of trying to understand things while we are part of the things we are trying to understand" (p. 16). When we teach using a TGfU approach, the teacher acts as a self-referencing conduit in the system of students who are learning to play the game, orchestrating students' learning by feeding back insights that enable students to engage in the game. Ultimately, like successful video games in which the programmer has structured the game to self-organize around occasioning moments in game play, the teacher in a TGfU approach must create this relationship to the game for students so that they can learn through these moments of game play.

Conclusion

Complexity thinking provides us with a way forward for understanding the needs of today's students as they grapple with an increasingly challenging and complex world. Building on notions of social constructivism, complexity thinking enables learners to recognize and develop from occasioning moments in game play. We have used complexity thinking not as an alternative to other discourses about learning, but rather as a discourse that arises among others as a way of helping us consider perspectives to inform learning in physical education that are physically, emotionally, and socially meaningful. Complexity thinking, as demonstrated through game play developed in video games and TGfU, offers possibilities for reawakening students from the lethargy they too often experience in formal learning situations, and reengaging them in significant and meaningful learning. The concept of the game as teacher invites instructors to think of themselves as computer programmers, creating nested-game structures that invite students to learn. The challenge in teaching games is to enable learners to access game play so that they are invested in playing again and again. The game-as-teacher concept invites learners to collectively take on more complex challenges, transferring skills developed in an easier game form to more challenging games, which leads to a sense of personal accomplishment and social connection.

Discussion Questions

1. As an adolescent did you find video games engaging? If yes, why was that?

2. Complexity thinking advocates a more organic metaphor for learning. What do you think a PE lesson would look like if a teacher encouraged students to learn using a complex lens?

3. What are the key features of a complex learning system?

4. Indirect instruction advocates learning from a problem or inquiry focus. How does complexity thinking connect to this instructional approach?

References

Bunker, D., & Thorpe, R. (1986). From theory to practice. In R. Thorpe, D. Bunker and L. Almond (Eds.), *Rethinking games teaching* (pp. 11-14). Loughborough, UK: University of Technology.

Chow, J.Y., Davids, K., Button, C., Shuttleworth, R., Renshaw, I., & Araujo, D. (2007). The role of nonlinear pedagogy in physical education. *Review of Educational Research, 77*(3), 251-278.

Clandinin, D.J. (2007). *Handbook of narrative inquiry: Mapping a methodology*. Thousand Oaks, CA: Sage Publications.

Clarke, A., & Collins, S. (2007). Complexity science and student-teacher supervision. *Teaching & Teacher Education: An International Journal of Research and Studies, 23*(2), 160-172.

Clarke, A., Erickson, G., Collins, S., & Phelan, A. (2005). Complexity science and cohorts in teacher education. *Studying Teacher Education, 1*(2), 159-208.

Davids, K., Button, C., & Bennett, S. (2008). *Dynamics of skill acquisition: A constraints led approach.* Windsor, ON: Human Kinetics.

Davis, B. (2008). Complexity and education: Vital simultaneities. *Educational Philosophy and Theory, 40*(1), 50-65.

Davis, B., & Sumara, D. (2006). *Complexity and education: Inquires into learning, teaching and research.* London: Lawrence Erlbaum.

Davis, B., Sumara, D., & Luce-Kapler, R. (2008). *Engaging minds: Changing teaching in a complex world.* New York: Routledge.

Davis, W.E., & Broadhead, G. (2007). *Ecological task analysis and movement.* Windsor, ON: Human Kinetics.

Gee, J. (2003). *What video games have to teach us about learning and literacy.* New York: Palgrave, Macmillan.

Gee, J. (2005). *Why video games are good for your soul: Pleasure and learning.* Toronto, ON: Common Ground.

Gee, J. (2007). *Good video games and good learning.* New York: Peter Lang.

Hopper, T. (1997). Learning to respond: Supervising novice physical educators in an action research project. *Sport, Education and Society, 2*(2), 163-180.

Hopper, T. (2003). Four R's for tactical awareness: Applying game performance assessment in net/wall games. *Journal of Teaching Elementary Physical Education, 4*(2), 16-21.

Hopper, T., & Bell, F. (2001). Can we play the game again? *STRATEGIES, 15*(1).

Hopper, T., Madill, L., Bratsch, C., Cameron, K., Coble, J., & Nimmon, L. (2008). Multiple voices in health, sport, recreation and physical education research: Revealing unfamiliar spaces in a polyvocal review of qualitative research genre. *QUEST, 60,* 214-235.

Hopper, T., Sanford, K., & Clarke, A. (2009). Game-as-teacher and game-play: Complex learning in TGfU and video games. In T. Hopper, J. Butler, and B. Storey (Eds.), *TGfU. . . Simply good pedagogy: Understanding a complex challenge* (pp. 201-212). Ottawa, ON: Physical Health Education.

Light, R. (2008). Complex learning theory—its epistemology and its assumptions about learning: Implications for physical education. *Journal of Teaching Physical Education, 27,* 21-37.

Mitchell, S., Griffin, L., & Olsen, J. (2006). *Teaching sport concepts and skills: A tactical games approach.* Champaign, IL: Human Kinetics.

Richardson, K., & Cilliers, P. (2001). What is complexity science? A view from different directions. *Emergence, 3*(1), 5-22.

Rovegno, I., & Kirk, D. (1995). Articulations and silences in socially critical work on physical education: Towards a broader agenda. *QUEST, 47*(4), 447-474.

Sanford, K., & Madill, L. (2008). Teachers and students learning through video game design. In R. Ferdig (Ed.), *Handbook of Research on Electronic Gaming in Education.* New York: Information Science Reference.

Sparks, A., Nilges, L., Swan, P., & Dowling, F. (2003). Poetic representations in sport and physical education: Insider perspectives [Article]. *Sport Education & Society, 8*(2), 153-177.

Thorpe, R., & Bunker, D.J. (1997). A changing focus in games teaching. In L. Almond (Ed.), *Physical education in schools.* London: Kogan Page.

8

Ecological Thinking and TGfU: Understanding Games as Complex Adaptive Systems

Brian Storey, MA • Joy I. Butler, EdD

I t's lunch time, the bell rings, and the children pour out of their box within a box onto sun-washed fields. The ball bucket is dutifully rolled into service by the monitors. A multiaged group swarms the bucket and digs for treasure. Cries of, "I found it! I've got the soccer ball!" are heard from the bunch. The treasure is rushed to the grassy area for release. Teams are struck along yesterday's lines, but there are newcomers. No problem, solution found: there are four newcomers, which means two will go on each team according to who knows them best. The game is on! Monitors mingle in the distance. A child falls, another helps her up, someone scores, someone else makes her best pass of the year. The game is lopsided, so a few players switch teams. Time slows and speeds up for each player as they slip in and out of focus on the ball, on each other, and on the game.

This description of a self-organizing and ever-changing game represents some of the joys and frustrations of childhood that we have all experienced in our own way. Some of us found these to be our most memorable moments of childhood, while others found them torturous and exclusionary. To assume that a spontaneous playground game would automatically lead to positive memories for everyone would be to ignore the evolutionary nature of multiplayer games. Whether formalized, as in the case of organized sports, or informally played, as in the opening example,

Teachers working from a reflective ecological perspective can never entirely dissociate their actions and decisions from those of their students or from the context in which they occur. On the contrary, teachers view themselves as embedded in the learning system in a coconstructed search for the unknown with the learner.

games are inherently complex learning systems. As such, they require a holistic perspective for understanding the learning that takes place within them. We turn to ecology—the study of adaptation and interconnection within ecosystems—to provide us with this holistic perspective and a different way to contextualize and examine teaching and learning games.

An ecological understanding of teaching and learning is based on values that encourage the search for meaning in the systemic and individual characteristics that both constrain and enable learning (Davis, Sumara, & Luce-Kapler, 2008). Teachers working from an ecological integration values orientation (Jewett, Bain, & Ennis, 1995) can never entirely dissociate their actions and decisions from those of their students or from the context in which they occur. On the contrary, teachers view themselves as embedded in the learning system in a coconstructed search for the unknown with the learner. This ecosystem of learning determines both the individual adaptations of the participants and the broader nature of their universe. Ideally, the school then becomes a context within which a wide spectrum of learners may be respected and integrated.

To develop an ecological perspective of games learning, we suggest that the following five sections of this chapter will help the reader understand what we believe to be important components of the perspective:

1. Understanding the role of games in society
2. Thinking ecologically as an orientation of values
3. Examining games as complex adaptive systems
4. Situating the approach of TGfU within an ecological view of learning
5. Identifying implications for teachers interested in the ecological-values orientation

Understanding the Role of Games in Society

The creation of a game is an implied contract to coadapt throughout the process of play. Games are sites of communal adaptation due to their social nature. Furthermore, the adaptive effects of games are cumulative for individual players, the group, and society. For example, learnings about cooperation and competition gained through playing childhood games may become adaptive beliefs or behaviors that carry forward into adulthood. Our beliefs about the importance of teamwork, effort, politics, and rules are just a few resulting values of our games experiences. In short, "sport [and games] function as an institution of socialization into the dominant cultural ideology" (Light Shields & Light Bredemeier, 1996, p. 369).

Although games can be classified as social institutions due to their historical and cultural meanings, the most important characteristic of their definition is that the individual intentions and histories of the agents (players, teachers, coaches, and officials) involved do not provide predictable or predetermined outcomes. The systemic uncertainty reserved for situations described as games necessitates a view of the future that is neither linear nor fixed. Culturally bound games with undetermined outcomes leave their potential for socialization open to the influence of the participants. How we play determines whether we replicate or reinterpret the inherent values in games and in the dominant ideologies of the surrounding culture.

Inherent value is defined as the objective property of the game itself, something that is part of its essential nature. For example, one inherent value of games is the uncertainty of the outcome and our collective enjoyment in observing and playing opponents who are evenly matched. Other inherent values of games are the interplay and relationship between cooperation and competition. A common western sporting notion of games is that one group of players (team) cooperates in an effort to compete against and beat another team (Siedentop, 2003), reinforcing a rather mechanistic, industrial mindset that "Our gain is your loss." From an alternative ecological perspective, no competition can exist between teams without cooperation; the act of setting up and agreeing to the challenge. In this scenario, opponents are appreciated in the collective striving toward higher goals.

Many teachers and coaches rally against extreme competitive notions of games in their zero-sum forms by insisting on fair play, good sporting behavior, and an environment that promotes socialization; however, these notions are often secondary to the greater competitive narrative that defines the majority of physical games in our society. The embodied understanding of children's game

From an alternative ecological perspective, no competition can exist between teams without cooperation; the act of setting up and agreeing to the challenge. In this scenario, opponents are appreciated in the collective striving toward higher goals.

experiences lays the foundation for our broader understanding of competition and cooperation in all games as adults. When our belief is that winning is the only way to gain status among our peers and approval from the attending adult, our experience of cooperation becomes perfunctory and manipulative. In extreme situations, notions of the team's greater good, the opponent's greater good, and individual differences are lost in the singular focus of winning.

If teachers accept that games are sites of communal learning and adaptation for the learners, then the purpose of games for society and the individual, from a values perspective, is an important consideration. If, on the one hand, we seek social efficiency (in which the purpose of our games is to foster competition and individualism in order to survive in our constructed economic and public spheres), then we do not need to rethink zero-sum children's games and common notions of winners and losers. If, on the other hand, we seek social reconstruction and want our teaching to create alternatives to the status quo, then alternative understandings of competition and cooperation (such as an ecological understanding) provide insights into potentially different outcomes of the communal adaptation that can occur during games.

Ecological Thinking as an Orientation of Values

Defining one's perspective on games-based physical education is presented in the previous paragraph as a deliberate and conscious choice. Some teachers are not aware of their perspective because it is a lens "they look through, rather than at, when teaching" (Jarvis-Selinger, Collins, & Pratt, 2007, p. 2). The choice of a lens for games teaching is defined both by the external constraints placed on the teacher and by what the teacher thinks the value of physical education is to the learners.

Games education has both inherent and intrinsic value for learners, and within this context, teachers make important choices about what they believe will be of most value and interest for students. These choices in turn impact the way that the curriculum is constructed and developed. These values have been usefully summarized by Jewett, Bain, and Ennis (1995), in the broader context of physical education, as five value orientations:

1. Mastery of disciplines
2. Self-actualization
3. Social reconstruction
4. Learning process
5. Ecological integration

Identifying the philosophical principles that underpin the curriculum allows the reflective part of praxis to take place. The values orientation of ecological integration best describes our understanding of games as complex learning systems.

In ecological integration, the teacher values the search for meaning and encourages learners to ask and examine critical questions. Ideally, learners see themselves as an integral component of an ecosphere, responding to the environment and thus determining the nature of that particular universe. The school is regarded as a context within which a holistic person may be integrated. It looks to the future. Evaluation techniques are selected to ensure that learners develop a holistic perspective (Butler, 2006, p. 248).

An understanding of games from a values orientation of ecological integration can be further developed by reconciling the characteristics of games and game-based learning with the established criteria for describing complex adaptive systems for learning.

Examining Games as Complex Adaptive Systems for Learning

Complexity thinking is the backbone of complexity science, which Davis and Sumara (2005a) describe as the study of how "autonomous agents can come together into more sophisticated, more capable unities and how, in turn, those grander unities affect the actions and characteristics of the agents that comprise them" (p. 454). From a games perspective, multiple players are required who have the potential for adaptation as a result of their involvement. In order to be considered a complex learning system, from an ecological perspective, the phenomena of study must be (a) comprised of codependent agents, (b) self-organizing, (c) open to disturbance, (d) a site of nested and coemergent learning, and (e) open to varying experiences or interpretations of time (Davis & Sumara, 2002, 2003, 2005a, 2005b; Doll, 1993; Mennin, 2007). Each characteristic of games seen through this orientation provides language and ideas for understanding the learning we facilitate and witness in our teaching. Table 8.1 and the following sections elaborate on each of these criteria for complex learning.

Complex Learning is Comprised of Codependent Agents

The agents of games and sport are its players, coaches, referees, and in some cases, parents. These agents process a lot of information and events that make up the complex adaptive system (Mennin, 2007). Players bring unique game experiences to a team, and learn to communicate

Table 8.1 Criteria of Complex Systems and Exemplary Game Characteristics

Complex-system criteria	Game characteristics
Comprised of agents	Players, coaches, and referees are all autonomous individuals who bring their own histories, abilities, and motivations to the game.
Self-organization	Games can be organized spontaneously (such as playground games). Players also spontaneously self-organize within games (group transitions from offense to defense).
Codependence	1v1 game: Competitor is the codependent for learning. 2v2 or greater games: Competitors and teammates are codependents required for learning.
Equilibrium, disequilibrium, and disturbance	Games have probable but not predetermined outcomes, making them open by definition. Disturbance is both consciously and unconsciously created by players, coaches, and teachers in different amplitudes.
Nested and coemergent learning	Improvement in the skill or tactics of one player or team creates disequilibrium for both teammates and competitors, forcing further adaptation or learning.
Fractal time (multiple experiences of time)	Athletes and children both describe competing and playing games as containing moments of slowed and accelerated time. Time is observed in many games forms as a constraint, but heartbeats, breaths, and concentration characterize the rhythms of games.

with teammates, adapt, and respond to opponents. In terms of complexity thinking, we can view the individual as a processing agent of complex adaptive information and the team as a processing unit for adaptive information. The team must both adapt to its own nuances and differences as a collection of complex adaptive agents and react and respond to the other set of complex adaptive agents within the opposing team. Together they create the complex adaptive system.

Codependence is not restricted to the members of a team; it extends beyond to the opponents in the contest. Without the opponent, there is no game. The two parties collaborate through implicit or explicit agreement to create the opportunity for the emotions, experiences, and ultimate learning that occurs within the complex adaptive environment we call the game. Such awareness necessitates a revised respect for the opponent. Without the opponent, players cannot improve. Too much disequilibrium, which results from skill, fitness, or cognitive differences between the teams, negates opportunities for both the dominated and dominators to experience meaningful challenge.

With this understanding, participants who work from a values orientation of ecological integration will no longer see the opponent as other or as the enemy. The opponent is a coconspirator in the agreement to create opportunities for adaptation. In order to test one's skill and thinking during a game, an equally matched opponent is one solution; an opponent or rule change that constrains the dominating team's performance is another. When a mismatch is obvious, some individuals and teams will spontaneously adapt their play to recreate the tension and enjoyment of near-equilibrium play, while others will project an approach of "take no prisoners." Learners' consciousness of their codependence on others, versus their domination of others, is central to an ecological perspective on games education, leading to a teaching focus that requires them to adjust, adapt, invent, and play games that maximize opportunities for all.

Complex Learning is Self-Organizing

Teams demonstrate self-organizing behavior as they adapt to their opponents and to each other to create patterns of play aimed at continually increasing their odds of success. In playground settings, children spontaneously create games without prompting in a desire to find adaptive circumstances that contain excitement and suspense. By setting up their own games, children self-organize their own growth opportunities.

The principle of self-organization states that new emergent structures and patterns will spontaneously emerge from old ones. This emergence, which comes from the inside of the agent, is based on feedback and information processed from the environment. When self-organization and learning as a biological adaptive process, whether cognitive or physical, is accepted as a foundational principle or learning, then educational emphasis necessarily shifts from teaching to learning (Davis & Sumara, 2005a; Doll, 1993; Mennin, 2007).

In playground settings, children spontaneously create games without prompting in a desire to find adaptive circumstances that contain excitement and suspense. By setting up their own games, children self-organize their own growth opportunities.

Complex Learning is Open to Disequilibrium and Disturbance

A stable system is one in which the agents maintain their position or status quo. In educational terms, they are not learning. In unstable systems, agents are adapting. Mennin (2007) refers to the stable system as being in equilibrium, while the unstable system is far from equilibrium. Doll (1993) refers to the two types of systems as *closed* and *open,* respectively.

Open systems are available for disturbances or perturbations, the challenges which force adaptation and pave the way for iterative learning in a game. These may be introduced by an outside force, such as a teacher or coach, or may spontaneously emerge as a result of game play.

Constraints are the environmental or external boundaries of the complex system. They may be represented by rules, physical space, or equipment. In games and sports terms, constraints range from fixed and bound, in organized sport, to open and changing, in inventive and playground games. Beyond the physical and cognitive constraints represented by space, equipment, and rules, the skill and ability of players combine to create distributed constraints on game play. If only one player on a volleyball court can spike the ball, then the tactics and strategy will represent this constraint through distributed player actions.

The adaptations of agents within the constraints of perturbation on structure and game play are not open-ended and unlimited. The player's potential for adaptation is bound by structure determinism (Davis and Sumara, 2005a). "The manner of response is determined by the agent's structure, not by the perturbation. That is, a complex agent's response is dependent on, but not determined by, environmental influences" (p. 464). The agent's structural determinism in games and sport affects both the rate of learning and the limits of the agent's ability. Agents new to a challenge and working far from their limits may show significant rates of adaptation, while experienced agents may appear to progress more slowly as they adapt near their physical, cognitive, and affective limits.

Complex Learning is Nested and Coemergent

When one agent changes, an inevitable spiral occurs that changes the potential of all other agents in the system (Mennin, 2007). Davis and Sumara (2005a) call this process *structural coupling,* referring to it as "co-evolution, co-specification, mutual specification, consensual coordination of action; the co-mingling of complex agents' ongoing histories; the intimate entangling of one's emergent activity with another's" (p.464). The important determinant from a complexity-thinking point of view is that learning only emerges in relation to others; without them, emergent learning is not possible (Luce-Kapler, Sumara, & Davis, 2002). Games depend on the spiral effects of learning when one player affects

> **A**n improvement in one player's passing affects another's ability to receive. From an ecological perspective of learning, this idea is expressed by the term receivable pass, in which the passer needs to be empathetic to the receiver's abilities in order to further the cause of the team.

others in a direct and immediate way. This factor makes games systems open and game outcomes unpredictable. An improvement in one player's passing affects another's ability to receive. From an ecological perspective of learning, this idea is expressed by the term *receivable pass,* in which the passer needs to be empathetic to the receiver's abilities in order to further the cause of the team.

Complex Learning is Open to Fractal Time and Flow

In contrast to linear time, represented by Cartesian seconds, minutes, and hours, experiential expressions of time used by humans and other organisms exist that are best expressed in a nonlinear fashion. Luce-Kapler et al. (2002) use the expression *fractal time* to describe this rhythmic experience:

> Fractal time, then, like fractal geometry, is a more complex form. It is commonplace to speak of life forms having their own clocks—a way that the passing of time is measured, whether it is a cell, a tree, or an ecosystem, in a recursive process that has an identifiable rhythm or pattern. In the mechanical interpretations of time, humans have regularized rhythms so that quantitatively every second, minute, and hour is the same length, but in doing so, human beings have lost the sense that one moment exists within another (p. 360-361).

The ebb and flow of energy, focus, and effort in the game wax and wane both individually and as a system. Games are described in terms of momentum and flow more commonly than in seconds and minutes. Flow "is a state of consciousness where one becomes totally absorbed in what one is doing, to the exclusion of all other thoughts and emotions. … More than just focus, however, flow is a harmonious experience where mind and body are working together effortlessly, leaving the person feeling that something special has just occurred. So flow is [also] about enjoyment" (Jackson & Csikszentmihalyi, 1999, p. 5). Games provide the participant with an experience of time that focuses on the rhythm of life and engagement. This rhythm is marked by breaths and heartbeats, engagement and retreat, exhilaration and disappointment.

Situating the TGfU Approach Within an Ecological View of Learning

The compatibility of TGfU and ecological teaching is rooted in the philosophy and learning theories that underpin both concepts. The original TGfU model presented by Bunker and Thorpe (1982) demonstrates a

Limitations for game category, game context, and game form can be grouped together as game-structure constraints under an ecological perspective (see figure 8.1).

game-centered approach (Waring & Almond, 1995), in which the underlying purpose of learning is to maximize appreciation, enjoyment, and cognitive and physical growth with the aim of participating in future games and sport. Game play is the beginning and end of the cyclical process. The model represents an iterative learning process in which new learning is constantly fed back into the spiral curriculum (Butler, 2006). The systems view of learning taken by TGfU is also inclusive in that it recognizes the diversity of participants and attempts to foster coevolution from heterogeneity. Ecological views of learning, such as TGfU, embrace the importance of all agents in a learning system.

TGfU provides a strong conceptual framework for understanding game categorization and for manipulating game structures. Specifically, the TGfU pedagogical principles of sampling, modification-representation, modification-exaggeration, and controlling tactical complexity (Butler, Oslin, Mitchell, & Griffin, 2008) provide the teacher with means for creating a constrained games environment. Limitations for game category, game context, and game form can be grouped together as game-structure constraints under an ecological perspective (see figure 8.1).

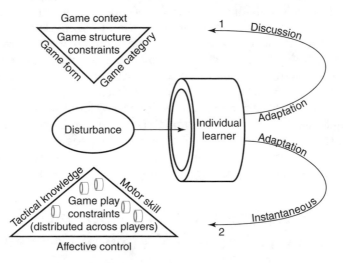

Figure 8.1 The balance of game structure, game play, and individual learner constraints leading to disturbance, learning, and a need to rebalance the game-structure and game-play constraints.

In addition to game-structure constraints, game-play constraints represent the combined knowledge, skills, and affective controls players embody at any given moment in a game. Game-play constraints are ever-present and fluid, changing with each subsequent adaptation a player makes (see figure 8.1). The constraints of ability distributed across players change every time a player adapts to a new challenge and begins to utilize a new ability, whether autonomously or consciously.

Game-structure and game-play constraints work in balance to create both spontaneous and planned disturbances (unexpected events). As players adapt, due to the disturbances created by one set of structural constraints, and integrate those adaptations into their game play, the balance is disturbed and a new game structure is needed to rebalance the system. Each learner's adaptations, although bound by his or her structural determinism, contribute to the iterative learning spiral that constantly changes the system. In TGfU pedagogy, discussion about tactics, strategy, skill, or game form is often the catalyst for changes to game-structure constraints (see figure 8.1, adaptation arrow 1). Changes to game structure may come in the form of a democratic process (Butler, 2006), or by way of teacher direction. Adaptation arrow 2 in figure 8.1 represents the fluid reintegration of learning fed back into a game in progress.

To illustrate a systems view of game-structure and game-play constraints working together to create disturbance and adaptation, we consider the rule that disallows players from deliberately using their hands (except for the goalie) in soccer (football). It may be a creative and worthy choice for a player to hit an overhead ball with a hand; however, it would be deemed a foul. The creative adaptation of the individual is subservient to the formality of the rules. Game-structure constraints require the player to use another part of the body to control the ball, such as the head.

The player's confidence in heading the ball, skill level, and presence of lack of knowledge of where to direct it further constrain the possible responses. These factors constrain not only the player, but also all the surrounding players to respond to a lofted ball. If the player cannot head a ball, the teammates will not expect that response, and therefore, will prepare for another type of pass. The moment the player learns to head the ball, both that person and the distributed game-play abilities of teammates on the field change in response to the new disturbance. This new skill not only affects game play instantly, in the form of new possibilities for passing and shooting, but also affects the game-structure possibilities of all subsequent games. New minigames can be formed to include heading or perhaps to improve the tactical use of skill by the team.

Teacher Implications: Teaching Focused on Emergent Learning

A values orientation of ecological integration and complexity thinking may provide a new lens through which to view our teaching in general and our TGfU lessons in particular; however, the lens does not change the purpose, only the view. TGfU advocates are concerned with the quality of teaching in physical education and the learning and the lifestyles that it inspires. An ecological view inspires systems thinking that differs from reductionist approaches and may hold specific and possibly intangible results for the future of learners, who participate in ecologically focused TGfU classes. System thinking requires teachers to manage the resources of the system in a sustainable way. Under this view, the notion of a good game comes to mean that the resources and motivation necessary for future games remain intact for most, if not all, of the agents involved.

> *Emergent-learning-focused (ELF) teaching is characterized by teachers' recognition that they are not only part of the system and therefore coevolving with learners, but are also expert observers of the system and its agents.*

An ecologically minded TGfU teacher becomes focused on capturing emergent learning, supporting it with a cognizing moment, and fostering subsequent iterations of that learning back into a new game structure. Emergent-learning-focused (ELF) teaching is characterized by teachers' recognition that they are not only part of the system and therefore coevolving with learners, but are also expert observers of the system and its agents. The ELF teacher determines when game-structure and game-play constraints are creating the right disturbances for players to lead to desired adaptations. In essence, an ELF teacher is able to recognize the components of the complex adaptive system outlined in table 8.1 and address the disturbances and constraints of the system to foster the agent's positive adaptations through pedagogy. This ability requires understanding of both the pedagogical and curriculum model (TGfU) being employed and an understanding of the value orientation driving their choices (ecological integration).

ELF teaching requires teachers to work within a set of probabilities that a game structure will lead to certain outcomes for learners; however, they also accept that games are open to perturbation and, therefore, that short-term learning outcomes cannot be guaranteed. A closed-system teacher with rigid boundaries and ideas of how learning should occur in physical education, perhaps in the form of strictly followed lesson plans, may be fundamentally at odds with the open-system structure and the emergent-learning opportunities that TGfU represents. In contrast, an ELF teacher may have difficulty following strict lesson plans beyond an initial setup of game form. For open-system teachers, creating a lesson plan is a visualization exercise for how the lesson might go. The plan contains a set of possibilities that could be incorporated into a lesson if the situation unfolds as visualized. Table 8.2 provides an overview of some TGfU interpretations of an ELF teacher's philosophy, knowledge, and skills.

Table 8.2   TGfU Interpretation of Teacher's Philosophy That is Emergent-Learning-Focused (ELF) on Knowledge and Skills

ELF teacher	TGfU interpretation
Epistemology	Knowledge and skills are not preformed Inert chunks of information, and do not directly transfer from teacher to student. Tactical knowledge and skills are both individually and socially constructed by the learner and are contextual in nature (Light, 2008).
Teaching philosophy	Ranges from a democratic view in which learners decide on the game-structure constraints (Butler, 2006) to a more teacher-directed process in which the teacher chooses the game category, context, and form (Metzler, 2005). Once game play begins, however, the teacher acts as catalyst for learners' emergent learning through facilitation and creation of perturbation.
Lesson design	Perturbation or disturbances force the adaptations of agents in the system; therefore, lessons must be open to perturbation. Lessons are not rigid scripts to follow to transfer learning. Lesson plans are visualization documents for a probable but nonfixed learning outcome.
Instructional skills	Competence is needed in all traditional instructional skills for physical education; however, they are used in concert with the appropriate learning phase of the TGfU lesson (see Metzler, 2005 for an overview of PE instructional skills).
Games and sport knowledge	The teacher must have knowledge of the principles of game categorization and an appreciation of the rules of specific games and sport. This knowledge is required for appropriate facilitation or direct creation of representative game forms.
Tactical knowledge	TGfU requires that teachers provide a framework for tactical language such as the one proposed by WIlson (2002). Emergent learning in the area of tactics and strategy may be demonstrated by learners; however, if they do not place a cognitive framework on top of their embodied experience, transfer may be limited according to the TGfU theory.

ELF-games teachers do not limit their observations and perturbations to the psychomotor or cognitive domains. The concepts of fair play, cooperation, and sportsmanship are as likely to emerge as the concepts relating to offense and defense and their associated skills. As each topic takes its moment in the foreground of a game, teachers receive a genuine learning opportunity to weave experience and cognition together. Under an ecological-values orientation, the game and its effect on the agents take precedence over the results. The principles of enjoyment, participation, learning, and cooperation in creating games overshadow temporary competitive states that players employ during game play. The creation and fostering of this belief in players and the facilitation of self-awareness of players' affective states is the responsibility of an ecologically minded ELF teacher.

Conclusion

We propose that learners will benefit if teachers adopt a values orientation of ecological integration toward games teaching and learning that embraces complexity thinking and the codependence of all participants in the complex adaptive systems known as games. We also suggest that the proliferation of an ecological perspective on game learning holds more promise than zero-sum views of games. Through the processes of embodied learning and socialization in sports, the suggested benefits of ecologically minded teaching of games may stretch past the boundaries of our fields and into the dominant culture in which games are embedded.

TGfU as practiced through a lens of ecological integration allows us to create physical-education lessons that are supportive of both sustainable and generative learning. Sustainability in our teaching is measured by the ability and motivation of the students in our classes to continue playing, and their generative learning is represented by their constant adaptation to changing game-structure and game-play constraints.

Discussion Questions

1. Based on a game of your choosing give an example that captures the five characteristics of complex learning systems that were used to align games and ecological learning theory.

   • Comprised of co-dependent agents

   • Self-organizing

   • Open to disturbance

   • Site of nested and co-emergent learning

   • Open to varied experiences or interpretations of time

2. We suggest that TGfU aligns with an ecological values orientation and this alignment has implications on how socialization occurs in sport. List 3 key messages about games that children who predominantly learn through a play-based ecological model may come to embody.

3. The emergent-learning-focused (ELF) teacher is required to set the constraints for a game-based learning experience, then let go and coadapt as children experience disturbances through play. How specifically does TGfU align with and inform this process?

References

Bunker, D., & Thorpe, R. (1982). A model for teaching of games in secondary schools. *Bulletin of Physical Education, 18*(1), 5-8.

Butler, J. (2006). Curriculum construction of ability: Enhancing learning through teaching games for understanding. *Sport, Education and Society, 11*(3), 243-258.

Butler, J., Oslin, J., Mitchell, S., & Griffin, L. (2008). The way forward for TGfU: Filling the chasm between theory and practice. *Physical & Health Education Journal, 74*(2), 6-12.

Davis, B., & Sumara, D. (2002). Constructivist discourses and the field of education: Problems and possibilities. *Educational Theory, 52*(4), 409-428.

Davis, B., & Sumara, D. (2003). Why aren't they getting this? Working through the regressive myths of constructivist pedagogy. *Teaching Education, 14*(2), 124-140.

Davis, B., & Sumara, D. (2005a). Complexity science and educational action research: Toward a pragmatics of transformation. *Educational Action Research, 13*(3), 453-464.

Davis, B., & Sumara, D. (2005b). Challenging images of knowing: Complexity science and educational research. *International Journal of Qualitative Studies in Education, 18*(3), 305-321.

Davis, B., Sumara, D., & Luce-Kapler, R. (2008). *Engaging minds: Changing teaching in complex times* (2nd ed.). New York: Routledge.

Doll, W. (1993). *A post-modern perspective on curriculum.* New York: Teachers College Press.

Jackson, S., & Csikszentmihalyi, M. (1999). *Flow in sports: The keys to optimal experiences and performances.* Champaign, IL: Human Kinetics.

Jarvis-Selinger, S., Collins, J., & Pratt, D. (2007). Do academic origins influence perspectives on teaching? *Teacher Education Quarterly, 34,* 67-81.

Jewett, A.E., Bain, L.L., & Ennis, C.D. (1995). *The curriculum process in physical education.* Dubuque, IA: Brown and Benchmark.

Light, R. (2008). Complex learning theory—its epistemology and its assumptions about learning: Implications for physical education. *Journal of Teaching in Physical Education, 27*(1), 21-37.

Light Shields, D.L., & Light Bredemeier, B.J. (1996). Sport, militarism, and peace. *Peace and Conflict: Journal of Peace Psychology, 2*(4), 369-383.

Luce-Kapler, R., Sumara, D., & Davis, B. (2002). Rhythms of knowing: Toward an ecological theory of learning in action research. *Educational Action Research, 10*(3), 353-372.

Mennin, S. (2007). Small-group problem-based learning as a complex adaptive system. *Teaching and Teacher Education, 23,* 303-313.

Metzler, M. (2005). *Instructional models for physical education* (2nd ed.). Scottsdale, AZ: Holcomb Hathaway.

Siedentop, D. (2003). Introduction of physical education, fitness and sport (5th ed.). New York: McGraw-Hill.

Waring, M., & Almond, L. (1995). Game-centered games: A revolutionary alternative for games teaching? *European Physical Education Review, 1*(1), 55-66.

Wilson, G. (2002). A framework for teaching tactical game knowledge. *Journal of Physical Education, Recreation and Dance, 73*(1), 20-26, 56.

Practice: Assessment, Coaching, Elementary and Secondary Teaching

chapter

9

Student-Involved Formative Assessment as a Cornerstone to the Construction of Game Performance

Jean-François Richard, PhD

From an authentic perspective, students would be involved in the process of self- and peer assessment in order to better integrate what they do and do not understand. This appropriation of content through assessment has been shown to have a great affect on learning in the context of games education (Richard, Godbout, Tousignant, & Gréhaigne, 1999).

Across North America and around the world, physical-education programs are guided by a similar mission: the global and integral development of school-age children using physical activities of various types for learning. Even though these missions differ slightly in wording and favored curricular approach, most programs seem to pursue the same core mission. More specifically, physical-education programs focus on the development of knowledge and competencies (such as physical literacy) that promote attitudes and behaviors that are favorable to a healthy and active lifestyle.

The notions of literacy and numeracy have been popular topics in educational literature during the last 20 years. These concepts are at the very core of students' future learning and are a determinant in the development of competencies in different subject areas. In the field of physical education and sport, the notion of physical literacy has received some attention from both a research and a practical perspective throughout the past quarter-century (Kirk, 1983; Whitehead, 2001). Essentially, a physically literate person can be defined in the following way:

To move toward the development of physical literacy, physical-education programs have to be structured, through their content and pedagogical approaches, in a way that nurtures the very essence of this ideology.

An individual who is physically literate moves with poise, economy, and confidence in a wide variety of physically challenging situations. Furthermore, the individual is perceptive in 'reading' all aspects of the physical environment, anticipating movement needs or possibilities and responding appropriately to these, with intelligence and imagination (Whitehead, 2001).

I would argue that the development of physical literacy for all children is an important and ambitious goal that we, as physical-education professionals, should pursue. To move toward the development of physical literacy, physical-education programs have to be structured, through their content and pedagogical approaches, in a way that nurtures the very essence of this ideology. Thus, to realize this goal, physical-education curricula must provide children with authentic and meaningful experiences.

Curricular Reform: Toward Authentic and Meaningful Learning

In most educational systems across the world, curricular reforms strive toward similar goals, which include improving overall student learning through the development of literacy and numeracy. Specifically, in physical education, the notion of literacy needs to be extended to include physical literacy. Regardless of the subject matter being taught, common elements are found in working toward these goals:

- Student-centered approaches to learning
- Durable and transferable learning through the presentation of authentic and meaningful classroom experiences

I believe that teaching approaches, such as Teaching Games for Understanding (TGfU), can lead to the development of physical literacy. TGfU is a student-centered approach to learning sport-related games which aims to foster durable and transferable learning, the very core of authentic learning.

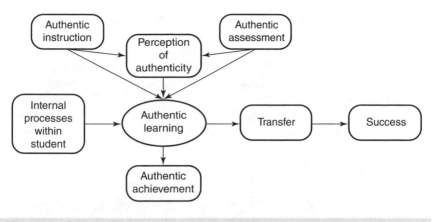

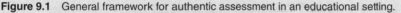

Figure 9.1 General framework for authentic assessment in an educational setting.

Reprinted, by permission, from J.T.M. Gulikers, T.J. Bastiens, and P.A. Kirschner, 2004, "A five dimensional framework for authentic assessment," *ETR & D,* 52(3): 67-86.

Gulikers, Bastiens, and Kirschner (2004) provide a general framework for authentic assessment in an educational setting (see figure 9.1). The essential components of authentic learning are authentic instruction and authentic assessment. These two components are predominant in the construction of teaching-learning scenarios that can lead to greater understanding and integration of content in real-life applications, thus leading to success (actual or perceived) for students. In the context of physical activity and sport, students who feel successful and competent have a better chance of appreciating certain activities and developing enjoyment from physical activity as a whole.

I believe that in the initial development of TGfU, Bunker and Thorpe (1982) intended to provide a solid example of authentic learning in the context of physical education—teaching games in a way that gives students a better chance to understand, learn, and succeed. Let us examine the organization and structure of scenarios for authentic learning. When planning to teach from a perspective of authentic instruction, the teacher must first consider what to teach (content) and how to teach it (authentic instruction). Second, the teacher must also look at how and in what context student performances will be assessed (authentic assessment). Assessment is critical for informing and improving the teaching-learning process.

> **I** believe that in the initial development of TGfU, Bunker and Thorpe (1982) intended to provide a solid example of authentic learning in the context of physical education—teaching games in a way that gives students a better chance to understand, learn, and succeed.

In order to meet the goals in any educational setting, a constructive alignment between instruction, learning, and assessment must exist (Biggs, 1996). The first step toward authentic learning is coherence and congruence among these three components. In any lesson or teaching unit, the teacher has to begin with clearly defined outcomes. These outcomes can influence the pedagogical approaches that will favor the teaching-learning process. The choice of an instructional approach, such as TGfU, will have a direct affect on the pedagogical strategies and tools used to assess learning. These choices all influence the students' experience of authentic learning.

The Role of Formative Assessment in the Development of Authentic Measurement Practices

Traditionally, assessment of student learning has been relegated to a secondary role in the teaching-learning process and has often been utilized merely for grading purposes (Burke, 1994). As educators, we are aware that the main purpose of assessment is the value it has for (a) the learner, (b) the promotion of learning, and (c) the affect on the teaching-learning process. Advocates for educational-reform movements across the world are asking for more meaningful approaches to student learning. Such approaches promote increased reflection on how students construct their performance (process) rather than on the end result (product). We need assessment strategies and tools that reflect these learning processes and assess more than simply the end result of performance (Burke, 1994).

Many scholars recognize the value of assessment as an instructional strategy to help guide teachers in the improvement of student learning (Schiemer, 1999; Veal, 1995). This notion of assessment as an instructional strategy represents the essence of formative assessment. In the context of authentic learning, formative assessment has a predominant role in the pursuit of developing authentic assessment practices.

In a now classic publication, Zessoules and Gardner (1991) define authentic assessment as being comprised of the two following characteristics:

- *Ecological validity.* Authentic assessment requires students to demonstrate relevant competencies through a significant, meaningful, and worthwhile accomplishment.
  - Example: Learning and assessing a skill in a game setting rather than in an isolated setting.
- *Students as active participants*
  - Example: Self-assessment and peer assessment

These two characteristics, when integrated in a regular and ongoing fashion within a teaching scenario, provide the essential elements for favorable learning conditions. Regular and ongoing formative information must be used to adjust future learning scenarios; this process is at the very core of formative assessment (Rink, 1998; Scallon, 2000). When a teacher makes adjustments

Regular and ongoing formative information must be used to adjust future learning scenarios; this process is at the very core of formative assessment (Rink, 1998; Scallon, 2000).

to future learning activities or to teaching strategies based on collected information, it is known as the *regulation of learning* (Allal, Cardinet, & Perrenoud, 1985). From a behaviorist perspective, the regulation of learning is typically teachers' responsibility as they analyze student performance through informal observation or the use of more formal procedures. Based on the situation in the teaching-learning scenario (lessons), teachers decide if modifications are needed in certain areas (content, approach, teaching progression, and so on) either in the moment or for the future. This regulation of the teaching-learning process is based on the teachers' analysis of the situation, and does not include any type of student involvement.

From an authentic perspective, students would be involved in the process of self- and peer assessment in order to better integrate what they do and do not understand. This appropriation of content through assessment has been shown to have a great affect on learning in the context of games education (Richard et al., 1999). Scallon (2000) refers to this paradigm shift in looking at assessment as going from a process of manual regulation (teacher-controlled) to one of automatic regulation (student involvement), which promotes a better integration of the material being taught. In the development of authentic-learning scenarios, formative-assessment tools must offer students information about what they need to improve in order to improve content integration and performance. The assessment strategies and instruments developed for these purposes must also be accessible to students for their own use for self- or peer assessment, thus actively involving students in the assessment process. Swiss researchers Allal, Cardinet, and Perrenoud (1985) put forward a continuum describing the teacher and student roles in the process for formative assessment (see table 9.1). When you examine this continuum closely, you can see that the more teachers want to involve students in the formative-assessment process, the more they will have to transform their conception of teaching and of classroom management. The higher you go in this continuum, the more dominant the students' role becomes, shifting the setting from one that is teacher controlled to one that is student involved. If teachers could function at least at level two on a regular and ongoing basis, students would benefit more from their learning experiences.

Table 9.1   Role of Teachers and Students in the Process for Formative Assessment

Level 1	The teacher assumes responsibility for the conception and organization of all assessment activities and prepares all the required material. She or he also administers all assessments and is responsible for all feedback to students.
Level 2	The teacher develops all assessments, organizes all assessment activities, and plays a central role in their coordination. Feedback to students is the responsibility of both teacher and students (self-assessment, peer assessment, and co-assessment).
Level 3	Students collaborate in the conception of assessment strategies and instruments. Students also assume an important role in the administration of formative assessment.
Level 4	The teacher explains the main goal of formative assessment and gives examples. Students conceive and develop strategies and instruments that seem useful for them in light of the pursued outcomes and are responsible for their administration. The teacher acts as a facilitator.

From Allal, Cardinet, and Perrenoud 1985.

Having put forward the key elements of authentic instruction and authentic assessment, including formative assessment, as essential components in the teaching-learning process, I will now present the application of such principles in the assessment of game performance. A shift toward problem-based approaches to games teaching, such as TGfU, has begun to influence the way we assess game performance. The game-centered theme of TGfU has enticed researchers and practitioners alike to develop assessment tools that do the following:

- Discourage the use of standardized tests that only measure students' technical performance
- Promote ways of informing student learning within authentic game situations

This chapter will present the key elements of authentic assessment through the description and pedagogical applications of the Team-Sport Assessment Procedure (TSAP).

Authentic Assessment in Games Education With TSAP

During the last decade or so, the evolution of TGfU as a pedagogical model has led to the development of assessment instruments that permit teachers to holistically assess game performances, rather than looking at performance as the sum or combination of fragmented elements of either technical or tactical execution. To this end, the Game-Performance

Assessment Instrument (GPAI) was developed as a comprehensive assessment tool for teachers to use and adapt in assessing a variety of games. Teachers can use the GPAI for different types of games across the classification system (for example, for both invasion and net/wall games) or within a particular classification (such as basketball or soccer). The different observational variables included in the GPAI help teachers code behaviors that demonstrate the ability to solve tactical problems in games by making decisions, moving appropriately (off-the-ball movement), and executing skills (see Griffin, Mitchell, & Oslin, 1997).

In this section, I will describe the TSAP and its various pedagogical uses for teaching invasion games. The TSAP has been shown to be of great pedagogical value in the teaching and learning of game competencies in various classroom settings at the upper-elementary-, middle-, and high-school levels. This pedagogical value results from the very nature of the instrument itself, which favors a peer-assessment setting for formative purposes. Thus, using this assessment procedure in a TGfU approach greatly enhances students' development and understanding of invasion games.

The TSAP, initially developed by Gréhaigne, Godbout, and Bouthier (1997), provides information that quantifies a player's overall offensive performance in selected invasion sports, such as basketball and soccer, and in net/wall sports, such as volleyball. The instrument reflects both technical and tactical aspects of game play (Gréhaigne et al., 1997). Individual variables, performance indexes, and performance scores are all macroindicators of both technical and tactical performance (see table 9.2) and are all related to successful game play (Gréhaigne et al., 1997).

Table 9.2   The Relationship Between Observation Items and Types of Information Collected

Observation items	Information collected
Received balls (RB)	Involvement of the player in the team's play (availability, accessibility to receive a pass)
Conquered balls (CB)	Information related to the player's defensive capacities
Offensive balls (OB)	Player's capacity to make significant passes to his or her partners (offensive capacities)
Successful shots (SS)	Information related to the player's offensive capacities
Volume of play (PB= RB+CB)	General involvement of the player in the game
Lost balls (LB)	A small number reflects a good adaptation to the game

Based on Gréhaigne, Godbout, and Bouthier 1997.

Name _____   Class _____

Observer _____   Date _____

Directions: Observe student's game play and place a tally mark in the appropriate box.

Gaining possession of the ball

Played balls (PB)	
Conquered ball (CB)	Received ball (RB)

Disposing of the ball

Lost ball (LB)	Neutral ball (NB)	Pass (P)	Successful shot (SS)

Figure 9.2   TSAP-observation grid for invasion games.

From J. Butler and L. Griffin, 2010, *More Teaching Games for Understanding: Moving Globally* (Champaign, IL: Human Kinetics). Based on Richard, Godbout, and Gréhaigne 2000.

The TSAP is based on two basic notions: (1) how a player gains possession of the ball (two variables) and (2) how a player disposes of the ball (four variables). According to these notions, a player's specific behaviors are noted and coded during game play on an observation grid (see figure 9.2). Two performance indexes and a performance score are then computed from the collected data (see table 9.3).

The TSAP is a peer-assessment instrument in which students not only serve as the data collectors but also play an active role in the interpretation of the collected data. The gathered information permits students and teachers to reflect on game-play data and to meaningfully discuss the game concepts being taught. Learning scenarios that permit students to be actively involved in the learning process through the engagement of assessment are extremely beneficial to learning, if they are well planned and if students are adequately prepared to use the assessment instrument at hand. Results from research have shown that students as young as 10 years (grade 5) were capable of using the TSAP with a good deal of precision and reliability (Richard, Godbout, & Gréhaigne, 2000). Due to the game focus, the TSAP combined with a TGfU model efficiently develops students' learning of game concepts (Gréhaigne & Godbout, 1998).

Table 9.3 Observational Variables, Performance Indexes, and Performance Score Computation Formula for the Team-Sport Assessment Procedure: Invasion Games

Observational variables: Operational definition

A. Gaining possession of the ball
   1) Conquered ball (CB)
      Players are considered to have conquered the ball if they intercepted it, stole it from an opponent, or recaptured it after an unsuccessful shot on goal or after a near loss to the other team.
   2) Received ball (RB)
      The player receives the ball from a partner and does not immediately lose control of it.

B. Disposing of the ball
   1) Lost ball (LB)
      Players are considered to have lost the ball when they lose control of it without having scored a goal.
   2) Neutral ball (NB)
      The player makes a routine pass to a partner which does not truly put pressure on the other team.
   3) Pass (P)
      The player makes a pass to a partner which contributes to the displacement of the ball toward the opposing team's goal.
   4) Successful shot on goal (SS)
      A shot is considered successful when it scores or when possession of the ball is retained by one's team.

The computation of performance indexes and performance score:
Volume-of-play index = CB + RB
$$\text{Efficiency index} = \frac{CB + P + SS}{10 + LB}$$
Performance score = (volume of play / 2) + (efficiency index × 10)

Based on the original work of Gréhaigne, Godbout, and Bouthier 1997.

Using the TSAP in Games-Related Teaching and Learning

Reprinted from *Teaching Games for Understanding,* with permission from the National Association for Sport and Physical Education (NASPE), 1900 Association Drive, Reston, VA 20191.

A major feature of the TSAP is its adaptability to different teaching scenarios. The full instrument has six different observational variables, which have been shown to reflect a student's global offensive performance in invasion games. When teaching more complex tactical problems at a higher grade level, such as at high school, the complete TSAP is recommended. Teachers might not want to use the complete TSAP if (a) learning outcomes do not require such a complex procedure (such as in upper-elementary- and middle-school programs) or (b) if they have little experience with peer assessment. In this case, starting with a simplified version will help set up both the teacher and students for success. Teachers must consider assessment logistics and management, observational complexity, and cognitive maturity when integrating students in the peer-assessment process. These factors will help determine the successful use of any assessment procedure in a classroom setting. For example, if a procedure is too complex to be used in a peer-assessment setting by a group of students of a certain age, the time and effort needed to prepare them for observation might not produce reliable or helpful results. In the case of the TSAP, Richard, Godbout, and Picard (2000) developed, experimented with, and validated modified versions in order to give teachers alternative assessment procedures based on learning objectives at different grade levels and on students' observational capabilities. These modified versions have been designed to be used at the lower grade levels (grades 5 to 8). For the purpose of this chapter, TSAP will be presented for use with invasion games, such as basketball, soccer, and handball.[1]

First Modified Version for Invasion Games

Volume of play (VP) = Number of possessions: conquered ball (CB) + received ball (RB)

$$\text{Efficiency index (EI)} = \frac{\text{VP}}{10 + \text{LB (lost balls)}}$$

Performance score = (VP/2) + (EI × 10)

In the first modified version, the number of observational variables is reduced by half. With regard to the volume of play, no distinction is made between a conquered ball (CB) and a received ball (RB). Only the total number of possessions and the number of lost balls (LB) are taken into consideration. The rationale behind this decision is twofold. First, we have noticed through different experiments with the TSAP that younger observers have a tendency to indicate most ball possessions as received, even if they are conquered or intercepted. Second, the difference between these two variables is not as important in relation to game concepts taught at the lower grade levels.

The modified version of the TSAP is simpler than the original version. The modifications allow teachers to progressively integrate students into the observation of game-play behavior without using a complex instrument. Also, the variables that were retained from this first modified version allow teachers and students to learn nuanced lessons about game-play concepts, such as getting away from a defender (represented by the volume of play) or ball circulation, which are mostly taught at the upper-elementary level (grades 5 and 6) in most physical-education programs. Through the efficiency index, students should realize that for their volume of play (the number of possessions), the goal is to lose as few balls as possible. This, in turn, reflects a good contribution to team success, whether passing the ball or shooting on goal.

Second Modified Version for Invasion Games

Volume of play (VP) = Number of possessions (CB + RB)

Efficiency index (EI) = $\dfrac{P + SS}{10 + LB \text{ (lost ball)}}$

Performance score = (VP/2) + (EI × 10)

As in the first modified version, this second version allows the teacher to place a specific pedagogical emphasis on the lessons related to objectives. In this case, the efficiency index's numerator is comprised of the number of passes and of the successful shots on goal. In this version, the pedagogical emphasis is on both gaining possession of and disposing of the ball. The efficiency index helps the teacher guide the student to know whether to pass the ball or to shoot on goal. This second modified version of the TSAP increases the number of observational variables to four. Consequently, it could be considered an intermediate version to the original TSAP.

Conclusion

Assessment can and should be a part of teaching and learning in every lesson. The information that different assessment strategies can provide for students and teachers is critical to the regulation of the teaching-learning process. As an authentic assessment instrument, the TSAP offers teachers the opportunity to promote the construction of game knowledge and skills through a procedure that actively involves students in the assessment process and helps them develop capabilities for automatic regulation in relation to their learning process. Authentic-assessment procedures can help instructors teach and students learn about how to make connections within and among games (intra and intertransfer). Students clearly

As an authentic assessment instrument, the TSAP offers teachers the opportunity to promote the construction of game knowledge and skills through a procedure that actively involves students in the assessment process and helps them develop capabilities for automatic regulation in relation to their learning process.

articulate that games are a meaningful part of physical education. Why? Playing a game provides structure and outcomes, which give meaning to performance. Students want to play games well. Having the chance to learn and to experience success in games is of the upmost importance if we, as physical educators, want to promote physical activity as a way of life.

The TSAP, integrated in a TGfU setting and combined with an authentic-assessment instrument, creates a context for authentic instruction that provides students with the necessary information to reflect and learn about themselves as games players. It also provides students with both means (process) and ends (products) that are interrelated. Through game-performance assessment, students will learn that each small element is valuable in itself but is also part of a coherent whole. Authentic-assessment instruments, such as the TSAP, can help teachers plan developmentally sound game experiences that can lead to more sport literate learners. Increased sport literacy moves us closer to our common goal of increasing overall physical literacy for all learners in physical education.

Discussion Questions

1. What are the fundamental characteristics of authentic learning?
2. What is the role of formative assessment in authentic learning?
    a. What are the advantages of using peer-assessment tools, such as the TSAP, in a teaching-learning context?
    b. What are some of the challenges in integrating peer assessment in a regular and ongoing fashion?
3. Does the data produced through the TSAP relate mostly to the product of performance? How can data from the TSAP be used to inform the process of students' performance?

Endnotes

[1] For information on the TSAP for volleyball, refer to Richard, Godbout, and Griffin (2002).

References

Allal, L., Cardinet, J., & Perrenoud, P. (1985). *L'évaluation formative dans un enseignement différencié* [Formative assessment in differentiated teaching]. Berne, Switzerland: P. Lang.

Biggs, J. (1996). Enhancing teaching through constructive alignment. *Higher Education, 32*, 347-364.

Bunker, D., & Thorpe, R. (1982). A model for the teaching of games in the secondary school. *Bulletin of Physical Education, 18* (1), 5-8.

Burke, K. (1994). *The mindful school: How to assess authentic learning.* Arlington Heights, IL: Skylight Training and Publishing.

Gréhaigne, J.-F., & Godbout, P. (1998). Formative assessment in team sports in a tactical approach context. *Journal of Physical Education, Recreation and Dance, 69*(1), 46-51.

Gréhaigne, J.-F., Godbout, P., & Bouthier, D. (1997). Performance assessment in team sports. *Journal of Teaching in Physical Education, 16,* 500-516.

Griffin, L.L., Mitchell, S.A., & Oslin, J.L. (1997). *Teaching sport concepts and skills: A tactical games approach.* Champaign, IL: Human Kinetics.

Gulikers, J.T.M., Bastiens, T.J., & Kirschner, P.A. (2004). A five dimensional framework for authentic assessment. *ETR & D, 52*(3), 67-86.

Kirk, D. (1983). Theoretical guidelines for teaching games for understanding. *Bulletin of Physical Education, 13,* 50-64.

Richard, J.-F., Godbout, P., & Gréhaigne, J.-F. (2000). Students' precision and reliability of team sport performance. *Research Quarterly for Exercise and Sport, 71*(1), 85-91.

Richard, J.-F., Godbout, P., & Griffin, L. (2002). Assessing game performance: An introduction to the team-sport assessment procedure. *Health and Physical Education Journal, 68* (1), 12-18.

Richard, J.-F., Godbout, P., & Picard, Y. (2000). La validation d'une procédure d'évaluation en sports collectifs. *Mesure et évaluation en éducation, 23*(1), 43-67.

Richard, J.-F., Godbout, P., Tousignant, M., & Gréhaigne, J.-F. (1999). The try-out of a team-sport assessment procedure in elementary and junior high school PE classes. *Journal of Teaching in Physical Education, 18* (3), 336-356.

Rink, J.E. (1998). *Teaching physical education for learning.* St. Louis: WCB McGraw-Hill.

Scallon, G. (2000). *L'evaluation formative (Formative assessment).* Montreal, QC: Les editions du Renouveau Pedagogique.

Schiemer, S. (1999). Designing student assessments: Rubrics 101. *Teaching Elementary Physical Education, 10*(1), 36-37.

Veal, M.L. (1995). The role of assessment in secondary physical education - A pedagogical view. *Journal of Physical Education, Recreation and Dance, 63*(7), 88-92.

Whitehead, M.E. (2001). The concept of physical literacy. *The British Journal of Teaching Physical Education, 32*(1), 127-138.

Zessoules, R., & Gardner, H. (1991). Authentic assessment: Beyond the buzzword and into the classroom. In V. Perrone (Ed.), *Expanding Student Assessment* (pp. 47-71). Alexandria, VA: Association for Supervision and Curriculum Development.

chapter 10

TGfU and Humanistic Coaching

Lynn Kidman, PhD • Bennett J. Lombardo, EdD

One of the [team] values that the boys decided on was enjoyment, and so I thought I had to create some real gamelike scrimmage-type activities. I still wanted to be able to highlight specific things that happened on the volleyball court and break the game down a little bit so [the players] [were] practicing one or two aspects. [The players] had to try to create and facilitate working on those things.

I think another measure [of games] could be... the social benefits that [students] experienced from it. I thought [the games approach] taught kids about values. I think it taught them the importance of [games] and I think they learned a lot socially. They learned how to get on with each other. At the start, there were some guys who couldn't handle one another, some personality clashes, and they learned how to get over those. Once they experienced [problem solving], they started to be able to implement [solutions] themselves. They could feel when they needed [the solutions] rather than me seeing when they needed [the solutions] and me going, "yeah right, now you need this." They had experienced [deciding on the solutions] in training, then we talked about [them]. Then, they were able to experience [decision making] in a game and implement it when they needed to. I don't think I had to call a time out and say, "You have to do this, this, and this. . . "

(continued)

(continued)

> We were able to attempt to teach the kids about intensity. . . to create scoring systems where the kids had to hammer those values. We just threw a ball on [the court] and they had to communicate their way in offense because [the game] was a disorganized situation. They had to try, from that novel situation, [to] create a good enough offense to put some pressure on the six who were on the other side. That's something that I don't think a lot of coaches do. [Players] do enjoy those games and it is easier to achieve commitment and intensity (our team values) when you are playing in a game, than it is in a drill training. I don't know how many Kiwi people are committed enough to pass 200 balls on the left side in a row and then pass 200 balls on the right side in a row.
>
> You've [as a coach] just got to keep checking where you are personally and keep reminding yourself what you are [coaching] for and whose campaign it actually is. I think when I first started out coaching, the reason was to win for myself.
>
> *Mark Norton, excerpts from A TGfU Developing Volleyball Coach*
> *(Kidman, 2005)*

The purpose of this chapter is to review and analyze the exciting potential of two approaches to providing leadership in movement settings; that is, the practice of humanistic coaching and Teaching Games for Understanding (TGfU). With acceptance of the TGfU approach on the rise, coaches who focus their efforts on the educational outcomes of the sport experience have been buoyed by the similarities in style and the conceptual nature inherent in the pedagogy of TGfU. This conceptual focus, which uses the sport experience as a vehicle to teach other concepts, is very attractive to the humanistic coach who is also an educator (Lombardo, 1987).

One of the major reasons people participate in sports is for the human-movement experience: the excitement and the indescribable feeling that comes with playing. Human movement is never static or robotic, but is expressive, creative, adaptable, and versatile. The best athletes are those who can respond to others' movement in novel situations, which appear continuously in sport. Some would claim that the best movers are those who can respond in the moment; that is, they have not only the high level motor abilities required of the task, but also the ability to perceive the necessary and important aspects of the required motor response, to focus on developing mental skills, and to make excellent and quick decisions (Kidman and Lombardo, 2010). Putting these elements together constitutes an individual who is physically, cognitively, mentally (affectively), and humanistically (fully self-aware) sound. Human movement and especially demanding, high-level, motor performance are dynamic actions that are always changing and modifying. The thrill of a great move cannot be underestimated.

Our interest in TGfU is based on how the approach emphasizes this human experience in sport. What exactly is the relationship between TGfU and humanistic coaching? Thorpe and Bunker (1989) developed TGfU as a means to enable students to learn in a more motivating and personalized environment than was occurring in physical education. Our focus here will be on the contextual realms of sport and coaching, specifically to highlight how TGfU has enabled athletes to revert back to play (the most humanistic form of movement) and how it meets holistic needs of an individual. We believe that true play is transformed once a leader intervenes and attempts to control or change individual athletes. Specifically, once a player's movement has been interfered with by another of significance, playing ceases and the athlete enters into a world of professional, adult-structured sport.

Athlete-centered coaching and *humanistic coaching* are terms that will be used interchangeably. They both refer to the total development of the individual (Lombardo, 2001) and focus on enhancing athlete self-awareness, and holistic (affective, cognitive, and physical) growth and development (Kidman and Lombardo, 2010). Humanism, based on Maslow's (1962) self-actualization theory and Rogers' (1969) work, focuses on the whole person and encourages athletes to reflect on the subjective, thrilling experience of sport (Lombardo, 2001). Sport is a vehicle to enhance personal development and understanding. It is an authentic experience that can influence the development of human character, which so many adults stress as an important life skill. Lynch (2001) reinforces that the vehicle of sport provides an educational experience for developing athletes to reach their full potential as human beings. TGfU is a model which perpetuates this affective notion and also contributes to the physical and cognitive development of athletes.

TGfU is a humanistic approach in that it requires performers to think and react, use intuition to solve athletic- sport-based problems, and therefore, become more fully self-aware. As such, the athletes' physical and affective cognitive responses (including movement), offered in response to game-related problems, must be listened to, reflected on, and respected by the coach conducting the TGfU session. The TGfU leader, according to the approach's pedagogy, must refrain from providing answers, and continue to probe and prompt the players, facilitating learning by modifying, reinforcing, and supporting. In short, the pedagogy of TGfU must encourage learners to discover for themselves possible viable responses to game situations that are organized by either the coach or the athlete.

Coaching humanistically means that when fulfilling the TGfU leadership role, coaches might (depending on the athletes' needs) use indirect

Coaching humanistically means that when fulfilling the TGfU leadership role, coaches might (depending on the athletes' needs) use indirect approaches, listen, respect athletes' responses, and probe (rather than informing or providing answers).

approaches, listen, respect athletes' responses, and probe (rather than informing or providing answers). Both humanistic coaching and TGfU leadership require patience, time, and opportunities for learners to struggle or complete numerous trials. To enable learning, athlete-learners need opportunities to discover possible responses for themselves. Although it would be much faster to give them direct instructions, as the proponents of traditional coaching (those who do not believe in the humanistic or the TGfU models) do, this approach would not result in the desired outcome: independent learners who possess not only the motor skills, but also the self-confidence and self-reliance, to figure things out for themselves. This approach can, quite possibly, lead to a reduction in the central power of the coach.

The Characteristics of the Professional Model of Coaching

Sport has been dominated by a system in which the needs and interests of the coach overtake those of the athletes. A system structured and ruled by adults, also known as the professional model of coaching, is one in which the coaches have the power to make all the important decisions and are mostly devoted to products or outcomes, rather than to the process of developing people. Kidman refers to the coach-centered approach in *Athlete-Centred Coaching* (2005) as a disempowering form of leadership, which takes ownership and responsibility of sporting experiences away from athletes. When coaching tactics and skills at training sessions, coaches traditionally tend to give athletes specific directions on how to fix a problem or perform specific moves. In some cases, coaches believe that unless they are seen to be telling athletes what to do and how to do it, they are not doing their job properly. They seem to feel that they need to conform to public expectations about being seen talking or yelling all the time. An educational understanding about athletes' learning will enable coaches to understand that they don't have to yell in order to facilitate the experience.

Workman (2001) describes humanistic involvement in sport as an emphasis residing "in recognizing the dignity, worth, integrity, responsibility, and wholeness in oneself and in others" (p. 85). She further suggests that competing in sport provides a personal test, and develops creativity, improvisation, and imagination. Workman says, "humanism in sport accentuates joy in movement, personal meaning in participation and positive interactions with all other participants, including the so-called 'opponents'" (p. 85). TGfU is embedded in this philosophy. However, what actually happens in the sporting environment may be a different story. Many sport environments (mostly run by adults) do not provide this authentic human experience.

Adults need to remember how to meet the athletes' humanistic needs, which include the following:

- Sport has a voluntary nature; children participate in sport because they want to.

- Athletes participate because of a strong intrinsic appeal; initially, enjoyment is the primary motivation.

- All participants develop in many ways and at many levels as a result of the sport experience, but each experience is unique to the individual player.

- Sport has an educational intent (Penney, 2006); namely, the development of people.

- Children possess a great variety of meaningful and relevant reasons for entering the sport experience.

Indeed, research suggests that children's reasons for playing sports are to have fun, be with friends, and experience thrills and excitement (Roberts, Treasure, and Hall, 1994). To enable athletes to participate for personal reasons, the role of an adult or coach becomes one of "releasing, facilitating, and assisting, not one of manipulating and coercing" (Lombardo, 1987, p. 47).

Sports within organizations contribute to this growth and development of an individual, so participation should promote both learning and enjoyment. Unfortunately, evidence exists that some of these needs are not being met (Lombardo, 2001). The following list outlines some of the problematic characteristics of a professional model of coaching:

- The coach, with an autocratic, authoritarian emphasis, is at the center (coach-centered) of the sport experience and is framed by a rigid, inflexible structure.

- Athletes' interests are secondary to those of the coach.

- Coaches are primarily concerned with winning and competition, making these the main focus of the athletes' experience.

- Objective results are emphasized over the subjective experiences of the performers; the product is valued more than the process.

- Learning is facilitated only as it relates to motor performance and winning. Learning and development in both the cognitive and affective domain are only incidentally or accidentally addressed. The professional model does not pretend to aspire to educational outcomes.
- The subjective nature of the experience is not celebrated. It would only be addressed as it directly relates to enhancing the pursuit of victory (team culture, athlete learning, trust, and honesty).

The current professional model of sport behavior highlights the expectations, especially from adults, to win at all costs. In their research on parents, Kidman, McKenzie, and McKenzie (1999) observed the following comment made to a son batting while playing cricket. The father told his son that he shouldn't have gone for a particular bowl after scoring 40 runs, stating, "How could you go after that shot? It was an idiot thing to do." The boy was nine years old. Bowlers at this age have difficulty even getting the ball to the stumps (wickets), yet this boy still managed to make 40 runs. The 40 runs were gained through robotic movements as the boy attempted to bat according to his father's instructions. The boy was never allowed to make his own decisions. Where is the learning in this case? We need to use a model like TGfU, which focuses on enabling learning in authentic situations, without the interference of adults.

To enable learning, coaches need to set up a learning environment and then stand back. For TGfU, coaches would set up a purposeful game before stepping aside to watch, learn if needed, and read the athletes. (How are they doing? Do they understand? Are they being successful?) The most difficult part of this process is refraining from jumping in. Once athletes are ready, coaches may decide to ask a question to determine understanding, to change the rules, or to let them play. *It depends* is the primary theory, meaning that the process depends on the athletes' needs and learning. When coaches consider the athletes first and enable their choice and control, the athletes are empowered. In other words, through training, empowered athletes and teams gain some choice in and control over what happens in their sporting life as well as in their general lives. They have this choice and control because the power is shared with them (Arai, 1997).

> *T*o enable learning, coaches need to set up a learning environment and then stand back. For TGfU, coaches would set up a purposeful game before stepping aside to watch, learn if needed, and read the athletes. (How are they doing? Do they understand? Are they being successful?)

The Pedagogy of TGfU

TGfU, which is widely employed at all levels of athletic communities and in physical-education programs, is an example of humanistic, athlete-centered coaching. It enhances performance through learning tactics and skills (including technique) in the context of a game. This model promotes and enables athletes to obtain lifelong learning in physical, cognitive, social, and emotional domains, using games as the vehicle for growth and development. If the TGfU movement is to maintain its momentum, it must broaden its scope to include such aspects as personalized learning and cognitive, social, emotional, and affective concepts (including a heightened sense of self). It must also maintain its focus on improving of players' game sense (tactical awareness, team culture, life skills, and so on).

After many years of the method's promotion, the value of TGfU for students or athletes has been rigorously researched. The research highlights the constructive approach (Griffin & Butler, 2005) as a learning theory, and skill-acquisition specialists (Turner, 2005) are keen to research cognitive-learning effects of the model. However, we want to revisit the early intention of the TGfU model as highlighted by Ketchmar (2005) of teaching for meaningful experiences and for delight in participation. The rationale for learning within a context of the sport game falls into constructivist learning, but humanistic coaching enables the athletes to construct sport experiences authentically and motivates them to gain the intrinsic desire to improve their movement capabilities, thus enabling the constructivist-learning process.

The rationale for learning within a context of the sport game falls into constructivist learning, but humanistic coaching enables the athletes to construct sport experiences authentically and motivates them to gain the intrinsic desire to improve their movement capabilities, thus enabling the constructivist-learning process.

However, in order to experience the many and wonderful outcomes, coaches must adhere to the pedagogy implicit in TGfU. Specifically, in contrast to the teacher or coach who situates learning in a context very similar to the game, the leader stand backs with minimal direction and permits the athletes to analyze, interpret, conjecture, and possibly complete several attempts to solve the motor or tactical problem through trial and error. At that point, the leader can reinforce, probe, prompt, restate the problem, or provide more information, but should refrain from solving the problem. Once the athletes have responded, the leader must truly and actively listen, reflect upon the response, and then move on. In this way, the learners are forced to become self-reliant and independent of the coach or leader, closely mimicking the numerous moments in which the coach cannot inform them of their next move that will occur during the heat of the moment in game play.

Humanistic coaching attempts to focus on and address a variety of educational outcomes for all the participants. In addition to promoting proficiency in the sporting activity, it includes many of the aspects inherent to the TGfU philosophy. The conceptual nature of TGfU is congruent with humanistic methodology; both attempt to engage athletes cognitively and physically, and both include a coach or leader who actively listens to the athlete's analytical thinking.

Humanistic or Athlete-Centered Coaching

The purpose of coaching is to enable athletes to learn in a way that works best for them. The first factor in this process is their individual physical and mental makeup, including where they are with technical and tactical development. Another factor is their ability to perform to their best in competition or when challenged (SPARC, 2006).

In a competitive situation, athletes will preferably stay in the moment and react based on their awareness of the situation or movement. Hopefully, they will have an appropriate goal and know how to get back on track when something goes astray. The learning that happens in training should develop this skill of self-correcting and self-coaching (SPARC, 2006). TGfU caters to this goal well by providing competition and authentic situational opportunities in which athletes can learn.

Lombardo (2001) highlights an oversight in ensuring that, as coaches, our mission is to create better human beings. He suggests that the experience in sport is about being authentic, true to oneself, human in every way. TGfU is a model that enables humanistic experiences to happen. Play is one of these intrinsic experiences, since it is spontaneous and expresses uniqueness. Current (professionally organized) sport programs can suppress this human need for play and spontaneity. Environments that demand conformity do not allow athletes to play sports. However, TGfU promotes play and perpetuates spontaneity, creativity, and innovation by helping athletes learn from constructing experiences. TGfU, given its indirect pedagogy (teacher or coach as facilitator), parallels and emphasizes similar humanistic concepts.

TGfU is humanistic by its very nature because it enhances athletes' motivation and thus intensity of performance through problem solving. Athletes increase their effort to match the meaningful challenges offered. These challenges also create opportunities for athletes to respond to pressure inherent in sport competitions. Achievement is also enhanced, since TGfU enables athletes to do something well, to problem solve, and to take ownership of their own learning and development. Of course, enjoyment is also enhanced because games are fun. Through games, athletes share success and failure; they learn how to trust each other and to care about each other's ways of competing and making decisions, which enhances team culture.

Coaches who have successfully embraced the humanistic model and TGfU can often be recognized by their ability to stand back (stay in the background instead of taking center stage) during coaching sessions. Specifically, these individuals have minimized their ego-involvement as they execute their coaching responsibilities. They feel little pressure to act like a traditional coach on the sideline—shouting directions, pointing, directing, and telling players what to do next. These individuals are at ease sharing the power and the decision-making with their athletes. Indeed, often these authentic leaders, who are fully comfortable with themselves, work diligently in practice or training sessions to prepare their athletes to take control of the team and to respond to the many decisions inherent during game play. Specifically, these coaches enable athletes to learn tactics, strategies, and techniques, so that they can occasionally run their own games. In situations like these, athletes are truly learning through playing.

As a model, TGfU can be used with the professional model of coaching in mind. That is, coaches may give direct feedback executing moves or techniques within the game, rather than using questioning or the game itself to solve problems. If this direct feedback occurs, it can perpetuate the coach-centered existence in which coaches maintain power and control without worrying about the process of developing fine human beings. TGfU is considered by some to be an outstanding tool, but when coaches dominate athletes' learning experiences, the opportunities for athletes to learn through the game are sometimes minimized or limited to the physical and motor domain, giving minimal attention to cognitive and affective growth or outcomes. The purpose of TGfU is to enable athletes' learning and ability to make physical, cognitive, and affective decisions. Athletes learn by playing the game and by solving game-related problems. If coaches can encourage and nurture athletes' self awareness, the athletes will learn to make informed decisions independently from the coach.

Leaving athletes to learn and facilitating this learning can be a different task to understand, but coaches who can withhold their knowledge enable athlete responsibility and learning (Whitmore, 2002). This withholding of knowledge, which is a sign of emotional intelligence and empathy, enables athletes to learn to solve problems, which transmits skills that they will retain longer and can likely employ in future situations (Cassidy, Jones, and Potrac, 2009). The athletes are the ones who must understand the game and make split-second, intuitive decisions in the heat of competition. Therefore, in TGfU, the coach facilitates responses to problems, but does not solve them for the athletes.

Kidman (2005) completed an action-research project with a group of high-school volleyball players in which she acted as a participant observer. The coach indicated that he wanted to develop TGfU and let go of control over the athletes. Some of the athletes were interviewed after the season to determine their perspectives on the approach. It is important to note that the athletes didn't understand the concept of TGfU, instead commenting on how they were trained, often using the word *drills* for what occurred in training. The following excerpt is an observation from Luke:

> [We played] a lot of gamelike drills, which was really good. It made it more fun as well. We all played because we wanted to play the game. If you are having fun, you work a bit harder and the level is higher as well. Other coaches, like at cricket, they throw a thousand balls at you or something and they play this shot over and over and over again. But it is not really helping, because if you are in a game then you are not going to get that ball that was thrown.

When asked whether the gamelike drills made a difference in how the team played at Nationals, Luke responded:

> I think it helped us know when to play together and. . . it taught us to be intense. It didn't necessarily improve our ability a lot because we had already done that when we were younger. We already had the skills. Doing those game drills taught us how to be intense all the time.

> I think that came from training as well. Like during drills or during game drills, sometimes [the coach] stops and explains things, explains why we are doing these things. He does that often enough that we know it and can see it by ourselves. I guess other teams don't do that. I think they just say, do this drill, [but the teams] really don't know why they are doing it.

Simon saw some real benefits in using games to practice unusual situations that might occur in competitions. The team's practice in novel situations could then be applied to those that they met in competitions:

> Our defense was good. We picked up the good hitters. Maybe because we did those drills, we could read the offense from the other teams better. When we were on offense, we knew where to hit the ball or [how to hit] around the blockers. So maybe that did help. It didn't feel like it because we did drills that

helped, but now that you look at it, you could probably say a few things helped us which gave us [practice] in situations.

Simon suggests that his coach allowed the players to take risks. Rather than jumping in when he did not like the risk, the coach left it to the boys to make the choice. They learned through trial and error in games. Simon appreciated the opportunity for decision making, which he compares favorably with more prescriptive coaching styles in the following anecdote:

> When I was on duty at the Nationals tournament, I heard a coach say to a player, "Don't you dare jump serve," because the game was close. The player then served and missed the serve, looked back at the coach with a sour face. The players need to make more decisions for themselves during the games. The coach can say where to serve, but not change how to serve during a game.

With TGfU, athletes can learn about the game and can practice skills and techniques within the context of a game rather than separate from it. Learning in context provides a sound understanding of the game and opportunities to apply skill and technique under pressure. When athletes are allowed to play or practice in a situation uncluttered by coaches telling them what to do and where to go, they are more productive in terms of learning in context, enhancing motivation through challenges, social interactions, and decision making (Kidman & Hanrahan, 2004), and working under pressure. The key here is that the coaches do not tell them what to do; the athletes work it out for themselves.

Creating Independent Athletes

Authenticity, the current topical term for defining real human practices, fits well with the idea of TGfU, which is the authentic practice of sport. Lombardo (2001) espouses humanistic coaching as a tool to give athletes the motivation to learn and achieve. Traditional models of coaching cater to the socializing influences and agencies of young people two generations ago. Today, coaching approaches must be modified to suit the socialization trends of the 21st century. TGfU caters to these trends, enabling athlete autonomy and freedom. These are developed by empowering athletes and encouraging them to be aware of and responsible for their performance. The movement experiences within the application of TGfU are humanizing in that they positively influence self-esteem, self-direction, independence, and opportunities that can "express intense movement of joy and supreme well-being" (Workman, 2001, p. 85).

*T*he movement experiences within the application of TGfU are humanizing in that they positively influence self-esteem, self-direction, independence, and opportunities that can "express intense movement of joy and supreme well-being" (Workman, 2001, p. 85).

A key to coaching is the ability to read the situation and decide when to stand back and let athletes play and when to jump in to give them thinking opportunities. Often, coaches lose sight of where the athletes want to head. Athletes have a need for their point of view to be understood, not evaluated or judged. Coaches who possess this quality are said to be empathetic. One of the major tools for athletes is self-awareness (Humm, 2010). To become self-aware, an element of self-evaluation must occur. Coaches must nurture and encourage athletes through this challenging process by allowing them to make mistakes and by inspiring independence and confidence. If athletes are dependent on the coach for total instruction, there can be an increase in stress to do exactly what is asked. They also won't easily be able to make decisions on the field or pitch.

Current cultures include several socializing agents that influence athletes significantly (such as unsupervised time for latch-key children, the presence of two working parents, and computer and video games). Unfortunately, in many instances, coaches have resisted changes, continuing to operate just as others did 40 years ago (which was more appropriate for the culture of that time). We need to recognize that parents and adults increase stress for children by neglecting to give them the tools to deal with problems (Marano, 2004). Even in the sport environment, the process of making meaningful decisions is taken away from athletes. Today, many children have trouble thinking for themselves.

Also, with the influx and continued creation of more and more technological advances, which minimize daily, frequent interactions between and among humans, it has become more imperative to engage athletes in a number of potentially humanistic sport ventures, which TGfU can provide! Sport, in which human interaction is a must and communication, empathy, and decision making are inherent in the action, might be a future focal point for growth and development of young people. TGfU can be a major part of this process.

Humanistic coaching promotes independence and reliance on others in sport contexts for the best performance. TGfU creates independent athletes who must perform their own way rather than depending on the instruction and direction of the coach.

Conclusion

Sport is important in the realm of modern society. It is important to review the benefits and to determine why each athlete participates or competes. The overreaching goals of coaches tend to be motor efficiency and winning (Lombardo, 1987), even though research shows that the main reasons athletes participate in sport are socialization, fun, and the pursuit of excellence.

So where is this humanistic athletic leadership? Based on humanism as we have seen it, we know great examples of best practice in the sporting context exist, but many of the practices still occur in a traditional, prescriptive way. Humanistic coaching is still dismissed as a fluffy, tree-hugging, dolphin-stroking, touchy-feely approach. As a fraternity, most coaches do not encourage athlete awareness, ownership, or responsibility. Many sporting and coaching organizations believe and state in their strategic plans that athlete-centered learning should be used to develop individuals, but often the nature of policy does not always lead to quality implementation. Administrative and organizational leaders seldom actually practice and enforce what they preach in these documents, displaying behaviors of conformity instead (Kidman and Lombardo, 2010).

This should be a major concern to all educators who proclaim vociferously that growth, development, and learning are their primary concerns. One needs only to examine closely the big-time level of sports at major institutions of higher learning to find examples of such hypocrisy. Yet we are more horrified by the implementation, if not entrenched establishment, of the tenets and practices of the professional model of sport for children aged 8 to 10.

Sporting and coaching organizations claim difficulty due to the commercialization trend which seems to have moved the focus from human learning to the bottom line, money based on results. Interestingly, research now is revealing that an athlete-centered approach actually enables better performance and winning (Allen and Hodge, 2006; Cassidy et al., 2009; Kidman and Lombardo, 2010), in which athletes are encouraged to become self-aware and take ownership and responsibility for their learning.

As long as sport is conducted in a manner which minimizes individuality and uniqueness, the humanistic experience will not happen. Until coaches begin to consistently emphasize objectives or outcomes other than victory, sports will not become a more humanized experience. Breaking away from the structured model is difficult because of expectations from outside influences from parents, spectators, and the media on coaches and athletes. Until recently, little attention has been given to implementing or practicing humanistic coaching. With TGfU, coaches are moving to an environment that is more motivational, using sport as an authentic learning experience, just as research rhetoric indicates should occur (Jones, 2006). TGfU is a humanistic approach that enhances athlete motivation by encouraging them to learn and understand. Motivation and enjoyment of the sport experience will keep athletes in sport and physical activity.

TGfU is an exemplar model of catering to the humanistic needs of athletes. Athletes benefit from physical learning opportunities, which are embedded in cognitive-learning outcomes and decision-making processes and encapsulated in the affective area for social and emotional needs. It values each person's experience as unique. It can be used to design practices around the desires and thrills of individual players. In essence, it is time to move sport back to its original intention: for fun, enjoyment, development through competition, and personal and social learning, which can all occur without interference, guidance, direction, and instruction from nonplayers. It is also time to use sport as a tool to focus on human qualities. If this latter objective is accomplished, sport will have fulfilled its potential. Specifically, sport has the potential to truly liberate players and enable them to access the essence of being fully human (Lombardo, 1987).

With the marriage of the TGfU approach and the humanistic tenets applied to sport and athletic leadership, it is quite possible that in the 21st century, sport will finally be able to fulfill its promise to participants. Specifically, the sport experience, given the combined efforts of these two major thrusts, will be able to contribute to the individual athlete in many and various ways: emotionally, intellectually, and physically. It will also facilitate the pursuit of motor excellence and the victory and success that should accompany such an event.

The recent and numerous accomplishments of TGfU have provided athlete-centered coaches with renewed confidence and inspiration that sport can, indeed, be transformed to become all that it should be to all participants. With the growing acceptance of the TGfU model, sport leaders will be better situated to address the whole individual and, in effect, humanize the sport experience for all participants. TGfU has all the elements required to sustain such a movement.

Discussion Questions

1. Which major characteristics of the TGfU model focus on the holistic needs of athletes?

2. Describe two coaching scenarios which demonstrate your holistic understanding of the TGfU model in action.

3. In what specific ways is the TGfU model humanistic?

4. Discuss several differences between adult-structured sports and sports organized from the participant's perspective.

5. How does the professional model differ from an athlete-centered model?

6. How can coaches create independent athletes? Be specific.

References

Allen, J.B., & Hodge, K. (2006). Fostering a learning environment: Coaches and the motivational climate. *International Journal of Sports Science and Coaching, 1*(3), 261-278.

Arai, S.M. (1997). Empowerment: From theoretical to the personal. *Journal of Leisurability, 24*(1), 3-11.

Cassidy, T., Jones, R., & Potrac, P. (2009). *Understanding sports coaching: The social, cultural and pedagogical foundations of coaching practice.* London: Routledge.

Griffin, L.L., & Butler, J.I. (2005). *Teaching games for understanding: Theory, research, and practice.* Champaign, IL: Human Kinetics.

Humm, R. (2010). How's your coaching? In L. Kidman & B.J. Lombardo (Eds.), *Athlete-centered coaching: Developing decision makers.* Worcester, UK: IPC Print Resources.

Jones, R.J. (Ed.). (2006). *Sports coach as educator: Reconceptualising sports coaching.* London: Routledge.

Ketchmar, R.S. (2005). Teaching games for understanding and the delights of human activity. In L.L. Griffin and J.I. Butler (Eds.), *Teaching games for understanding: Theory, research, and practice* (pp. 199-212). Champaign, IL: Human Kinetics.

Kidman, L. (2005). *Athlete centred coaching: Developing inspired and inspiring people.* Christchurch, NZ: IPC Print Ltd.

Kidman, L., & Hanrahan, S.J. (2004). *The coaching process: A practical guide to improve your effectiveness.* Sydney, AU: Cengage Learning.

Kidman, L., & Lombardo, B.J. (Eds.). (2010). *Athlete centered coaching: Developing decision makers.* Worcester, UK: IPC Print Resources.

Kidman, L., McKenzie, A., & McKenzie, B. (1999). The nature and target of parents' comments during youth sport competitions. *Journal of Sport Behavior, 22*(1), 54–68.

Lombardo, B.J. (1987). *The humanistic coach.* Springfield, IL: Charles C Thomas.

Lombardo, B.J. (2001). Coaching in the twenty-first century: The educational models. In B.J. Lombardo, T.J. Carvella-Nadeau, K.S. Castagno, & V.H. Mancini (Eds.), *Sport in the twenty-first century: Alternatives for the new millennium* (pp. 3-10). Boston: Pearson Custom.

Lynch, J. (2001). *Creative coaching: New ways to maximize athlete and team potential in all sports.* Champaign, IL: Human Kinetics.

Marano, H.E. (2004). A nation of wimps, *Psychology Today* [Online]. April 15, 2008 Available: http://www.psychologytoday.com/articles/200411/nation-wimps.

Maslow, A. (1962). *Towards a psychology of being.* Princeton, NJ: D. Van Nostrand.

Penney, D. (2006). Coaching as teaching: New acknowledgements in practice. In R.L. Jones (Ed.), *Sports coach as educator: Reconceptualising sports coaching* (pp. 25-36). London: Routledge.

Roberts, G.C., Treasure, D.C., & Hall, H.K. (1994). Parental goal orientations and beliefs about the competitive-sport experience of their child. *Journal of Applied Social Psychology, 24*, 631–645.

Rogers, C.R. (1969). *Freedom to learn: A view of what education might become.* Columbus, OH: Charles Merrill.

Sport and Recreation New Zealand (SPARC). (2006). *Athlete-centred coaching philosophy effective coaching resource*. Retrieved June 16, 2009 from www.sparc.org.nz.

Thorpe, R.D., & Bunker, D. (1989). A changing focus in games teaching. In L. Almond (Ed.), *The place of physical education in schools* (pp. 42-71). London: Kogan Page.

Turner, A.P. (2005). Teaching and learning games at the secondary level. In L.L. Griffin & J.I. Butler (Eds.), *Teaching games for understanding: Theory, research, and practice*. Champaign, IL: Human Kinetics.

Whitmore, J. (2002). *Coaching for performance: Growing people, performance and purpose* (3rd ed.). London: Nicolas Brealey.

Workman, G.J. (2001). Humanistic ideology in sport: Time for a change. In B.J. Lombardo, T.J. Carvella-Nadeau, K.S. Castagno, & V.H. Mancini (Eds.), *Sport in the twenty-first century: Alternatives for the new millennium* (pp. 84-87). Boston: Pearson Custom.

chapter

11

TGfU as a Coaching Methodology

Adriano De Souza, MA • Steve Mitchell, PhD

The nature of competition in sports demands faster assessment of game needs (offensive or defensive systems) and faster adaptation, consequently faster player-to-player, player-to-coach, and coach-to-player interactions. Players who are encouraged to share their opinions and find solutions during practices have the opportunity to develop their game performance in an environment that is open for creativity, which is much needed when finding ways to achieve success in game play. Placing players in the center of the process for performance development and giving them autonomy to participate in problem-solving situations unleashed one after another during game play can help them more effectively make adjustments and find success in real competition.

Although Teaching Games for Understanding (TGfU) now has an increased presence in public-school physical education in numerous countries, it is perhaps used less frequently as a coaching methodology in some countries as compared to others. It has been formally adopted in Australia and New Zealand, in the shape of Game Sense (Light, 2005), but TGfU thinking is less evident than might be expected in written coaching materials and on Web sites based in Canada, the United Kingdom, and the United States. The adoption of TGfU as a coaching methodology may depend on several factors, such as technical skill-based orientation to sport and coaching, individual preferences for coaching style, the prevalence of strong governing bodies for sports, and coaching-education requirements. The purpose of this chapter is to examine the use of TGfU as a coaching methodology and to identify coaching preferences, characteristics, and behaviors necessary to successfully implement a TGfU approach in formal coaching settings. Furthermore, we will identify differences between using TGfU in coaching and in teaching, and will describe the potential affect of TGfU on coaching practices and player performance. Finally, we will discuss issues of planning and assessment in a TGfU setup for a season, and for practice and match settings.

TGfU as a Coaching-Style Preference

When referring to TGfU in sports coaching and traditional sports coaching, two distinct coaching styles might be seen:

1. Coach A has an approach of designing practices with games that present tactical and strategic problems, gives players a voice, and places high responsibility on the players for decision making, choices, and changes within the game.

2. Coach B designs practices which are based on drills out of game context, focuses highly on developing techniques, makes little use of game situations to develop players and team performance, and usually takes control of every problem-solving step in practices and matches, allowing very little room for players' voices and opinions.

Both styles will have different outcomes because of the environment they promote. An environment which values players' ideas will probably develop creative and independent players, and an environment which is centered on solutions from coaches will develop dependent players.

Both teaching and coaching practices involve planning, delivering, sharing, developing information, creating knowledge, assessing, and readjusting lesson or practice plans for future training sessions. Teaching-style preferences are molded over time during the formal-education period of young teachers, based on undergraduate courses in areas of education or in specific majors, such as art education, physical education, and music education. Supported by an ecological paradigm (Bronfenbrenner, 1979), teaching-style prefer-

An environment which values players' ideas will probably develop creative and independent players, and an environment which is centered on solutions from coaches will develop dependent players.

ences are also a consequence of young teachers' life experiences, including the learnings and developments they gained among the surrounding adults in their lives, including parents, teachers, neighbors, and friends, as well as from influential books and media. Likewise, coaching-style preferences (CSP) will be molded the same way. Coaches' personal histories will influence their coaching-style preferences in two very distinct ways. The first, at one end of the spectrum, is a formal influence that occurs when former players search for college education in physical education or sports-coaching education in undergraduate programs. These coaches usually continue their formal education in graduate schools in the area of sports pedagogy, sports coaching, or related areas. The second influence at the other end of the spectrum is informal, meaning that the coaching-style preferences were developed mainly by observing their former coaches for their advice, their styles, and the sports media they listen to (which is specialized for covering stories, but not in teaching and coaching).

These two types of influences will have very distinct consequences for one's CSP. Coaches with CSP developed from formal education tend to use more updated methods, to value past, present, and future research in the field, and to make their choices based on argued references that will benefit their coaching. On the other hand, coaches with CSP developed by a playing career and by observation of former coaches tend to replicate the coaching or teaching approaches they personally experienced when they plan, implement, and assess their practices and matches.

Coaches that develop their CSP through former coaches and personal playing experience tend to exhibit several, sometimes negative, tendencies. First, coaches would probably make most or all of the choices about solutions for tasks or game problems themselves. Secondly, coaches might blame players for not achieving certain goals and punish them with physical, demanding exercises such as push-ups, sit-ups, and sprints. They might also use social or emotional punishment, like not talking to players and excluding them from discussions, instead of talking to them and using the opportunity to find solutions. Ultimately, punishment is chosen in place of opportunities for both players and coaches to reflect on and change behavior. McCaughtry and Rovegno (2003) demonstrate how beginning physical-education teachers change their teaching and assessment approaches as they begin to reflect about their practices, using their mentors' expert knowledge of pedagogical content. Since coaching is about planning, teaching, administering, and assessing, similar results could be found in formal-coaching education.

Coaching-style preference is one of the most significant factors that will influence the outcome of every practice session. The influence on the outcome happens because coaching-style preferences guide the way practices are designed, how tasks are delivered, how results are assessed, and how problems are solved when goals are not achieved in practices or matches. The end result is that the game-play style of players and the team will be products of how coaches plan and administrate team environments like practices, matches, and evaluation sessions. Also, coaches conduct continued assessments and promote adjustments, based on individual coaching-style preferences. Because coaches control practice environments, team culture is a result of every interaction, explicit or hidden (the choices that coaches make about not talking to athletes and judging their actions instead of interacting with them), that coaches have with players, which may also lead to interaction among players.

Traditional Coaching Approaches

When discussing possibilities about teaching games in 1982, Bunker and Thorpe described traditional physical-education classes that intended to teach games, but were not effective for the following reasons:

1. A large percentage of children achieved little success because of the emphasis on performance.
2. The majority of school leaders knew very little about games.
3. The players who were supposedly skillful in fact possessed inflexible techniques and poor capacity for making decisions.
4. The performers developed dependence on the teacher or coach.
5. The teachers failed to develop the students as thinking spectators and themselves as knowing administrators at a time when games and sport were an important form of entertainment in the leisure industry.

A traditional approach to coaching is similarly connected to the traditional teaching model for physical education described by Bunker and Thorpe (1982). A traditional coaching approach has the following characteristics:

- A large use of drills to teach sports techniques outside of game context
- A high amount of time dedicated to trying to teach skills outside of game context
- A low amount of time dedicated to developing game skills and tactical and strategic knowledge within the game context
- A low amount of time dedicated to teaching and developing game knowledge (tactics and strategies)
- The development of a large number of players who believe that knowing sports means knowing the sports skills only

- The development of a large number of players who are too dependent on coaches, reaching a higher level of playing with little ability to tactically problem solve or adapt to situations without the coaches' help
- The development of a large number of players who cannot make fast and effective tactical and strategic changes during games
- The coach assumes the role of problem solver, thereby depriving players of opportunities to develop game knowledge
- The coaches demand high creativity from players during matches but do not allow them to develop game-play creativity in practices
- Players do not reflect on personal and team performance

We can draw inspiration on how to reflect on performance from children and teenagers who do not play in traditional settings, since they talk informally with peers about their win or loss after the games are over. They find other places to play, even if it is in a street or a backyard. This game environment gives them the opportunity to develop their knowledge of tactics and strategies and helps them to gain an appreciation of the game and its needs—ultimately encouraging the development of motor, cognitive, and emotional skills, all of which are needed to achieve success in games. Coaches who use a traditional approach rapidly take away players' autonomy in making their own choices about problems that require a tactical or strategic adjustment. In this approach, the coach retains the power for making choices and solving problems. Typically, such coaches are quick to complain that their players are not creative when it comes to making tactical or strategic changes, finding ways to score, or preventing their opponents from scoring, yet they fail to acknowledge that they hardly allow their players to think for themselves and to learn how to make effective choices during practices or games.

TGfU as a Contemporary Approach to Coaching

Arguing for a different approach to teaching games and sports, Bunker and Thorpe (1982) proposed the approach in physical education that we know as TGfU (see figure 11.1), emphasizing learning about the game and how to make game play successful. They argued that this approach would benefit the students for the following reasons:

1. Students would develop game awareness and would become better decision makers.
2. Students would engage more in game play because they would understand more about the game.

Figure 11.1   The original TGfU model from Bunker and Thorpe 1982.

Based on D. Bunker & R. Thorpe, 1982, "A model for teaching of games in secondary schools," *Bulletin of Physical Education, 18*(1), 5-8.

3. Students would attach greater value to skill development after they see the need for it in real-game situations.
4. Students would become more informed consumers of games and sport.

TGfU has been applied to coaching in New Zealand and Australia as the concept of Game Sense, and in the United States, Canada, and parts of Asia under the name Tactical Games Teaching. In Portugal, the book *Jogos Desportivos Colectivos* (Graca & Oliveira, 1998) offers ideas about keeping games players at the center of the teaching process as well as allowing them to play games during the process of learning and development. In Brazil, the approach called Jogo Possivel (Paes, 2001) also uses similar ideas. Despite differences in name, these techniques all share a learner-centered approach, allowing players to participate actively in the process of solving problems and making decisions (Mitchell, 2005). Within a TGfU approach, coaches design practices and present problems for players, allowing them time to solve the problems and make their own choices before giving an answer. Here, coaches value the players' abilities to make different choices and adjustments in the process of achieving success; capabilities which are ultimately

> *Within a TGfU approach, coaches design practices and present problems for players, allowing them time to solve the problems and make their own choices before giving an answer.*

paramount when using TGfU in coaching sports or teaching physical-education classes.

Mageau and Vallerand (2003) provide strong support for the importance of players' autonomy (ability to self-govern, freedom to make choices and decisions), competence (state and understanding of being competent), and relatedness (being connected by a reason) to the activity. They bring coaches into the picture, emphasizing that they must allow room for players' autonomy, ownership, and participation in the learning and development process in sports settings. Their approach, autonomy-supportive coaching, has many of the delivery and management (administrative) aspects necessary to effectively plan and conduct practices and to develop players who can efficiently adapt, create, innovate, and take advantage of certain moments in a game.

TGfU for Teaching Versus TGfU for Coaching

The differences between TGfU for teaching and TGfU for coaching stem from the demand for competitiveness and fast adaptation. The nature of playing to achieve success demands faster assessment of game needs (offensive or defensive) and faster adaptation; therefore, faster player-to-player, player-to-coach, and coach-to-player interactions are necessary. In this environment, coaches will work with the same approach as physical-education teachers do; however, coaches can use TGfU coaching processes (see figure 11.2). When conducting a practice session, coaches might use more of the inquiry approach and more complex questions about abstract tactics and strategies than teachers might use with TGfU for physical education.

The nature of competition necessitates using different characteristics of TGfU in coaching than in teaching. Time and the opponent's ability to change tactics and strategies become stronger constraints that players must deal with as they emerge in fierce competition. As indicated in table 11.1 (pp. 195-196), the coaching context, with its inherent level of competition and the need to balance results with performance, allows for increased possibilities for game assessment, problem solving, creativity, and game-plan development. Game assessment is constant on the

Game assessment is constant on the part of both players and coaches, whether in practice or in competitive situations. Continual reflection and decision making relative to both on-the-ball and off-the-ball performance puts players and the game at the center of the performance-learning process.

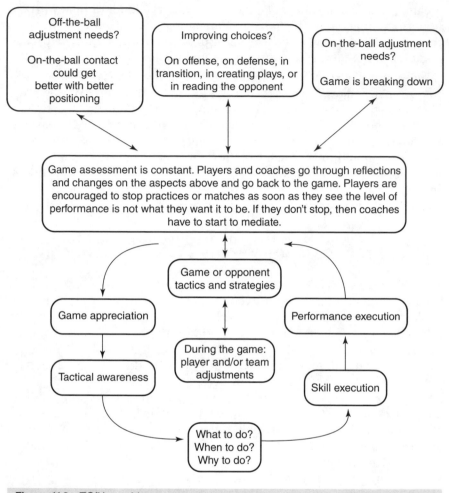

Figure 11.2   TGfU coaching processes.

part of both players and coaches, whether in practice or in competitive situations. Continual reflection and decision making relative to both on-the-ball and off-the-ball performance puts players and the game at the center of the performance-learning process.

In a traditional approach, coaches concentrate on assessing, making decisions, and solving problems themselves. Consequently, players take longer to effectively develop game intelligence and make decisions. TGfU in coaching can help players more skillfully, intelligently, and frequently change game strategy and tactics to score and to stop opponents from scoring.

Game reading, adaptation, and adjustments require great cognitive effort and effectiveness from the players. Players must constantly assess, create, predict, innovate, and change in a short amount of time with the opposition, making problem solving an almost instant process. Imagine that team A is playing against team B (in any sport of your choice), and team A is on offense. Team A tries to score by developing various methods and strategies. At the same time, team B tries to prevent the offense from scoring by reading and adapting its defensive positioning and movements according to team A's offensive maneuvers. While offensive- and defensive-building opportunities take place, players are constantly solving problems and making different tactical and strategic choices in ever-changing game situations.

If coaches want to develop teams with self-motivated players who are able to adapt, create, innovate, take advantage of certain moments of the game, and recognize when those moments happen, TGfU could help

Table 11.1 Differences in Teaching and Coaching With TGfU

	Teaching within TGfU	**Coaching within TGfU**	**Playing after practicing with TGfU. This is what is expected from the players.**
Planning	Teachers develop games to teach offense, defense, and transition systems while developing skills on and off the ball.	Coaches design games to develop the offense and defense systems according to the style they want. These games will also give the players opportunities to develop their skills on and off the ball while playing. Coaches also design games to match their styles of offense and defense games according to their opponents.	The opponents bring the offensive, defensive, and transition game. The players must figure these out as a team and problem solve in the search for success. Players are expected to assess game needs, make adjustments on and off the ball, and keep deciding whether to make adjustments in order to achieve success with time constraints. They will play against teams that can also change and adjust.
Delivering	Teachers change the game's rules, area, and number of players to teach offense, defense, and transition systems while developing skills on and off the ball.	Coaches change the game's rules, area, and number of players to teach, develop, and advance (progress) the complexity of offense and defense systems while developing skills on and off the ball.	Opposing teams provide each other with game constraints that will make each improve their offense, defense, and transition games in search of success.

(continued)

Table 11.1   *(continued)*

	Teaching within TGfU	Coaching within TGfU	Playing after practicing with TGfU. This is what is expected from the players.
Administrating	Teachers encourage students to problem solve and to make their own choices to improve their game performance. These choices are related to their tactical, strategic, and motor skills. Teachers ask questions to help students solve problems.	Coaches encourage players to problem solve and to make their own choices to improve their game performance. These choices will force players to change and to adapt their tactical, strategic, and motor skills. Coaches ask questions to help players solve problems and make adjustments to reach success in the task.	Players solve problems and make their own choices to improve their game performance according to the needs of the game and their opponents' qualities. These choices will affect their tactical, strategic, motor, emotional, and behavior skills. Time is a constant constraint and keeps building pressure for one team or another, depending on which is ahead in the score and many other aspects, such as championship placement, record, and so on.
Student-player assessment	The idea is to assess learning. Teachers can ask questions to evaluate learning of individual students or of the group.	The idea is to assess game performance and why the team is either achieving success or not. Coaches ask questions to evaluate the learning of individual players or of the team.	Coaches ask questions to help players solve problems. Coaches give ideas and sometimes bear the responsibility of tactical choices.
Outcome assessment	Learning is assessed according to questions posed by teachers or students: Are the students able to participate in game play and develop individual skills needed (motor, cognitive, and social)?	Learning and performance are assessed according to questions posed by coaches or players: Are the players able to participate in game play, develop individual skills needed (motor, cognitive, and social), and counter the performance of the opponent?	Coaches and players assess team and individual game performance. Assessment is done through group reflection and questions placed by players or coaches regarding game performance: What was done? Why was it done? Could we have done it differently?

them administrate practices that facilitate these learnings in real-game situations. As an example of using games to develop game performance, Lourenco and Ilharco (2007) describe professional soccer coach, Jose Mourinho: "Mourinho trains nothing but the game, what happens in practice will happen in the real game...the tactics, the technique, the emotions, the leadership" (p. 62). When coached from a TGfU approach, players learn and train to perform in demanding environments designed to enhance game skills, plus some strategic and tactical aspects of game play (competition), with goal-oriented practices. This training allows players to go through situations that require problem solving, ultimately making them more ready when it comes to real competition. This helps eliminate the problem of inadequate transfer of skills from practice to game settings.

> *If coaches want to develop teams with self-motivated players who are able to adapt, create, innovate, take advantage of certain moments of the game, and recognize when those moments happen, TGfU could help them administrate practices that facilitate these learnings in real-game situations.*

A Framework for TGfU in Coaching

During a season, when planning and assessing practices and actual competitions (games and matches), several questions may arise. Practices are based on a player-centered, empowering, and tactical approach to coaching within the TGfU model, although though the extent to which players are allowed to make decisions might depend on whether the context is focused on the season, game, or the practice.

TGfU Within a Season Plan

When brainstorming to plan a season, coaches will meet with their staff to think about what to do for preseason, regular season, preparation for matches, and specific training aspects, as well as which tactics and strategies to use throughout the season. Traditionally, coaches involve only their staff in these processes and do not allow player participation. Enhancing player participation guides the approach of TGfU; coaches can ask their players for opinions in the planning process. Instead of brainstorming about how to plan and what to do, coaches would pose specific questions to players to guide their planning:

- What do you (players) want our game to look like at the end of the season?
- What do we need to do to achieve the quality of play that you want at that point?
- What do you want our game to look like at the beginning of the season?

- What do we need to do to achieve the quality of play that you want at that point?
- What are the strengths of our team?
- What are the weaknesses of our team?
- What do we need to improve on defense?
- What do we need to improve on offense?
- What do we need to improve in transition?
- What information about our opponents do you remember and can share with us at this time?
- How do you think we should play against each one of our opponents? Could you help us to design practice according to whom we would play?
- What do you (individually) want to improve?

These questions do not have to be addressed all at once, but they will help players reflect on their personal and team game and share what they think. This starting point to get valuable information will show players that the coaching staff values their opinions, which is an important step if coaches want players to be creative and involved in the performance-building process. This survey can be done through e-mail, but live discussions that involve the entire team and coaching staff would be even better, including players in brainstorming for solutions that will develop the team's culture.

TGfU Within a Practice Design

Several questions can serve as guidelines when starting to design practices using the TGfU approach. Coaches should keep in mind that the more players are allowed to participate in solving problems and making decisions for practice tasks, the more quickly they will learn to find solutions during games and matches.

Question 1—How can we design practices to develop aspects of performance like decision making, problem solving, creativity, and awareness?

Answer—Practices will be designed with games and drills to fulfill the development of tactical knowledge and skills, which are both necessary for the game; therefore, skills will not be practiced in isolation. Instead, they will be followed by another skill execution, because in a game situation, players have to move and touch the ball again in consequent play after they touched the ball the first time. Players will have opportunities to develop their ability to effectively solve problems and make decisions that are based on cognition, information processing, past experiences, and knowledge.

Question 2—How can coaches design practices that will give players opportunities to develop game-specific motor skills and tactical knowledge when they are most needed (during games)?

Answer—Practices will demand players to master their on-the-ball skills while keeping the ball in play in confined areas. Games and multiskill drills demand that players perform holistically, using their motor, behavioral, social, emotional, and cognitive abilities.

Question 3—How can coaches design practices that will give players opportunities to become better decision makers?

Answer—Coaches need to support players to solve problems, rather than giving them answers all the time. In fact, coaches will share responsibilities with the team, encouraging players' participation in finding effective ways to attack or defend. Players' opinions will be heard and taken into consideration along with the coaches' opinions. In the end, the head coach will make decisions after analyzing pros and cons for any given situation. Players will learn that they can participate in the decision-making and problem-solving process, building a sense of belonging and ownership.

Players learn to perform in demanding environments with games designed to enhance certain skills and tactical aspects of play. Coaches use goal-oriented drills in practices that closely mimic game situations so players are ready when it comes to real competition. Coaches design and administrate practice environments that hold players accountable for their performance. Coaches can use the following guidelines when planning practice:

Start by asking yourself which part of the game you want to practice: offense, defense, or transition. Then, ask yourself how to recreate this element in a game to allow the players to practice their choices and skills in context. When creating the game, define the playing area, the number of players, their responsibilities, the scoring system, and how the game will be initiated to help the players understand what to do and to give the practice a rhythm close to that of a real game.

After this, think about questions that will help you guide the players' thought process, letting them find answers when they do not achieve success in the game.

When redesigning future practices, keep in mind that it takes time for players to adjust to learning and to create solutions; therefore, sometimes you should progress slowly and repeat certain games so that players become proficient in what they are trying to do.

A coach who chooses a TGfU approach goes through the process of learning to adjust rules and task goals to increase or decrease difficulty and

> **P**layers need both repetitions of movement and chances to repeat problem-solving situations in order to gain experience in a shorter amount of time.

to disrupt players' performance to help them search for balance again. Players need both repetitions of movement and chances to repeat problem-solving situations. This approach gives players experience in a shorter amount of time and makes them adjust both individually and as a team to new game needs and strategic and tactical possibilities.

TGfU Within Game Planning

If coaches want to make sure that their players understand the game plan, they must not give all the information before starting play. Leaving information out allows players to take control, but coaches may ask provoking questions that help them understand the plan, such as the following:

- What do you see your opponents doing in this offensive situation?
- What can you do to stop them?
- What type of defense does your opponent play in this situation?
- What can you do offensively to take advantage of this?

If coaches would like their players to remember game plans and make changes when needed, they also need to use questions to help players reflect on possibilities. Allowing time for questions contributes to the players' game retention and working memory. In this process, the players will most likely come up with the answers coaches are seeking while maintaining ownership of the process.

Other questions for reflection might include the following:

- In this offensive case, if this situation happens (explain the situation), what do we have to do?
- If they close our first option, what would we need to change to keep being successful?

This inquiry approach helps players think about the game, reflecting on their own to develop ideas rather than receiving ready answers. Therefore, when it comes to game situations, players will have an idea of what they can do if the game changes.

TGfU in Practice and in Games or Matches

When conducting practices and coaching matches, coaches need to observe, encourage, and allow the players to think and participate in the problem-solving process. Their responses should carry very little negative emotion and affect. Communication to the players should be direct, simple, and concise. Coaches should communicate what they need to see done and wait for players to do it, rather than constantly reminding players what to do, which ultimately makes players less accountable and

When conducting practices and coaching matches, coaches need to observe, encourage, and allow the players to think and participate in the problem-solving process.

dependent, rather than autonomous and creative. Coaches can use the following questions to prompt reflection:

- What happened there?
- Why did that happen?
- What went wrong in that instance?
- What do you think you could have done differently?
- Where did the ball go?
- What could you do to change where you hit the ball and make it more effective?

In practice, a certain amount of time should pass between players' attempts to solve problems and the next time the coach steps in to remind them what to do. Coaches should allow the players to go through the natural consequences of making poor decisions—usually the loss of a point, possession, and consequently, the game. They should guide the players through reflection and game assessment, either as a team or individually. This process can take a little time to master, but when players do, they develop their game intelligence and ability to make effective decisions. For effective practice and game management, coaches can use a checklist to ensure successful application of TGfU principles. For example, the following steps would be helpful:

- Design practices with activities (games) as close to game situations as possible.
- Give players room and time to respond in practice and in games or matches. They have ideas that differ from those of the coaches. Since they are the ones who play the game, they may have quality insights to help improve game tactics.
- Give players room to participate in decision making and problem solving in practice settings through discussion. They will learn that they can and must be creative in building solutions for the game problems that their opponents will create.

- Give players voice and participation through time-outs. Giving the athletes the freedom to ask to stop practice, if they see that they are not achieving the performance they want or if they feel that they could not overcome their opponents, will help them effectively solve problems and make decisions.
- Allow players to meet as a group after practices and bring information about what they think should be developed or practiced. Players may have needs and ideas that the coaches do not realize.

Performance Assessment in TGfU

Assessment within a TGfU approach directly reflects the coaches' observations of practices, games or matches, and the season. This team process, which goes beyond number or percentages of success or errors in ball contact, should focus on players' and coaches' perceptions of game results and on opinions about the offensive, defensive, and transitions systems. Most importantly, it focuses on helping players make effective decisions and solve problems in game play.

Practice Assessment in TGfU

When using a TGfU approach, coaches need to think about assessment as they design practices. Good assessment facilitates an environment in which players can informally assess their game performance by stopping practice for time-outs and by taking time to solve problems and to make new choices to improve their game performance. The approach focuses on outcomes and on doing things effectively. Coaches can use the following questions to guide players:

- Are we achieving our goal?
- If so, what is making us successful?
- If not, what can we change to make our performance more successful?

After this, players start to play and practice again, verifying whether changes help them achieve their goals or stopping to problem-solve again if they do not see improvement. The overall idea is to help players to understand that they can be creative and can use ideas to change their individual and team performance.

Game Assessment in TGfU

Tools for assessing game performance in physical education exist that include the element of decision making. Mitchell, Oslin, and Griffin

(2006) have developed the Game-Performance Assessment Instrument, and Gréhaigne, Richard, and Griffin (2005) have developed the Team-Sport Assessment Procedure, both of which can be used by teachers, coaches, or athletes in peer-assessment situations. In 2001, the Brazilian junior-national volleyball team used informal assessment in their preparation for the world championship (Rizola Neto, Souza, Scaglia, & Oliveira, 2002). Performance was assessed by the players and the coaches, and involved players reflecting on their team-game performance after the matches with a short questionnaire. The following process was used:

- After each formal competition, players answered a win-or-loss questionnaire to account for the outcome of the match.
- Coaches did not talk with the players about any of their own thoughts about the match so that the papers reflected the opinion of the players. Players were also asked not to talk with each other about the match before writing down their ideas.
- Players returned the questionnaires to the coaching staff.
- Members of the coaching staff read the answers and prepared a debriefing meeting with the players.
- In the meeting, coaches protected players' identities by mentioning only ideas and points of view.

With this process, coaches valued players' ideas and points of view, showing the players that their thoughts counted. With time, players started to talk more tactically, their opinions started to be more assertive in the game, and tactical and strategic conversations became more productive. Coaches observed players becoming more game intelligent, with an increased ability to problem solve, to change their game play as needed, and to follow directions when coaches had input.

Season Assessment in TGfU

At the end of the season, coaches usually prepare their assessment and present it to players in the form of numbers, statistics, and percentages. Remember that very little is normally asked of the players. They become mere receptors, passive participants in the process. However, when using a player-centered approach like TGfU, coaches could benefit from asking the players' opinions about the season and ideas for the future, touching on practice content and design, practice assessment, the speed of team development ("Did we develop at a good pace?"), match preparation, match or game administration, and match or game assessment. This shows players that their opinions and voices are important in the process, makes them reflect and think of things they could have done differently to improve results, and helps them bring forth ideas for making the next season better and even more successful.

Conclusion

In this chapter, we strongly encourage coaches to allow players to share ideas and input in practice and game environments, as well as to design practices that challenge the players to solve problems while developing their motor, cognitive, emotional, and social skills, which are necessary for game performance. The thought processes and cognitive ability needed to solve problems and make effective play choices in games can be developed in practice with increased autonomy for players (coaches make room for players' ideas) and in game situations. Players can only reflect about the game while playing by going through both successful and unsuccessful experiences without constant input from a power figure (coach or team captain). Players who are dependent on coaches for performance will have difficulties when playing against teams that make frequent tactical and strategic changes.

Remember that games, as well as other complex systems, are in constant change due to choices made by players. New game situations with different performance needs emerge second after second, minute after minute. Defense situations change to offense opportunities throughout game play; therefore, sports teams can benefit from having players with the freedom, autonomy, and, most importantly, the ability to solve problems under time constraints and to make good use of scoring and defending opportunities in games. The ability to reflect on a given play or game result and to come up with effective changes is necessary for teams to play better defensive, offensive, and transition games. A group of players that can change and adapt their game tactics and strategies will be able to evolve their team performance when faced with the offensive or defensive constraints presented by opponents.

A group of players that can change and adapt their game tactics and strategies will be able to evolve their team performance when faced with the offensive or defensive constraints presented by opponents.

Asking questions and withholding answers for a while when tasks are not being achieved or points and goals are not being scored opens up opportunities for players to develop their problem-solving abilities and vision to change. Giving players time to reflect, come up with their ideas, and solve problems will help them increase their game knowledge. Giving them the opportunity to participate in the planning process helps players perform better under time constraints because they can predict plays and make game choices that dictate their opponents' answer in each play.

We conclude this chapter with some convincing, verbatim testimony from a high-school volleyball coach regarding the efficacy of TGfU as a coaching approach. In response to a few straightforward questions, Dana Brashear gave clear responses indicating that using TGfU, which she previously learned in a coaching clinic, helped her improve her team's performances (personal communication, November 17, 2008):

> **Question 1**—What was it like to use the approach from a coaching perspective? List both good feelings and concerns.
>
> *Answer—I loved using the approach—it felt like teaching; giving the students (athletes) a chance to make predictions, draw conclusions, and analyze the game. I felt as if there was more purpose to both practices and competitions—the kids were more focused on what they needed to accomplish. The only concern that I have is using the approach with young players who are just learning the basics. I can see using it, but not to the extent that I did this year. You would have to know your team, and its weaknesses and strengths.*
>
> **Question 2**—List some key moments in which you caught yourself saying, "Wow… they are now understanding it and doing it."
>
> *Answer—One of the key moments in which I was thinking, "They are getting it," was in practice when my setter was running the drill to identify the large blocker and was setting away from the block—her team was losing, but not due to her setting, just lack of concentration. During every drill, I would give them a 20-second time-out opportunity (both sides), and the setter called the time-out and shared more information in the 20 seconds than I had seen her share in the two years that she had been our setter.*
>
> *Another moment was at one of our very important conference matches. We play in one of the strongest conferences in the state (usually the state champ comes out of our conference or region). It was the fifth game, and we were down by a point. I called a time-out and the girls were talking strategy the whole time. [They were] nice and calm, but strategic and intense. I knew at that moment that they were "getting it." We ended up losing the game by 2 points, but when I received their sheets the next day, I knew that they were understanding the concept of analyzing and processing the match, both during and after.*
>
> **Question 3**—List moments when you caught yourself saying, "Wow… this is what I wanted to teach them—to figure it out by themselves."

Answer—We are trying to create problem solvers, both on the court and in real life. I felt that there were several moments where I was proud to be their coach, on and off the court. One thing that we tried to hit home was turning defense into your offense and having them figure out how they were going to do that. We always struggle on transition and release positioning, and at the end of the season, there was just so much communication from our left sides—I had one [player] who was a senior who had started for 3 years; great kid and smart player. She has always been a communicator, but the other girl was very timid and was not as vocal. When I heard the timid girl initiating the conversation both during practice and during our region-final game, and [the communicative girl] right with what she was saying, I knew the approach was working and I had them buying in.

Question 4—How would you describe the process of the team becoming more effective in their decision making?

Answer—I felt that when we started the season, we were just playing the ball over the net to play it over, and not thinking through where the other team's weaknesses were or being strategic with placement. We were just playing to survive. After addressing this, after they all felt it on their sheets, things changed. They were much better at picking out the other team's weaknesses and playing around our weaknesses. The decision making of our hitters and setters changed drastically from the beginning of the season to the end. They finally figured out that sharing information about the other team only makes us stronger. I have always said that volleyball is a simple game, hit it where they are not, and don't be readable—if you hit hard one play, mix it up the next. Don't be predictable—we were not predictable at the end of the season, making much better decisions with where to put the ball.

This method made us a closer team through communication and strategic talk. It also had the girls talking about the matches all day before we played. They knew how to talk about what the other team may do, and what our game plan was before stepping out on the court. It made them trust one another—that they were all on the same page. This method also increased the communication between players and coaches. They felt more comfortable telling me things through writing than they would have [if they were] sitting in front of me, telling me how they felt about the match.

Discussion Questions

1. What would be the characteristics of a practice session, which promotes problem-solving and players' autonomy?

2. List aspects that have influenced your coaching style preferences. Are these preferences supporting a practice environment where the coach is the one who provides all the answers for game performance problems or do the players have room for input and creativity?

3. Explain why coaching style preference is one of the most significant factors that will influence the outcome of every practice session.

4. Usually coaches are the ones who assess game performance and give their rationale to the players. Explain the benefits of players' participation in game performance assessment.

5. How can the repetitions of problem solving and strategizing in practice help the players with what is going to happen in the real game?

References

Bronfenbrenner, U. (1979). *The ecology of human development: Experiments by nature and design.* Cambridge, MA: Harvard University Press.

Bunker, D., & Thorpe, R. (1982). A model for the teaching of games in secondary schools. *Bulletin of Physical Education, 18*(1), 5-8.

Graca, A., & Oliveira, J. (Eds.). (1998). *O ensino dos jogos desportivos coletivos.* (3rd ed.) Lisbon, Portugal: Universidade do Porto.

Gréhaigne, J.-F., Richard, J.-F.., & Griffin, L. (2005). *Teaching and learning team sports and games.* New York: Routledge Falmer.

Light, R. (2005). Making sense of games sense: Australian coaches talk about game sense. In L. Griffin & J. Butler (Eds.), *Teaching games for understanding: Theory, research and practice* (pp.169-181). Champain, IL: Human Kinetics.

Lourenco, L. & Ilharco, F. (2007). *Lideranca: As licoes de Mourinho.* Lisbon, Portugal: Booknomics.

Mageau, G., & Vallerand, R. (2003). The coach-athlete relationship: A motivational model. *Journal of Sports Sciences, 21,* 883-904.

McCaughtry, N., & Rovegno, I. (2003). Development of pedagogical content knowledge: Moving from blaming students to predicting skillfulness, recognizing motor development, and understanding emotion. *Journal of Teaching in Physical Education 22*(4), 355-368.

Mitchell, S. (2005, December). *Different paths up the same mountain: Global perspectives on teaching games for understanding.* Keynote address presented at the third international TGfU conference, Hong Kong, China.

Mitchell, S.A., Oslin, J.L., & Griffin, L.L. (2006). *Teaching sport concepts and skills: A tactical games approach* (2nd ed.). Champaign, IL: Human Kinetics.

Paes, R.R. (2001). *Educação física escolar: O esporte como conteúdo pedagógico no ensino fundamental.* Canoas, Brazil: ULBRA.

Rizola Neto, A., Souza, A.J., Scaglia, A.J., & Oliveira, P.R. (2002). *Atletas com autonomia aprendem a construir resultados. [Athletes with autonomy learn how to build results]. Relato de experiencia da preparacao especifica de inteligencia para o jogo realizado com a selecao brasileira feminina juvenil de voleibol em 2001.* In W.W. Moreira and R. Simões, Anais Segundo Congresso Cientifico Latino Americano FIEP/UNIMEP. Piracicaba, Brazil: Unimep.

chapter

12

A Model for TGfU in Elementary-School Physical Education

Inez Rovegno, PhD

The content of our field symbolizes what we stand for and what we have to offer the education of children. Our graduates will have to make decisions about what children will experience, in what sequence, and about how skillful they want children to become. These are tough decisions; never before in our history have we had so many directions from which to choose. For example, we can choose among:

Adventure
Aerobic dance
Aerobic exercise
American country dance
Basic movement
Basketball
Basketball basics
Bean bags
Beginning ball skills
Breaking up space sensibly
Challenging climbing capacities
Creative dance
Creative dramatics
Creative movement
Educational dance

Educational games
Educational gymnastics
Eyes and fingers in motion
Fitness trails
Folk dance for fun
Football fantastics
Fun with ropes
Hoopnastics
Huckleberry beanstalk
Modern educational dance
Movement/dance
Movement/games
Movement/gymnastics
Parachute play
Partner gymnastics

(continued)

(continued)

Rhythmic movement for fun and fitness	Sticks and wands
Rope courses	Sticks, paddles, and things
Rope jumping	Tennis tactics
Simple soccer skills	Tinikling for fun and fitness
Sittercises	Ultimate Frisbee
Softball strategies	Volleyball requisite skills
	Working in your on-target zone

How do you react to this list? "My reaction is that any profession which defines its content to include so great a range needs to reevaluate its purpose for being and, ultimately, its justification as a required subject in a child's curriculum" (Barrett, 1985, pp. 9-10). This list, created by Barrett, was based on session titles from physical-education conferences at the time. A similar list could easily be generated today.

This chapter outlines a model of TGfU for all elementary-school grades. Following Kate Barrett's point, I believe that the games portion of the elementary curriculum should not embrace every fad and activity devised from an equipment catalog; rather, it should focus on developing skillful games, players with a deep understanding of substantive game structures and tactics, and the thinking and social skills that support equitable, just, and caring game environments.

> **I** believe that the games portion of the elementary curriculum should not embrace every fad and activity devised from an equipment catalog; rather, it should focus on developing skillful games, players with a deep understanding of substantive game structures and tactics, and the thinking and social skills that support equitable, just, and caring game environments.

The ideas presented in this chapter emerged from my long-term collaboration on the movement approach with Dianna Bandhauer, an elementary-school physical educator in Lecanto, Florida, United States. In developing this model, I reflected on our practice (which tactics and skills we teach to children and when), my research on teaching and learning game play at the elementary level (Rovegno & Bandhauer, 1994; Rovegno, Nevett, Brock, & Babiarz, 2001; Rovegno, Chen, & Todorovich, 2003), and the situated-cognition and constructivist theories on which the research projects were based.

Themes in Early TGfU Papers

To start, I will review what I perceive as the big themes from early TGfU papers (Bunker & Thorpe, 1982; Thorpe, Bunker, & Almond, 1986) that described TGfU as a secondary-school model. I will then discuss those themes in relation to elementary physical education. These themes include the following instructions:

1. Modify equipment and game structures to enable learners to play games.
2. Teach for understanding of tactical game play. Games are not an add-on for practicing skills. Games curriculum should help learners to do the following:
   - Develop flexible, adaptable skills
   - Acquire tactical knowledge
   - Make tactical decisions in game situations
   - Play and learn independently from the teacher or coach
3. To address the above goals and to solve the problem of lack of motivation, use a progression that starts with game play and tactics. Teach skill technique only if necessary and when students recognize the need for technique improvement to enhance game play.
4. Make content meaningful and relevant to students.
5. Teach game appreciation.

Theme 1: Modifications

The first theme, modifying equipment and game structures, is well accepted in elementary physical education and has been for many years. It needs no elaboration from me. We have been less successful in convincing undergraduates and practicing secondary-school physical educators that modifications of equipment and game structures are important for all grade levels (McCaughtry & Rovegno, 2003). With its emphasis on matching equipment and games to the needs of learners, I believe that TGfU can and will make a significant contribution to improving the quality of secondary physical education in the same way that modifications improved the quality of elementary physical education.

Theme 2: Teaching for Understanding

The second theme, to me, is most critical as a guideline that can be applied at the elementary level since it addresses what I believe to be a weakness in many physical-education programs for elementary students. The content of skillful game play is rich and complex to teach. Unfortunately, many of us have seen teachers who have a games-and-activities curriculum at the elementary level that is neither substantive nor informative about actual game play. Rather, the teacher explains the rules and the children play. Children enjoy these simple, fun, and recreational activities, but they do not learn important content. By important and substantive content, I mean games that teach skills and tactics that are foundational to major sports and physical activities.

Moreover, as Thorpe et al. (1986) claim about secondary school curriculum, we need to question the common practice that adding on games to the end of lessons to allow children to practice skills is an effective way to produce skillful players. To leave out the tactical elements, the ways players must adapt their skills to game situations, and the meaning of game structures is to eliminate the very content necessary to help children become truly skillful players. In order for games curriculum to be educational, it can't be a long list of trivial activities. Rather, children must have the time to learn and practice important skills and tactics within modified games and gamelike situations and to develop the deep and well-connected knowledge that will support skillful game play.

Theme 3: Progression

The third theme, progression, is critical to any curriculum. A progression that begins with game play and tactics is the hallmark of TGfU. The problem at the elementary level, which does not occur at the secondary level, is that children need to be able to perform skills at a level that will allow them to play a game. In the lower-elementary grades, in particular, children often can't perform skills well enough to play games. If you can't catch a ball, you can't play a game that requires catching. I don't believe anyone would seriously debate this issue.

The extent to which children's skills must be developed before you add game play (Rink, 2001) is a subject of debate. In the past, folks have claimed that children's skills must be strong enough so they won't regress in a more difficult context, such as a game (Roberton, 1977). I would like to counter that claim and propose the following progression, which is based in part on Rink's familiar four-step progression (2005) and Barrett's (1977) three-phase process of games teaching.

- *Level 1: Basic skills.* Students learn the basic movement patterns of the skill until they can control the ball often.
- *Level 2: Tactical game skills.* Students learn how to vary and adapt the basic skill using movement concepts from the Laban framework, which teachers select in relation to specific contexts of tactical

games (target, net/wall, invasion, and fielding games, such as softball or cricket) and teach in gamelike situations.

• *Level 3: Game play.* Students use skills and tactics in games.

In level one, children learn the basic pattern of skills and practice until they can control the ball most of the time. I propose a relatively low standard: student should demonstrate just enough control to move to level-two tasks. I don't worry about a little regression, since our research suggests it might represent development in relation to specific task and environmental constraints (Chen, Rovegno, Todorovich, & Babiarz, 2003); however, if children play a game or practice a level-two task and their skills regress to the point where the game falls apart or they get emotionally upset or stressed, then the game or task is inappropriate for that child.

In level two, children learn how to vary and adapt the basic skill using movement concepts from the Laban framework in relation to specific game contexts. For example, in invasion games, children need to be able to throw or pass balls in the wide variety of ways listed in table 12.1, which uses the Laban framework to identify and label the content.

Table 12.1　Analysis of Throwing and Passing in Invasion Games at the Elementary Level

Body aspects	Pass or throw balls: • Throw and pass while standing still and while traveling. • Throw balls of different shapes and sizes with 1 hand and 2 hands. • Combine motions with other skills, such as catching then immediately throwing or passing, and dribbling and then passing.
Effort	Pass or throw balls: • Use different amounts of force and speed. • Use large and small amounts of space (effort-space).
Space	Pass or throw balls: • From all areas of personal space, from all 3 levels. • To targets at different levels. • To different distances. • In different directions.
Relationships	Pass or throw balls: • That can be easily caught by teammates. • That avoid the defender guarding/marking the passer. • To the open space ahead of a moving receiver, to an open space in a goal, or to score. • To a receiver when it is advantageous to catch the ball in relation to defenders and/or scoring opportunities. • To a receiver who is free and in a position to improve the team's opportunities to create space, move the ball closer to the goal, or score.

We label level-two objectives as *tactical skills* because it is the tactical context of games that gives skills meaning. This context also dictates the kinds of variability and adaptability children need to develop to play games skillfully, which is a topic I discuss later. In level three, students use skills and tactics in modified games. As I will illustrate later, tactical information can be presented in all three levels.

Table 12.2 illustrates the typical amount of time spent at each grade level working at content from levels one, two, and three. The symbol x represents time spent on basic skills, o represents the time spent working on level-two content, and + represents the time spent in level-three game play.

This is a skill-specific model. Some skills develop relatively quickly and some take considerably more time. Notice that I assume children will still be developing some basic skills in fifth grade (aged 10 to 11). It has been Dianna's and my experience that basic skills, such as striking backhand and overhead with a tennis racket, still need to be practiced even in fourth and fifth grades.

Notice also that even kindergarten lessons can include games in the second half of the year. For example, after teaching tossing for accuracy, Dianna gives kindergartners the option to play a simple game. One child stands on a plastic spot and attempts to toss a bean bag into a hula hoop on the ground about 1.5 meters away, while a defender tries to prevent the score. She has children play the game and then asks them, "When is it harder to toss the bean bag in the hoop?" Different children answer, "When he waves his arms," and "When she stands between me and the hoop." The defensive tactic Dianna is teaching is positioning on the goal side of the offense. Some children are not emotionally ready for games in

Table 12.2   Amount of Time Spent at Each Grade on Content From Levels 1, 2, and 3

Grade	Amount of time spent on each level of skills and play
K	x x x x x x x x x x x o o o o o o o o o o o o o o o o o o o +
1	x x x x x x o o o o o o o o o o o o o o o o o o o o o + +
2	x x x x o o o o o o o o o o o o o o o o o o o o + + + + + + +
3	x x o o o o o o o o o o o o o + + + + + + + + + + + + +
4	x o o o o o o +
5	x o o +

x = Level 1: Basic skills
o = Level 2: Tactical skills and movement concepts
+ = Level 3: Game play

kindergarten and Dianna has those children continue to practice tossing the bean bag into the hoop.

In first grade, she presents, as an option, the second step in the progression. She tells children they can set up two spots about 2 meters apart. If they choose, the offense can run from one spot to the other to toss the bean bag. The defender learns to shift to remain goal-side of the offense. In second grade, she extends the progression to two spots and two hula hoops. Thus, the offense can shoot at either hoop from either spot. The defender must not only defend two hoops but also two shooting spots. This adds more complex tactical decisions for both offense and defense players.

In terms of the model, my point is that tossing underhand to a large target requires a skill that children develop early. Striking skills, on the other hand, take much longer to develop.

In regard to the development of striking skills, I went back and reviewed how movement-approach curriculum writers recommend teaching tactics for net game (Logsdon, Alleman, Straits, Belka, & Clark, 1997; Logsdon, Barrett, Ammons, Broer, Halverson, McGee, & Roberton, 1984). Scholars recommend teaching net-game tactics using throwing skills with deck tennis rings or handmade newspaper rings tossed like a Frisbee over badminton-height nets. Some units use balls. I have no research to support this, but based on our reading and our experiences teaching children, net-game tactics can be developed earlier and to a more sophisticated level using throwing skills. Moreover, we think teaching net-game tactics for creating and denying space is an excellent way to introduce these concepts in invasion games (Rovegno & Bandhauer, 1998). Even though space is used differently in net and invasion games, children can more easily visualize space in net games and can understand that tactical space is the relationship of players to boundaries and players to other players.

Thus, I support the early teaching of tactics for net/wall games using skills other than striking. However, I have to ask, "When will children be given the time they need to develop striking skills with different body parts (as in volleyball) and with rackets? When can modified net games grow up to become tennis, racquetball, or volleyball if we focus simply on net-game tactics using throwing skills, neglecting the hours of striking-skill practice needed to play?" As I will discuss later, the elementary-school years are excellent for practicing skills.

Theme 4: Meaning and Relevance

The progression in TGfU to begin with tactics and game play likely make content meaningful and relevant to students, thus improving students' knowledge and game performance (Oslin & Mitchell, 2006). Consequently, the progression addresses well, in my opinion, the problems Thorpe et al.

(1986) note about a large percentage of unmotivated students who have poor game skills, inflexible techniques, and few capabilities to make tactical decisions.

The arguments for a tactic-skill progression to address problems with motivation and relevance make sense at the secondary level. However, they lose power at the elementary level because what young children find meaningful and relevant differs greatly from adults and secondary students.

In addition, children's levels of cognitive and social development affect their understanding of games. To understand game tactics, like secondary students do, children must understand not only their own perspective but also the perspectives of opponents and teammates. Research going all the way back to Piaget suggests that this ability to understand multiple perspectives develops across the elementary years, as does the ability to share and cooperate, which are two necessary social aspects of games (Roberton & Halverson, 1984).

To understand game tactics, like secondary students do, children must understand not only their own perspective but also the perspectives of opponents and teammates.

We have not conducted much research on the development of children's game play or on the development of children's concept of space, tactical relationships, and the role of social development in game play. However, most of us have experience teaching or observing children play games and sports. I personally would be very happy never again to see 5- and 6-year-olds in community soccer leagues playing a meaningless game of soccer in which all the kids run and try to kick the ball (sometimes kicking each other) like a bunch of bees swarming around a hive.

I do not want to argue that games are inappropriate for children; quite the contrary, children can and do find games meaningful. However, the meaning they find in and about games is different from that for older children and adolescents, and I think we can exploit these differences. First, children's conceptions of games are much broader. To a child, practicing skills can be a game. Dianna described one first grader hitting a ball off a batting tee: each time he made a solid hit, he yelled, "I won!" It was a game. When a 7-year-old comes in from recess and says, "We played soccer," this does not mean they organized 11-a-side soccer. It is more likely that two kids kicked a soccer ball back and forth, dribbled the ball around the space, chased each other, and possibly shot at imaginary goals.

Moreover, we don't need real games to motivate children to practice skills. The good news is that children find well-designed tasks for practicing skills to be engaging and interesting. Ang Chen and his colleagues have been conducting research on situational interest, which teachers create by getting students engaged in tasks that they find interesting at that moment, even in an activity they might not find personally interesting (Chen, 2001; Chen, Ennis, Martin, & Sun, 2006). Haichun Sun's recent study at the elementary level suggests teachers can get children interested in learning about a new skill or activity by presenting tasks that challenge them, demand their attention, give them opportunities to explore, or are instantly enjoyable (Sun, Chen, Ennis, Martin, & Shen, 2008).

> **T**hose of us who work at the elementary level must take the idea from TGfU that the skills and tactics we teach need to be relevant and meaningful, regardless of the age of the students.

Although motivation might be less of a concern at the elementary level, meaning and relevance are not. Those of us who work at the elementary level must take the idea from TGfU that the skills and tactics we teach need to be relevant and meaningful, regardless of the age of the students.

Flexible, Adaptable Skills and Tactical Knowledge

I am going to give you some examples from our research on expert teachers about how tactical knowledge can be presented to help children understand the meaning and relevance of performance techniques for skills (Rovegno et al., 2003). We studied four expert instructors teaching dribbling with the hand. They all began their unit by asking children to tell them the performance cues that they learned in grades K through 2 (aged 5 to 8). Each teacher taught approximately three cues and none of them taught the exact same three cues. The following list outlines the four cues the instructors taught and the tactical information they presented:

Performance cues for dribbling with the hand

- Push, don't slap the ball; push with your fingerpads. Your fingerpads are like your eyes, they watch the ball; your eyes watch defenders and teammates.
- Dribble at your waist; dribbling higher makes it easy for defenders to steal the ball.
- Keep the ball to the front-side so defenders can't easily reach the ball; your body protects it.
- Keep your eyes and head up so you can see defenders and teammates.

Notice that only part of one cue ("Push, don't slap the ball.") was not linked to tactics. Although the children were too young to play so-called real basketball, they could and did find performance cues meaningful because teachers helped them recognize the link to basketball tactics.

It is important to mention that the teachers did not simply rely on tactics to make performance cues meaningful. They told stories and used images and metaphors to help children understand and remember performance cues. The point I want to make here is that these four teachers taught skills and tactics simultaneously. Tactics provided meaning and relevance for performance techniques.

Flexible, Adaptable Skills and the Laban Framework

In addition, the teachers used a wide variety of practice tasks, applying concepts from Laban's framework and linking them to tactics to provide meaning and relevance. Moreover, these tasks were aimed at developing flexible, adaptable, tactical skills within gamelike situations. The following list summarizes the movement concepts they taught:

Movement concepts

- Dribble in straight, angular, and curved pathways. Go straight when there is no defender because you can get to the goal faster; use angular and curved pathways to go around and to avoid defenders.
- Change hands while you dribble to protect the ball by putting your body between it and the defender.
- Dribble at medium and low levels because it is harder for the defender to steal the ball at these heights.
- Dribble and stop quickly or change directions to avoid defenders.
- Dribble traveling at slow, medium, and fast speeds. Travel slow and dribble low in a crowd; travel fast when there are no defenders.
- Change speeds while dribbling to fool defenders. Dribble at fast speeds to avoid or move around defenders.

The teachers taught the preceding concepts for tactical movement using a variety of games and gamelike tasks. For example, they taught several dribbling games that were similar to tag. Children also designed their own dribbling games, which helped them practice the tactical skill of dribbling against defenders. Children's games, as opposed to real basketball, provided the context for understanding and practicing dribbling tactics.

Dribbling activities are only one example of skill variations that illustrate the value of Laban's framework and movement concepts for teaching flexible, adaptable, tactical skills. I could do the same with other basic skills. Moreover, I would like to make an even stronger claim. I think that it makes sense to teach Laban's movement concepts only within the context of games, dance, or gymnastics, and only in the service of developing skillfulness within these contexts. Some people suggest teaching the movement concepts as generic content; for example, doing lessons on levels, directions, and pathways as cognitive content without a focus on refining skills. I don't think that this is good use of what little time we have in the curriculum. When movement concepts are taught as cognitive content, they lose meaning and can become trivial. The context of games, dance, or gymnastics gives the movement concepts meaning and relevance.

For example, lessons on dribbling in different pathways are excellent for teaching tactics in second and third grades (ages 7 to 9). An excellent dance lesson for first graders (ages 6 to 7) could use different pathways to represent weather patterns, with children traveling slowly and moving their arms and bodies in soft, gentle, curved pathways to represent clouds, or running in angular pathways and making forceful, jagged shapes to represent lightning. In gymnastics, however, pathways are not rich or important content. As Dianna said, when you do curved pathways, all you get are sloppy little rolls. If our goal is to teach for understanding, then I think we need to teach movement concepts as authentic content within games, dance, or gymnastics. Teaching rich, authentic content helps children understand in deep and meaningful ways.

Theme 5: Game Appreciation

Thorpe et al. (1986) discuss the importance of game appreciation. However, few curriculum writers discuss or propose units specifically on this topic. Dianna and I label *game appreciation* as teaching children about game structures (Bandhauer & Rovegno, 1992). This includes teaching them about boundaries, rules, consequences for breaking rules, scoring goals, numbers of players, equipment, and how changes in game structures affect game play. I want to strongly suggest that at the elementary level, we need to approach teaching game structures as seriously and systematically as we approach tactics and skills. Secondary students might not need lessons on game appreciation. They might understand the meaning of a boundary and its role in offensive and defensive play. Young children, however, do not. We regularly see children in grades K through 2 set boundaries and then ignore them completely. To children, game rules are simply one more rule imposed by adults; they are no different than the rule to walk quietly in lines in the hallway. Children do not meaningfully relate game rules to game play.

I am going to briefly describe two units Dianna and I use to teach children about game structures, typically starting in third grade, to illustrate

> *I want to strongly suggest that at the elementary level, we need to approach teaching game structures as seriously and systematically as we approach tactics and skills.*

not only the methods for teaching game appreciation but also the rich and extensive content that the process can entail. The first is through tag using flag-football flags (Bandhauer & Rovegno, 1992) and the second is through dribbling with two students playing against one another (1v1).

We start with boundaries using the pedagogical technique of modification-exaggeration (Thorpe et al., 1986). With tag, children form groups of five with one tagger and play outside in a large field with no boundaries. With dribbling, the defender remains in a hula hoop while the other player tries to dribble 5 meters from one end line to another. We have the children set very wide sidelines. The children play several times, rotating positions. These games are designed to fail. The tagger can't pull the football flag from anyone because without boundaries, the runners simply take off in any direction. In dribbling, the defender can't touch the dribbler because the defender is confined to the hoop and the sidelines give the dribbler ample room to move away. We then have children discuss their opinions of the game. The consensus is that the games are neither fair nor fun.

Next, we have the children make boundaries that are too small and play the game several times, rotating positions. Again, the games are designed to fail. We discuss the games again and children readily discuss how boundaries that are too small favor defenders and boundaries that are too big favor the offense. For games to be fair and fun, the boundaries must allow for balanced opportunities between offense and defense.

Finally, we let the children experiment to find the boundaries that are perfect for them. They use a *play-discuss-play cycle* until they have perfect-sized boundaries and a good game. In a play-discuss-play cycle, children play the game, stop to discuss problems, revise the game or tactics, and then play the game again. We use the following characteristics to define a good game:

- The game must have flow; it doesn't stop continuously.
- Balance exists between offense and defense.
- The social interactions are positive. Players understand the rules and do not argue.
- The children are learning content that is the objective of the lesson.

It doesn't take long, however, before problems occur with children stepping out of bounds. We then move to segment two: teaching children about game rules, consequences for breaking rules, and safety rules. Children design rules for going out of bounds, consequences for breaking the rules, and some sort of scoring system. Using the play-discuss-play cycle, the children modify their game rules until they have a good game working. We then shift the discussion to tactics. We ask, "Which tactics allowed you to be successful on offense? On defense? How did you use boundaries on defense to help you? How can you prevent the defense from trapping you in the corner or against the boundary?" Children play the games and practice the tactics they identified.

In the third segment of the unit, with tag, we give children the option to add one or two bases and multiple flags. We begin by asking them to predict how the bases will affect game play and tactics. In dribbling, children work in pairs, both dribbling and trying to knock the ball away from the other. Using the play-discuss-play cycle, the children first set perfect boundaries, rules, and consequences for breaking rules; determine ways to score, deciding if they want to keep track of the score or not; and design rules for safety. This process takes several play-discuss-play cycles as children learn about the effect of using bases in tag and fouling in dribbling and decide how to design rules that solve these problems. Again, once the games are working well, we shift the discussion to the tactics of the games, such as which tactics helped them succeed on offense and defense and how the new game structures affected their tactics.

In the fourth segment of the unit, children design goal-oriented tag and dribbling games while learning about tactics and game structures. Again, using the play-discuss-play cycle, the children first design and refine their rules and boundaries and then, once the games are working, they discuss tactics and how they are affected by game structures. By the end of the unit, the children understand basic game structures and their role in game play (game appreciation), and basic tactics for invasion games. The following list outlines the game structures and tactics children discuss and learn in the tag unit:

- For a game to work, reasonably even opportunities for offense and defense must exist.
- Boundaries that are too large favor the offense.
- Boundaries that are too small favor the defense.
- Rules can be (and often are) changed to make games better.
- Rules make games fun and fair.
- Rules are needed for safety.
- When you break a rule, there are consequences that give the advantage to the opponents.
- Common consequences for invasion games include awarding points, losing tries, moving a player to a position that gives the opponents an advantage, and awarding penalty shots or plays.
- Locating a base near a boundary limits the use by the offense; locating a base in the middle of the playing area makes it harder for the defense to guard.
- You need to make rules to limit runners' time on base.

- Some games need a *no-play* zone around bases or goals to keep the offense or the defense from getting too close and having too much of an advantage.

This next list includes the offense tactics for invasion games that children discuss in the tag unit:

- Avoid being tagged by running on different pathways, changing directions quickly, running fast, and dodging.
- Avoid being tagged by running behind a blocker.
- Stay away from the boundaries, especially the corners, to avoid being trapped.
- Especially stay away from the boundaries when you have both flags.
- You can protect your flag by turning your body, doing jump spins, and keeping the flag between the boundary and your body.
- If you are about to be tagged and can't score, run to a base or safety zone.
- Decoys and sacrifices can enable some runners to score.
- To score, sometimes you need to help players who are trapped or have lost their flags.
- To beat a zone defense, shift zones quickly or get the zone to shift too far to one side to create space for your team on the other side.
- To beat one-on-one defense, use teammates and other defenders as *picks*, or blockers, to create space for you.
- If you lose your flag, block for your teammates.
- A blitz (running all at the same time) counteracts a zone defense.
- Crossing pathways counteracts a one-on-one defense.

Finally, this list describes the defense tactics the children discuss for invasion games.

- Tag someone (pull the flag) by watching the runners, anticipating their direction, and watching their eye and body movements.
- Tag by cornering, trapping, or limiting a runner with a boundary.
- *Double teaming* means working with teammates to corner or trap a runner. The boundary acts as another defender by denying space.
- Stay with the person you are guarding until he or she loses the flag, unless another player needs you to double team.
- In a zone defense, each defender guards a zone of space.
- In person-to-person defense, each defender guards one person on the other team (1v1).

- Defenders have to guard both the goal and the safety zones (bases).
- With one-on-one defense, select who you will guard ahead of time based on matching abilities.
- With one-on-one or zone defense, if you are beaten, run back and help out a teammate.
- With one-on-one or zone defense, if a teammate is beaten and his or her opponent is about to score, leave your opponent and try to stop the person about to score.
- With zone defense, concentrate the defense at the goals or locations where scoring will most likely occur.
- Zone defenses are layered (some defenders are in front and some in back).
- Try to cut off the angle the offense will run on to score.
- Avoid running behind the runner in a circle without changing your pathway. This tactic, called *doggie chases the tail,* will not help you pull flags.

I think that this is a pretty impressive list of invasion-game tactics for third grade (ages 8 and 9). I must note that it is easier to work on these tactics in tag because the children do not have to worry about throwing and catching balls. However, they have acquired a tactical vocabulary and a basic understanding of invasion-game structures and their relationship to tactics.

Once you add balls, the tactics you can teach are more limited. Neither Dianna nor I teach zone defense outside of games like tag and knock the pin down because children's offensive skills are less developed than their defensive capabilities. In our research on the development of tactics in fourth grade children, we spent 12 lessons working solely on cutting to get free to receive a pass and sending lead passes to receivers in basketball-type games of 1v3, 2v3, and 3v3 with no dribbling or shooting (Rovegno et al., 2001). Although we saw significant improvements in cutting and passing, the children had not mastered these tactics after 12 lessons. Our research suggests the most basic cutting and passing tactics of invasion games probably take several years to master.

Child-Designed Games and the Goals of TGfU

Dianna and I choose to teach game structures (game appreciation) by helping children design games. Child-designed games are a curricular option that we cherish for many reasons. In keeping with the goals of

TGfU, probably the most important reason is that experimenting and solving problems while designing games helps children acquire in-depth knowledge of game structures and tactics that is meaningful to them. Child-designed games also help develop thinking and social skills through group work. Working in groups requires children to learn how to cooperate and make decisions, how to explain and justify their ideas, and how to consider the needs and opinions of others.

Moreover, it gives them the power to be in charge of their games and to work independently from teachers, another goal of TGfU. In one of my first research studies at Dianna's school, I interviewed one of the older classroom teachers. She explained why she liked Dianna's physical-education program:

> Our first couple of years here we had recess . . . [it] was an exercise in [saying], "No, stop chasing, let him alone," or watching kids just stand around looking at each other and talking. Well, recess kind of was legislated away from us for a little while. We reinstated recess and suddenly it was like an explosion of activity. Nobody just stands and talks. They're all doing something. They're all inventing things. I can't believe these kids are any different than other kids or different than the ones years ago, but these kids have less trouble finding something to do when they're given free time. The only difference that I can see is that they've been taught how to [design games] in PE, and I think that's a positive result. They love it, and they're all friends when they're done, and it's their game. They somehow make up the rules, and I'm not breaking up fights, and I'm not forced to go over to somebody and say, "Come on . . . I want you to do something. Don't just stand here and look at each other" (Classroom teacher).

Developing Related Thinking and Social Skills for TGfU at the Elementary Level

Finally, I want to discuss content not typically examined in relation to secondary models of TGfU; that is, thinking and social skills. Because children's cognitive and social levels have not developed as much as those of secondary students, thinking and social skills affect the playing of games and, I believe, are critical for TGfU at the elementary level. In our research, we found that expert teachers broke down and explicitly taught thinking and social skills (Rovegno et al., 2003). Based on this study and other research, we developed a three-step framework for breaking down and teaching the following skills in a progressive way:

- Critical thinking
- Decision making and problem solving
- Creative thinking
- Self-regulation and metacognition
- Taking a learning-mastery orientation rather than an ego-orientation
- Taking an effort-based learning orientation, rather than believing success comes from ability
- Developing empathy and caring
- Developing social justice (fairness)
- Developing community and cooperation
- Valuing diversity and respecting difference

Some of these are more general, but in terms of tactics, I think critical thinking, decision making, problem solving, and creative thinking all directly support children's abilities to select tactics with teammates and to use tactics in game situations.

I can't possibly present the entire framework in the space allotted, so I will just share a few examples of three components: critical thinking, decision making, and fairness. The framework has three steps for teaching thinking and social skills that enable both instructors and children to learn how to progressively incorporate these skills in physical education.

One possible first step for teaching critical thinking and decision making is to put feedback in the form of a question, so that children have to analyze and critique their movement to answer. For example, you can ask the following questions:

- You really improved this time; what did you do better?
- As you were dribbling, the ball hit your toes. What do you think you need to do to prevent that?
- Your tactic worked initially, but then it fell apart. What happened and what was your thinking about this tactic?

One of the first steps in teaching young children about fairness is to have them identify actions that are not fair to others, such as taking equipment that is not their own, hogging the ball, and not returning equipment nicely.

The second step in teaching critical thinking and decision making can include having children think critically, self-evaluate, and make a decision about what they need to focus on. For example, after children have learned two to four critical cues for a skill or tactic, they can select and work on the one cue they think will most help them improve. When

I suggest this to undergraduates and teachers, sometimes they worry that children will choose the wrong cue. It has been my experience that this doesn't happen very often. Children typically select the cue I would have selected for them. They will, of course, make mistakes in learning to think critically and make decisions. However, if you respond by asking them about their process in making the decision ("What was your thinking on that? Why did you decide to select that cue?"), they will either self-correct or give you a reasonable explanation. You can give children feedback on their thinking in the same way that you give them feedback on their tactics and skills.

Other second steps include having children think critically and make decisions about which task to practice, which ball to use, and how to set up the equipment and the environment. For example, teach them several tasks (for skills or tactics), and then have them decide which task to practice, based on the selection criteria that will best help them improve at this particular point in time. Again, you might need to give them feedback on their decisions, especially encouraging children who make difficult but good decisions.

Second steps in teaching about fairness can be to put children in pairs and have them design a challenge course, which is an obstacle course for practicing a tactical skill. A simple challenge course we used in one study included giving children a choice of 6 to 8 pieces of equipment, such as cones, jump ropes, and hula hoops, and then letting them design a challenge course for practicing dribbling on straight, curved, and angular pathways to avoid pretend defenders (the cones and hoops). You can start the discussion by asking, "What can partners do to be fair? What is not fair?" If the children do not discuss the following criteria, we say, "The challenge course must be challenging for everyone, but also allow both of you to succeed. If the course is too difficult for one of you, it isn't fair. If it is too easy for one of you, the course isn't fair either. You need to find ways to make the course fair for both partners." We will set the same criteria later for teaching children how to modify games to ensure a fair balance between offense and defense.

As discussed earlier, a third step for teaching decision making, critical thinking, and fairness is to teach children to work together to design game rules and boundaries and to modify their games until they find a model that works. Next, have them critique their game play and discuss which tactics worked and which did not work.

Conclusion

In my opinion, many elements of TGfU can transform and improve physical education for elementary students. Teaching the substance of game play (tactical elements, game structures, flexible and adaptable tactical skills, and decision making) and ensuring that this content is meaningful and relevant to children is critical for helping children become competent and skillful movers in a variety of physical activities that will enhance their health and help them develop the knowledge, cognitive and social skills, and values that facilitate a lifetime of participation. We need to modify the tactic-skill progression of TGfU when children cannot perform skills to a level that allows for game-like play. In addition, game play itself has different meanings for children; we do not need real game play to motivate children to practice either basic or tactical skills, especially if teachers make the content meaningful and relevant. For young children, tactics can provide meaning and relevance for performance cues and movement concepts, which they can practice in gamelike situations and in child-designed and modified games. Finally, we advocate systematically teaching game appreciation as part of TGfU by helping children design their own game boundaries, rules, and structures.

> *Teaching the substance of game play (tactical elements, game structures, flexible and adaptable tactical skills, and decision making) and ensuring that this content is meaningful and relevant to children is critical for helping children become competent and skillful movers in a variety of physical activities that will enhance their health and help them develop the knowledge, cognitive and social skills, and values that facilitate a lifetime of participation.*

Dianna and I have been fans of TGfU for more than 20 years. We have found much in TGfU that relates to how we have taught the movement approach at the elementary level. We thank all of the TGfU authors and researchers who have given us rich food for thought about teaching games and tactics. The time is ripe for taking what we know and applying that knowledge to K-12 curricula.

Discussion Questions

1. What constraints of the school setting contribute to children playing games without first learning the tactics or how to adapt skills to game situations?

2. What constraints discourage teachers from using child-designed games?

3. Identify good games and child-designed game tasks for each grade level that facilitate the development of skillful games players.

4. What supports and teacher-education experiences would help teachers and undergraduates learn to teach TGfU at the elementary level?

5. What can teacher educators and in-service providers do to help teachers critique fads and elementary curriculum that is based on activities devised from equipment (for example, beanbag activities, parachute activities, and wand activities) rather than from substantive skills and tactics?

References

Bandhauer, D., & Rovegno, I. (1992). Teaching game structure and strategy. *Teaching Elementary Physical Education, 3*(6), 7-9.

Barrett, K.R. (1977). Games teaching: Adaptable skills, versatile players. *Journal of Physical Education and Recreation, 48*(7), 21-24.

Barrett, K.R. (1985). The content of an elementary school physical education program and its impact on teacher preparation. In H. Hoffman & J.E. Rink (Eds.), *Physical education professional preparation: Insights and foresights* (pp. 9-25). Reston, VA: AAHPERD.

Bunker, D., & Thorpe, R. (1982). Model for the teaching of games in secondary schools. *Bulletin of Physical Education, 18*(1), 5-8.

Chen, A. (2001). A theoretical conceptualization for motivation research in physical education: An integrated perspective. *Quest, 53,* 59-76.

Chen, A., Ennis, C.D., Martin, R., & Sun, H. (2006). Situational interest: A curriculum component enhancing motivation to learn. In S.N. Hogan (Ed.), *New Developments in Learning Research* (pp. 235-261). Hauppauge, NY: Nova Science Publishers.

Chen, W., Rovegno, I., Todorovich, J., & Babiarz, M. (2003). Third grade children's movement responses to dribbling tasks presented by accomplished teachers. *Journal of Teaching in Physical Education, 22*(4), 450-466.

Laban, R. (1975). *Modern educational dance* (3rd ed.). London: Macdonald & Evans (originally published in 1948).

Laban, R., & Lawrence, F. C. (1981). *Effort: Economy of human movement* (2nd ed.). Boston: Plays (originally published in 1947).

Logsdon, B.J., Alleman, L.M., Straits, S.A., Belka, D., & Clark, D. (1997). *Physical education unit plans for grades 3-4* (2nd ed.). Champaign, IL: Human Kinetics.

Logsdon, B.J., Barrett, K.R., Ammons, M., Broer, M.R., Halverson, L.E., McGee, R., & Roberton, M.A. (1984). *Physical education for children: A focus on the teaching process* (2nd ed.). Philadelphia: Lea & Febiger.

McCaughtry, N., & Rovegno, I. (2003). The development of pedagogical content knowledge: Moving from blaming students to predicting skillfulness, recognizing motor development, and understanding emotion. *Journal of Teaching in Physical Education, 22*(4), 355-368.

Oslin, J., & Mitchell, S. (2006). Game-centered approaches to teaching physical education. In D. Kirk, D. Macdonald, & M. O'Sullivan (Eds.), *The handbook of physical education* (pp. 627-651). London: SAGE.

Rink, J.E. (2001). Investigating the assumptions of pedagogy. *Journal of Teaching in Physical Education, 20,* 112-128.

Rink, J.E. (2005). *Teaching physical education for learning* (5th ed.). Boston: McGraw-Hill.

Roberton, M.A. (1977). Developmental implications for games teaching. *Journal of Physical Education and Recreation, 48*(7), 25.

Roberton, M.A., & Halverson, L.E. (1984). Developing children—Their changing movement. In B.J. Logsdon, K.R. Barrett, M. Ammons, M.R. Broer, L.E. Halverson, R. McGee, & M.A. Roberton (Eds.), *Physical education for children: A focus on the teaching process* (2nd ed., pp. 24-86). Philadelphia: Lea & Febiger.

Rovegno, I., & Bandhauer, D. (1994). Child-designed games—Experience changes teachers' conceptions. *Journal of Physical Education, Recreation and Dance, 65,* 60-63.

Rovegno, I., & Bandhauer, D. (1998). Teaching game strategy: Building on the basics. *Teaching Elementary Physical Education, 9*(1), 19-23.

Rovegno, I., Chen, W., & Todorovich, J. (2003). Accomplished teachers' pedagogical content knowledge of teaching dribbling to third grade. *Journal of Teaching in Physical Education, 22,* 426-449.

Rovegno, I., Nevett, M., Brock, S., & Babiarz, M. (2001). Teaching and learning basic invasion-game tactics in fourth grade: A descriptive study from situated and constraints theoretical perspectives. *Journal of Teaching in Physical Education* [Monograph], *20,* 370-388.

Sun, H., Chen, A., Ennis, C., Martin, R., & Shen, B. (2008). An examination of the multidimensionality of situational interest in elementary school physical education. *Research Quarterly for Exercise and Sport, 79,* 62-70.

Thorpe, R., Bunker, D., & Almond, L. (Eds.). (1986). *Rethinking games teaching.* Loughborough, UK: University of Technology.

chapter

13

Development of Creativity in the Scope of the TGfU Approach

Daniel Memmert, PhD

In the past, children used to play in fields and roads without coaches and systematic training schedules. Today, they often have to stand in line and wait for their turn to throw or kick. In addition, they are bombarded with instructions and corrections from their coaches. As a result, in Western Europe, there are very few creative ballplayers left. Creative behavior is more likely to emerge when children play different kinds of sport games early on, especially if they play more than they practice. Creative solutions arise from the presence of multiple objects or options. Consider the following example: if a player can only focus his attention on two players, A and B (narrow breadth of attention), only one relationship, AB, can be discovered. This means that the player can only consider these two players, A and B, in his decision-making process. With three players—A, B, and C—there are three potential relationships—AB, AC, and BC—to be discovered (mean breadth of attention), which can therefore play a role in the decision-making processes. With four elements (wide breadth of attention), there are six potential relationships, and so on... (Martindale, 1981).

The approach of Teaching Games for Understanding (TGfU) (Bunker & Thorpe, 1982), the Tactical Games Model (Mitchell, Oslin, & Griffin, 2006), Play Practice (Launder, 2001), Game Sense (Light, 2004) and, finally, the Tactical-Decision Learning Model (Gréhaigne, Wallian, & Godbout, 2005) are well-established approaches for teaching and coaching because they offer students ways of learning both tactical and technical skills in different games (Gréhaigne, Godbout, & Bouthier, 1999). All these approaches focus initially on teaching and developing an understanding for the tactical dimensions (what to do) of game play before moving on to the development of the technical skills (how to do it) associated with the game. Thus, the primary aim of these teaching and coaching approaches is to teach tactical problem solving in different types of invasion games, such as, basketball and soccer. Furthermore, these approaches advocate contextual, real-world, game-simulated practice to develop both the tactical and technical skills needed to be an effective games player (Holt, Strean, & Bengoechea, 2002; Mitchell, Griffin, & Oslin, 1995; Turner & Martinek, 1992).

In this chapter, in addition to tactical and technical skills, I will present and discuss another competency that children should learn which has not been an intentional component of TGfU: creativity. Creative behavior means that a player can produce surprising and flexible solutions to tactical problems. Michael Jordan and Steve Nash are examples of basketball players who use highly unusual and even original passes. Even when actually intending to pass the ball to player A, they are able to perceive at the last minute if player B is suddenly unmarked and better positioned and pass the ball to him instead.

Therefore, the purpose of the chapter is to offer creative behavior as a new aspect of teaching and research on the training and development of tactical creativity in invasion games. First, I will define the term, *tactical creativity*. Second, I will introduce a theoretical framework for developing tactical creativity that distinguishes between a macro (content) level and a micro (method) level. Third, I will present empirical evidence that supports macro rules for environmental conditions and, fourth, micro rules for the methodical aspects of the respective training units. Finally, I will discuss the results within the TGfU framework and consider the potential for further research for teaching and coaching.

What is Tactical Creativity in Invasion Games?

The distinction between expert decision making and creativity may lie in the theoretical distinction between "divergent thinking" and "convergent thinking" (Guilford, 1967). *Convergent thinking* refers to the ability to find the ideal solution to a given problem. In invasion games, this is similar to tactical decision making or simple game ability. In contrast, Sternberg and Lubart (1999) define creativity as "the ability to produce work that is both novel (original, unexpected) and appropriate (useful)" (p. 3). On a behavioral level, *divergent thinking* can be defined as the unusualness, innovativeness, statistical rareness, or uniqueness of solutions to a related task. In invasion games, this concerns tactical creativity that produces varying, rare, and flexible decisions in different situations (Memmert & Roth, 2007). Two central ideas about creativity will be discussed next.

> *In invasion games, divergent thinking concerns tactical creativity that produces varying, rare, and flexible decisions in different situations (Memmert & Roth, 2007).*

First, in order for players to generate possible decisions and original solutions, they must be able to perceive all the pertinent information from their environment (positions of teammates and opponents, players emerging unexpectedly, and so on) and take it into account in their action plan. Creative soccer or basketball players, for example, set themselves apart by perceiving opportunities in the game as they emerge. For example, the creative Dutch soccer player, Arjen Robben, seems to take in all relevant stimuli of a complex environment and subsequently uses this information to pass the ball to a player without even looking at him (i.e., "no-look passes").

Second, training units should focus on developing tactical creativity. By improving divergent abilities for tactical thinking early in the training process, the teaching of ball games and the measurement of its success can focus on relevant competencies that cannot be developed and improved upon in later training phases. For example, many psychological studies have shown that creativity has to be learned and stored early on in life (for a review, see Milgram, 1990). After childhood, the influence of training for creativity becomes weaker. Research from the neurosciences suggests that stagnation in creative development

> *Many psychological studies have shown that creativity has to be learned and stored early on in life (for a review, see Milgram, 1990).*

may occur after the age of eight (Huttenlocher, 1990). Children up to age seven exhibit the greatest absolute number and density of synapses in the primary visual cortex as well as the greatest rates of resting glucose uptake in the occipital cortex. These indicators are associated with creativity (Ashby, Valentin, & Turken, 2002; Bekhtereva, Dan'ko, Starchenko, Pakhomov, & Medvedev, 2001).

In recent years, I have conducted numerous studies dealing with the development of tactical creativity. The empirical evidence can be summarized into a preliminary framework.

Theoretical Framework: A 3-by-3 Environment-Training Model of Tactical Creativity

I suggest a preliminary theoretical framework (table 13.1) that is informed by several individual studies (Memmert, 2007; Memmert & Furley, 2007; Memmert & Roth, 2007; Memmert, Baker, & Bertsch, in press). This framework can be seen as a first step in the development of divergent tactical thinking and creativity in invasion games for children between 6 and 8 years. The 3-by-3 environment-training model distinguishes between a macro (content) level and a micro (method) level. The former points toward the environmental conditions (macro rules) and the latter toward the methodological accents in the respective training units (micro rules) that can be steered by the teacher.

On a macro level, environmental conditions are created and curriculum designs are implemented to correspond to the following three criteria:

- Diversification (macro rule 1)
- Deliberate play (macro rule 2)
- Deliberate practice (macro rule 3)

On a micro level, three methodic principles for conducting training units also exist:

- By using certain instructional options and by giving external (implicit) cues, attentional focus in team ball sports can be controlled (micro rule 1).
- With a large attentional focus, unexpected and potentially better alternatives can be perceived, used, and learned (micro rule 2).

Table 13.1 Theoretical Framework for 3-by-3 Environment-Training Model of the Development of Tactical Creativity

Macro level (content)	Micro level (method)
• Diversification	• Quantity of instruction
• Deliberate play	• Breadth of attention
• Deliberate practice	• Status of motivation

- In the future, it would also be possible to consider instructions that cause certain motivational feelings for the children (micro rule 3).

Factors on a Macro Level: Environmental Conditions

In this section, I describe the macro (content) level of the 3-by-3 environment-training model, which specifies the environmental conditions of the creative development of children. I discuss in detail the factors of diversification, deliberate play, and deliberate practice.

Diversification

Involvement in a diverse range of sport and physical activities may be valuable for the development of creativity. Current theoretical approaches (Sternberg & Lubart, 1995) support the view that gathering diversified experience over a number of years is ideal for the development of creativity. Diversification is supported by theoretical models (Simonton, 1999; Sternberg, 1999) and by empirical evidence from research on creativity-related context variables (Csikzentmihalyi, 1999; Martindale, 1990; Simonton, 1996).

Involvement in a diverse range of sport and physical activities may be valuable for the development of creativity.

Recent research suggests that in some sports, participation in other activities could play a functional role in the development of experts (Baker, 2003; Baker, Côté, & Abernethy, 2003). For instance, Baker et al. (2003) found a negative correlation between early breadth of exposure to other sports and the amount of sport-specific training required to obtain expert-level proficiency in basketball, netball, and field hockey, suggesting that early involvement in other sports facilitates the acquisition of skills necessary for high-level performance. General cognitive skills, such as pattern recognition, are transferable across domains with similar offensive and defensive structures (Abernethy, Baker, & Côté, 2005).

Memmert and Roth (2007) showed that experience and understanding of many different sport and game situations have a positive influence on the development of divergent tactical cognition. The efficacy of various training approaches in invasion games for the development of tactical creativity was investigated. Nonspecific experiences seem to be a promising alternative to specific training programs. Unlike motor competencies, it seems possible to train tactical creativity independently from sport-specific situations. Finally, Memmert and Roth conclude "that non-specific and specific concepts are on a more or less similar level in terms of creativity development. As the comparisons of the percentage increase in the treatment phases have shown, the non-specific approaches can even prove to be more workable in the long term" (p. 1429).

Deliberate Play and Deliberate Practice

As Côté and Hay (2002) suggest, the sampling years (ages 7 to 12) are characterized by a high frequency of deliberate play. Self-determination theory and Vallerand's hierarchical model of motivation in sport support the notion that early deliberate play has a positive effect on intrinsic motivation over time (Ryan & Deci, 2000; Vallerand, 2001). The aforementioned treatment study (Memmert & Roth, 2007) also shows the positive effects of specific training concepts, and contrasts the role of different forms of sports involvement and practice conditions in team-sport athletes who exhibit a range of creativity (Memmert et al., in press). The results suggests that deliberate practice (Ericsson, Krampe, & Tesch-Römer, 1993) and unstructured playlike involvement (Côté et al., 2003) both play crucial roles in the development of creative behavior in basketball, handball, field hockey, and soccer. Within this approach, *deliberate play* refers to noninstructed involvement in play-oriented and at-first-sight unstructured activities. *Deliberate practice,* on the other hand, offers targeted and task-centered training programs based on instruction.

This evidence provides a basis for the convergence of two prevalent research paradigms, expertise research and creativity research, that have not yet been discussed in the same context. These two paradigms suggest that practice experiences and early play are important influences on the development of creativity in sport. In this case, specific experiences over a long time (10 years or more) are necessary to attain expertise (Helsen, Starkes, & Hodges, 1998). At the same time, current theoretical approaches and empirical research regarding the development of creativity (Sternberg & Lubart, 1995) support the view that gathering diversified and even nonspecific experiences (such as unstructured play) over time is ideal for the development of creative thinking.

Factors on a Micro Level: Training Conditions

In this section, I describe in detail the micro (method) level of the 3-by-3 environment-training model with the factors quantity of instruction, breadth of attention, and status of motivation. Thus, it points to the methodological aspects in the training sessions that can be influenced by the teachers themselves.

Quantity of Instruction

Following the paradigm of *inattentional blindness* (the failure to detect an unexpected object if attention is diverted to another task or object) by Mack and Rock (1998), Memmert and Furley (2007) conducted a series of experiments on attention focusing to analyze the influence of special instruction on tactical decision making in team-ball sports. In the first experiment, juniors, aged 14, were instructed to focus their attention on their direct opponent in a handball-specific test on making tactical decisions. Their primary task was to name the position of their opponent at the end of the trial. At the same time, they also had to make a tactical choice, identifying a player who was totally open, that would most likely lead to a goal, or secondary task. Forty five percent of the participants failed to notice the open team member in experiment 1. These results are similar to the findings of Most, Scholl, Clifford, and Simons (2005).

In experiment 2, participants were confronted with the exact same tasks; in order to investigate the influence of instructions on the tactical decision, one group received more tactical instructions and the other group received fewer. The results indicated that the group who received more specific instructions prior to the tactical decision made inferior tactical decisions. The procedure in experiment 3 was exactly the same as in experiment 1, with the slight difference that in the decision-making test, the open team member was waving his hands in order to signal that he was unmarked. Only one participant failed to notice the open team member. Thus, inattentional blindness did not occur anymore.

It is important—particularly in invasion games where the generation of tactical response patterns and original solutions are critical, such as soccer, hockey, or basketball—that young players receive fewer instructions if the goal is to develop creativity, since this may increase their capacity to deal with unexpected situations.

Simple instructions led to a reduced focus in attention, and the essential characteristics of a situation (open players) were not taken into account in decision making (Memmert & Furley, 2007). For this reason, it is important—particularly in invasion games where the generation of tactical-response patterns and original solutions are critical, such as soccer, hockey, or basketball—that young players receive fewer instructions if the goal is to develop creativity, since this may increase their capacity to deal with unexpected situations.

Breadth of Attention

Breadth of attention is the term used to refer to the number and range of stimuli that a subject attends to at any one time. A six-month longitudinal study examined different kinds of breadth-of-attention programs during training sessions on the development of divergent thinking in team sports (Memmert, 2007). A real-world, sport-specific task was used to measure creative performance. A control group, which focused on training a wide breadth of attention, and a treatment group, which focused on training a narrow breadth of attention, were compared. The creative performance of the attention-broadening training group improved significantly. In the attention-broadening training group, the teachers only defined the idea and the rules of the games; they gave no special tactical advice or any kind of feedback regarding attention focus. As a result, the children learned to have a wide breadth of attention in complex situations.

The children in the attention-narrowing training group performed the same kind of exercises as the participants in the other training group. The only difference concerned the role of the teachers. The trainers gave the children in this group explicit tactical instructions and corrections for each game type. As such, the only variations in the two training models were the instructional guidelines. In contrast to the teaching models of the attention-broadening program, this attention-narrowing program discouraged the children from learning to direct their attention toward different kinds of stimuli. As a result, they were not able to take in and associate all the present stimuli and information that could have led to original or unique solutions.

The training experiment presented here supports the view that less instruction by the coaches during game play leads to a wide breadth of attention, and therefore facilitates greater improvements in tactical creativity. These findings support previous research on environmental stimulations that narrow attention (Kasof, 1997). A wide breadth of attention, on the other hand, makes it possible to associate different stimuli that may initially appear to be irrelevant.

Status of Motivation

In the meantime, numerous experiments from general psychology provide compelling documentation that a happy mood (positive affect) can inspire creative performances (Isen, 2000), stimulate the production of innovative ideas (Isen, Daubman, & Nowicki, 1987), and further the generation of unusual free associations (Hirt, Levine, McDonald, Melton, & Martin, 1997). Beyond this, Friedman and Förster have presented further research that shows the influence of attitude on the achievement of positive successes in creative performances (Friedman & Förster, 2000, 2001).

These results are currently associated with different motivationally oriented theoretical models from social psychology (Regulatory-Focus Theory, Higgins, 1997; Theory of Personality Systems Interactions, Kuhl, 2000), which indicate that creative performances can be directly influenced by the simplest of instructions, such as the emotional manipulation of participants. Higgins (1997) proposed two modes of self-regulation in order to regulate pleasure and suffering (to direct behavior toward promotion or prevention targets). More specifically, a focus on accomplishments and aspirations is labeled as a promotion, and a focus on safety and responsibilities is called a prevention. According to this approach, the performance on a given task may depend on the fit between people's regulatory focus (promotion or prevention) and people's chronic regulatory orientation (promotion or prevention) (Higgins, 1997). This idea of better performance and a more positive effect through regulatory fit has already received some empirical support in the domain of cognitive tasks (Keller & Bless, 2006).

In a first step, Plessner, Unkelbach, Memmert, Baltes, and Kolb (2009) showed that performances during a penalty-shooting task also benefited from a regulatory fit. In that study, soccer players shot five penalties. Players with a relative-prevention focus (measured by a questionnaire) performed best when the task was framed as a prevention task (they received the instruction, "Your obligation is to miss no more than two times"), while players with a relative-promotion focus (measured again by a questionnaire) performed better when the task was framed as a promotion task (they received the instruction, "Your aspiration is to score at least three times"). Therefore, when the task framing fit the players' chronic focus, they scored more goals compared to the conditions that didn't fit.

In sum, it can be noted that the connection between personality variables and motivational instructions (promotion or prevention framing) have a direct effect on sports (technical-tactical) performances. Moreover, such considerations seem to have the potential for optimizing divergent (tactical) performances.

All findings show that different environmental influences and organizational conditions nurture original, creative, tactical solutions in invasion games.

Discussion

All findings show that different environmental influences and organizational conditions nurture original, creative, tactical solutions in invasion games. While the mainly (environmentally characterized) external circumstances in games cannot, for the most part, be influenced directly, the training options for children can be targeted and controlled. So, what does this mean for the TGfU approach? How can the 3-by-3 environment-training model for the development of creativity in young children be integrated into the TGfU approach?

First of all, I must once more highlight that the 3-by-3 environment-training model is presently only valid for 6- to 8-year-old children. Therefore, it can be seen as a preliminary stage of the TGfU approach. So far, little research has been conducted at this age level (Mitchell, 2005). Hence, it fills a gap and generates new ideas for teaching invasion games to children younger than 8 years. In the following points, the individual factors of the 3-by-3 environment-training model for the development of creativity are discussed in relation to the TGfU approach:

• *Diversification*. The TGfU approach has developed (relatively) exact forms of play; instruction manuals and practice examples that are intended to make children develop specific tactical ability in conjunction with technical skills (Mitchell et al., 2006). The factor of diversification in the 3-by-3 environment-training model suggests presenting forms of play from different sports alternately and at shorter intervals to children between 6 and 8 years of age. The rationale for this position is that during games, a wide range of environmental variability is present; therefore, in training diversification is important and perhaps even necessary for the development of creativity.

• *Deliberate play and deliberate practice*. These factors have direct parallels in the TGfU approach. Deliberate play is given top priority, since it is the central focus of the approach for teaching invasion games (Launder, 2001; Gréhaigne et al., 2005). As Kidman (2008) noted, "The game is the teacher". Central to this idea is that forms of play and practice that have been developed so far, taking into account adaptations for age, can be applied to the development of creative behavior in younger children. Through deliberate and self-controlled play in ecologically valid situations, the children should improve their tactical creativity.

• *Quantity of instruction*. The concepts in TGfU which are in line with the environment-training model stress the idea that programs for younger children must put special emphasis on giving fewer instructions. This means, forms of play chosen from the TGfU approach must be constructed in such a way that the situations speak to the children. The teacher gives only the idea and the rules of the games, nothing more (no special tactical advice or any kind of feedback). Hence, the aim of the training for children between the ages of 6 and 8 should be that the trainer gives the children few instructions, and thus offers them the possibility of seeking out and perceiving unexpected and perhaps better solutions. In this way, discovery learning (Bakker, Whiting, & Van der Burg, 1990), self-controlled learning (Wulf & Toole, 1999), and engaged learning (Renzulli, 1994) are possible. Moreover, greater emphasis is placed on implicit-learning processes whose positive effects have long been discussed in the fields of psychology (Reber, 1989), motor-function research (Magill, 1998), and sports science (Farrow & Abernethy, 2002).

• *Breadth of attention.* This focus requires the greatest modification of the TGfU model when extending it to younger children. Although questions by coaches and teachers in the TGfU focus direct attention to different areas of the game, the aforementioned studies suggest that for children aged 6 to 8, less attention-guided instruction leads to a wider breadth of attention. A wide breadth of attention makes it possible to associate different stimuli that may initially appear to be irrelevant. Hence, younger children would benefit from coaches who line up forms of play and practice without posing any specific questions to the children during or after each game.

• *Status of motivation.* The final factor of the 3-by-3 environment-training model for development of tactical creativity is implicitly contained in the TGfU approach. Since the model emphasizes play, it is associated with certain informality. "Learning is more effective when children enjoy what they are doing" (Renzulli & Reis, 2000, p. 380). However, future sports-related studies must show which mechanisms can help optimize the motivational states of children so that the unique and original solutions can be generated. The results from social psychology already indicate that this exercise is worthwhile and likely to add value.

Conclusion

Children must absorb and process a large amount of information within a very short time in all sport games. They must pay attention to sensory impressions that are, at first, totally new and unexpected. This raises the question of how children can become more proficient at perceiving constant minor and major changes in situations, which have been caused by the interaction of their opponents and team members, if their attention has only been directed to a few specific aspects of the situation by the coach. Since it is not possible for coaches to mention all possible solutions for a situation or for children to remember them all, coaches are challenged to find ways to increase their players' proficiency at identifying tactical solutions. Considered together, the findings discussed in this chapter highlight the fact that the 3-by-3 environment-training model can play a useful role in promoting the development of creativity in younger children. Our research suggests that keeping conditions playful encourages greater learning for young children in team-sport games.

Discussion Questions

1. Define tactical creativity in invasion games.
2. List the factors and components for the 3-by-3 environment-training model for the development of tactical creativity.
3. List the three macro rules concerning the environment conditions for developing tactical creativity in young children.
4. List the three micro rules concerning the training conditions for developing tactical creativity in young children.
5. Compare and contrast the TGfU approach and the 3-by-3 environment-training model for the development of tactical creativity.

References

Abernethy, B., Baker, J., & Côté, J. (2005). Transfer of pattern recall skills may contribute to the development of sport expertise. *Applied Cognitive Psychology, 19,* 705–718.

Ashby, G. F., Valentin, V.V., & Turken, A.U. (2002).The effects of positive affect and arousal on working memory and executive attention: Neurobiology and computational models. In S. Moore & M. Oaksford (Eds.), *Emotional cognition: From brain to behaviour* (pp. 245–287). Amsterdam: Benjamins.

Baker, J. (2003). Early specialization in youth sport: A requirement for adult expertise? *High Ability Studies, 14,* 85–92.

Baker, J., Côté, J., & Abernethy, B. (2003). Sport specific training, deliberate practice and the development of expertise in team ball sports. *Journal of Applied Sport Psychology, 15,* 12–25.

Bakker, F.C., Whiting, H.T.A., & Van der Burg, H. (1990). *Sport Psychology. Concepts & application.* Lanchester, UK: Butties.

Bekhtereva, N.P., Dan'ko, S.G., Starchenko, M.G., Pakhomov, S.V., & Medvedev, S.V. (2001). Study of the brain organization of creativity: III. Positron-emission tomography data. *Human Physiology, 27,* 390–397.

Bunker, D., & Thorpe, R. (1982). A model for the teaching of games in secondary schools. *Bulletin of Physical Education, 18,* 5–8.

Côté, J., Baker, J., & Abernethy, B. (2003). From play to practice: A developmental framework for the acquisition of expertise in team sports. In J.L. Starkes & K.A. Ericsson (Eds.), *Recent Advances in Research on Sport Expertise* (pp. 89–110). Champaign, IL: Human Kinetics.

Côté, J., & Hay, J. (2002). Children's involvement in sport: A developmental perspective. In J. Silva & D. Stevens (Eds.), *Psychological Foundations of sport* (pp.484–502). Boston: Merrill.

Csikszentmihalyi, M. (1999). Creativity. In R.A. Wilson & F.C. Keil (Eds.), *The MIT encyclopedia of the cognitive sciences* (pp. 205–206). Cambridge, MA: MIT Press.

Ericsson, K.A., Krampe, R., & Tesch-Römer, C. (1993). The role of deliberate practice in the acquisition of expert performance. *Psychological Review, 100,* 363–406.

Farrow, D., & Abernethy, B. (2002). Can anticipatory skills be learned through implicit video-based perceptual training? *Journal of Sports Sciences, 20,* 471–485.

Friedman, R.S., & Förster, J. (2000). The effects of approach and advoice motor actions on the elements of creative insight. *Journal of Personality and Social Psychology, 79,* 477–492.

Friedman, R.S., & Förster, J. (2001). The effects of promotion and prevention cues on creativity. *Journal of Personality and Social Psychology, 81,* 1001–1013.

Gréhaigne, J.-F., Godbout, P., & Bouthier, D. (1999). The foundations of tactics and strategy in team sports. *Journal of Teaching in Physical Education, 18,* 159–174.

Gréhaigne, J.-F., Wallian, N., & Godbout, P. (2005). Tactical-decision learning model and students' practices. *Physical Education & Sport Pedagogy, 10*(3), 255–269.

Guilford, J.P. (1967). *The nature of human intelligence.* New York: McGraw Hill.

Helsen, W.F., Starkes, J.L., & Hodges, N.J. (1998). Team sports and the theory of deliberate practice. *Journal of Sport & Exercise Psychology, 20,* 12–34.

Higgins, E.T. (1997). Beyond pleasure and pain. *American Psychologist, 52,* 1280–1300.

Hirt, E.R., Levine, G.M., McDonald, H.E., Melton, R.J., & Martin, L.L. (1997). The role of mood in quantitative and qualitative aspects of performance: Single or multiple mechanisms? *Journal of Experimental Social Psychology, 33,* 602–629.

Holt, N.L., Strean, W.B., & Bengoechea, E.G. (2002). Expanding the teaching games for understanding model: New avenues for future research and practice. *Journal of Teaching in Physical Education, 21,* 162–176.

Huttenlocher, P.R. (1990). Morphometric study of human cerebral cortex development. *Neuropsychologia, 28,* 517–527.

Isen, A.M. (2000). Positive affect and decision making. In M. Lewis & J. Haviland-Jones (Eds.), *Handbook of emotions* (2nd ed.) (pp. 417–435). New York: Guilford.

Isen, A.M., Daubman, K.A., & Nowicki, G.P. (1987). Positive affect facilitates creative problem solving. *Journal of Personality and Social Psychology, 52,* 1122–1131.

Kasof, J. (1997). Creativity and breadth of attention. *Creativity Research Journal, 10,* 303–315.

Kidman, L. (2008, May). *Teaching games for understanding (TGfU) is widely used at all levels of athlete communities.* Key note presentation at fourth international TGfU conference, Vancouver, Canada.

Keller, J., & Bless, H. (2006). Regulatory fit and cognitive performance: The interactive effect of chronic and situationally induced self-regulatory mechanisms on test performance. *European Journal of Social Psychology, 36,* 393-405.

Kuhl, J. (2000). A functional–design approach to motivation and self–regulation: The dynamics of personality systems interactions. In M. Boekaerts, P.R. Pintrich, & M. Zeidner (Eds.), *Handbook of self–regulation* (pp. 111–169). San Diego: Academic Press.

Launder, A.G. (2001). *Play practice: The games approach to teaching and coaching sports.* Champaign, IL: Human Kinetics.

Light, R. (2004). Coaches' experiences of games sense: Opportunities and challenges. *Physical Education & Sport Pedagogy, 9,* 115–131.

Mack, A., & Rock, I. (1998). *Inattentional Blindness.* Cambridge, MA: MIT Press.

Magill, R.A. (1998). Knowledge is more than we can talk about: Implicit learning in motor skill acquisition. *Research Quarterly for Exercise and Sport, 69,* 104–110.

Martindale, C. (1981). *Cognition and consciousness.* Homewood, IL: Dorsey.

Martindale, C. (1990). *The clockwork muse: The predictability of artistic styles.* New York: Basic Books.

Memmert, D. (2007). Can creativity be improved by an attention-broadening training program? An exploratory study focusing on team sports. *Creativity Research Journal, 19,* 281–292.

Memmert, D., & Furley, P. (2007). "I spy with my little eye!" Breadth of attention, inattentional Blindness, and tactical decision making in team sports. *Journal of Sport & Exercise Psychology, 29,* 365–347.

Memmert, D., & Roth, K. (2007). The effects of non-specific and specific concepts on tactical creativity in team ball sports. *Journal of Sport Science, 25,* 1423–1432.

Memmert, D., Baker, J., & Bertsch, C. (in press). Play and practice in the development of sport-specific creativity in team ball sports: A preliminary examination. *High Ability Studies.*

Milgram, R.M. (1990). Creativity: An idea whose time has come and gone. In M.A. Runco & R.S. Albert (Eds.), *Theory of Creativity* (pp. 215–233). Newbury Park, CA: Sage.

Mitchell, S.A. (2005). Teaching and learning games at the secondary level. In L.L.Griffin & J.I. Butler (Eds.), *Teaching games for understanding: Theory, research and practice* (pp. 71–90). Champaign, IL: Human Kinetics.

Mitchell, S.A., Griffin, L., & Oslin, J.L. (1995). An analysis of two instructional approaches to teaching invasion games. *Research Quarterly for Exercise and Sport, 66,* A–65.

Mitchell, S.A., Oslin, J.L., & Griffin, L.L. (2006). *Teaching sport concepts and skills: A tactical games approach* (2nd ed.). Champaign, IL: Human Kinetics.

Most, S.B., Scholl, B.J., Clifford, E.R., & Simons, D.J. (2005). What you see is what you set: Sustained inattentional blindness and the capture of awareness. *Psychological Review, 112,* 217–242.

Plessner, H., Unkelbach, C., Memmert, D., Baltes, A., & Kolb, A. (2009). Regulatory fit as a determinant of sport performance. *Psychology of Sport & Exercise, 10,* 108–115.

Reber, A.S. (1989). Implicit learning and tactic knowledge. *Journal of Experimental Psychology: General, 118*(3), 219–235.

Renzulli, J.S. (1994). *Schools for talent development: A practical plan for total school improvement.* Mansfield Center, CT: Creative Learning Press.

Renzulli, J.S. & Reis, S.M. (2000).The schoolwide enrichment model. In K.A. Heller, F.J. Mönks, R.J. Sternberg, & R.F. Subotnik (Eds.), *International handbook of giftedness and talent* (pp. 367–382). Amsterdam: Elsevier.

Ryan, R.M., & Deci, E.L. (2000). Self-determination theory and the facilitation of intrinsic motivation, social development, and well-being. *American Psychologist, 55,* 68–78.

Simonton, D.K. (1996). Creative expertise: A life-span development perspective. In K.A. Ericsson (Ed.), *The road to expert performance: Empirical evidence from the arts and sciences, sports, and games* (pp. 227–253). Mahwah, NJ: Erlbaum.

Simonton, D.K. (1999). Talent and its development: An emergenic and epigenetic model. *Psychological Review, 106,* 435–357.

Sternberg, R.J. (Ed.). (1999). *Handbook of creativity.* Cambridge, UK: Cambridge University Press.

Sternberg, R.J., & Lubart, T.I. (1995). *Defying the crowd.* New York: Free Press.

Sternberg, R.J., & Lubart, T.I. (1999). The concept of creativity: Prospects and paradigms. In R.J. Sternberg (Ed.), *Handbook of creativity* (pp. 3–15). Cambridge, UK: Cambridge University Press.

Turner, A.P., & Martinek, T.J. (1992). A comparative analysis of two models for teaching games. *International Journal of Physical Education, 29,* 15–31.

Vallerand, R.J. (2001). A hierarchical model of intrinsic and extrinsic motivation in sport and exercise. In D.G. Roberts (Ed.), *Advances in motivation in sport and exercise* (pp. 212–235). Champaign, IL: Human Kinetics.

Wulf, G., & Toole, T. (1999). Physical assistance devices in complex motor skill learning: Benefits of a self-controlled practice schedule. *Research Quarterly for Exercise and Sport, 70,* 265–272.

chapter 14

Unpacking Tactical Problems in Invasion Games: Integrating Movement Concepts Into Games Education

Kath Howarth, PhD • Jennifer L. Fisette, EdD
Michele Sweeney, EdD • Linda L. Griffin, PhD

The teaching of movement concepts develops a deeper understanding of tactical problems in invasion games. When teachers intentionally and explicitly focus on movement concepts, learners will form a more cohesive appreciation of games, which require skill, spatial awareness, degrees of effort, and relationships between people and objects.

Games are complex because they are based on skills, strategy, and chance that are open and unpredictable (Siedentop, 1990; Light, 2005). Both scholars and practitioners agree that the complex interactions of tactical decisions, skills, and social dynamics make games particularly difficult to teach well (Graham, Holt/Hale, & Parker, 2004; Kirk, Brooker, & Braiuka, 2000). However, these same complications make games meaningful and pleasurable. To guide instructors in teaching complex sport-related games, Mitchell, Oslin, and Griffin (2006) simplified the six-component model for Teaching Games for Understanding (TGfU) to a three-part version known as the Tactical Games Model (TGM). The latter model utilizes modified game play, develops tactical awareness and decision making, and incorporates basic tactical problems, frameworks, and levels of complexity. However, little focus has been placed on potential of applying the movement concepts developed by Rudolf Laban (1963) to these models. Laban's movement analysis defines movement in terms

Introducing the explicit consideration of movement concepts to the complex cosmos of games play will enhance students' awareness and understanding of the underlying principles of games. Furthermore, it will equip players with another set of tools to use in making tactical decisions, which they can then apply to learning new games.

of four concepts – body, space, effort, and relationship. Although these concepts have been part of the pedagogical language of physical education for half a century, they have yet to become fully integrated into the language of games teaching. We argue that connecting movement concepts to games understanding will deepen students' awareness of what it means to play games that require skill, spatial awareness, degrees of effort, and the relationships between people and objects.

The purpose of this chapter is to expand the reader's thinking about games teaching by including movement concepts in models for understanding games (TGfU and TGM). We propose that introducing the explicit consideration of movement concepts to the complex cosmos of games play will enhance students' awareness and understanding of the underlying principles of games. Furthermore, it will equip players with another set of tools to use in making tactical decisions, which they can then apply to learning new games.

In the TGM and TGfU models, games are organized according to a classification system that helps teachers and coaches think about the complexities of and the similarities and differences between games (Mitchell, Oslin, & Griffin, 2006). In both models, games are categorized by the primary means of scoring and are classified as target, striking or fielding, net/wall, and invasion games. These classifications rank game complexity in relation to the varying demands of body or skill when matched against concepts of space, effort, and relationships (Light, 2005; Rovegno, 2008). For example, in target games, such as golf or bowling, the space in which players move is constant. However, space in invasion games is ever changing.

The concepts of body awareness (what the body does), space awareness (where the body moves), effort (when and how the body moves), and relationship (with whom the body moves) describe the various movements players experience in games.

The concepts of body awareness (what the body does), space awareness (where the body moves), effort (when and how the body moves), and relationship (with whom the body moves) describe the various movements players experience in games. Graham et al. (2004) use skill themes as a proxy for body awareness and use a grammarian's model to depict skills as action verbs and movement concepts as adverbs that express concepts of effort, space, and relationship. The skill of running can be described in many complex and different ways simply by attaching a movement concept adverb. For example, players can run in different directions (forward or backward), at different levels of effort and intensity (fast or slow), and in different relationships to others (away from or toward an opponent).

TGfU and TGM are learner-centered approaches designed to develop tactical understanding through carefully constructed, modified game play (Mitchell, Oslin, & Griffin, 2003). TGfU has usually been considered a thematic model for games curriculum and pedagogy for middle-school and high-school students (aged 11 through 18). Recently, scholars have proposed that the models are appropriate for students as young as second grade (age 7) (Mitchell et al., 2003; Mitchell, 2005). Rovegno (2008) has stretched the idea even further, suggesting that the themes represented through TGfU, especially the notion of teaching tactical skills and thematic understanding for games, can be taught as early as kindergarten (age 5). Movement concepts provide an additional thematic structure within which tactical skills develop. A game-playing skill—catching, for example—is described as tactical because it develops within the context of a game or a gamelike setting. When further described according to a movement concept, such as space, the tactical skill of catching can be performed by individual players in the different areas of personal space around their bodies. Using the relationship concept, catching can then be practiced while moving away from an opponent to create a passing lane, which is more challenging than catching in the static setting of personal space. When modified by the effort concept, catching can be performed at different speeds, such as accelerating or suddenly stopping to lose a defender.

All four movement concepts can be used in a progression to develop tactical skills. But in invasion games, space—awareness of it, movement through it, manipulation of opponents within it, strategies to control it—is arguably the key movement concept for successful performance. Therefore, for the purpose of this chapter, we will focus on developing a sequence of activities that utilize the movement concept of space in invasion games. We suggest that the language and understanding of movement concepts should be an intentional component of games education in both TGfU and TGM models. Integrating them would enable students to learn from the ebb and flow between movement concepts and tactical awareness in game play. For example, instead of telling students to "get open," which implicitly introduces the concept of movement in space, we suggest explaining what it means—creating a passing lane by moving from personal to general space. When both movement and tactical concepts are consciously taught, students learn skills from the fluid process of play rather than from isolated drills.

Both TGfU and TGM primarily emphasize the game and its tactical problems, followed by game appreciation, decision making, movements, and the skills players need to solve tactical problems in performance (Mitchell et al., 2003). However, as Rovegno (2008) asserts, movement concepts should be taught as authentic content within games, thus helping children to understand in meaningful ways. Therefore, a different model will be required if TGfU and TGM are to explicitly place more attention on

> **W**hen both movement and tactical concepts are consciously taught, students learn skills from the fluid process of play rather than from isolated drills.

movement concepts in the early stages of teaching invasion games. In the next section, we offer a new model to assist in the planning of learning experiences that are developmentally appropriate for the integrated teaching of tactical and movement concepts.

Teaching Tactical and Movement Concepts: A Model for Teachers

Since learners' characteristics shape the game form and influence the design for teaching tactical and movement concepts, the proposed model is similar to the TGfU and TGM frameworks (figure 14.1) in that it places learners at the center. The model has three planning steps for teachers. First, with knowledge of the students' characteristics in mind, the teacher selects the tactical concept to be learned or the tactical problems to be solved in the lesson. Next, the teacher considers what students need to understand about the ways in which movement concepts relate to the tactical problem. Finally, the teacher contemplates the factors that must be considered when designing a game or game form that explores the selected tactical and movement concepts.

Table 14.1 outlines a number of decisions teachers must make about learners during the planning phase (Howarth & Bailey, 2009). This matrix presents a set of guiding questions within the three learning domains (psychomotor, cognitive, and affective), which teachers can use to locate the level of students' skills, knowledge, and social responsibility.

The next element to consider is students' understanding of movement concepts while playing invasion games. Table 14.2 on page 250 provides a matrix for the movement concept of space. The matrix focuses on a developmental progression for spatial understanding that ranges from simple to complex. It demonstrates how the demands of spatial aware-

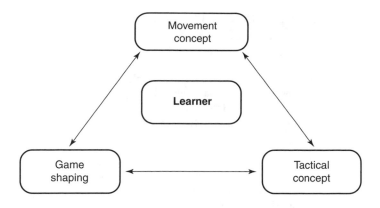

Figure 14.1 Model for teaching tactical and movement concepts.

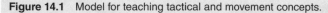

Table 14.1 Student Characteristics: Central Questions for Teachers

Psychomotor skills	Cognitive skills	Affective skills
What relevant skills have learners already acquired?	What do learners know already about this game (skills, rules, tactics, and so on)?	Can learners run a small game without teacher assistance?
What relevant skills have your learners been introduced to but have not yet mastered?	What knowledge can learners transfer from other games?	Can learners work on skills alone, with a partner, and in small groups?
What strengths do learners have (relative to size of space, equipment, and so on)?	Do learners understand safety issues?	Can learners organize themselves and safely collect and set up equipment?
What skills do learners have in regard to the use of spatial awareness, effort, and relationships?	What do learners already know about space awareness, effort, and relationships in game play?	Can learners work on movements alone, with a partner, and in small groups?

ness become more complex for learners when the number of players is increased or the playing area is made larger.

Having assessed their students' individual characteristics and knowledge of movement concepts, teachers can then plan an appropriate form through games shaping (see table 14.3) (Howarth & Bailey, 2009). For example, teachers decide on the number of players depending on the tactical content of the lesson and student characteristics. When the lesson focuses on defense, the teacher may want to increase the number of defenders so that players are more likely to experience success. Similarly, decisions about the space used for the game depend on the skill and

Table 14.2   Movement Concept Matrix for Space

Space situation	Space type	Action
Alone (1)	Personal space Directions Levels Pathways	• Hold the object and carry it into general space • Forward, sideways, backward • High, medium, low • Linear, curved, zigzag
With a partner or teammate (1+1)	General space Personal space Levels Pathways and directions	• Distance: short and long passes • Stationary to moving through space together • Signaling, receiving, and sending at low, medium, and high levels • Player and object and goal or target
Against an opponent (1v1)	General space Personal space Levels Pathways	• Distance from opponent: large and small spaces • Areas: large for attack advantage, small for defense advantage • Use low, medium, and high signals to protect the object • Straight line if unmarked, zigzag to dodge, curve to evade
Two attacks versus one (2v1)	General space Distance between players Directions Pathways	• Distance between attacks • Sides: free side, marked side • Support right, left, forward, back, angle • For players: straight, V-cut, hook • For object: flat, arc, bounce, through, angle • Shapes (of players): e.g., triangle in give-and-go pattern
Two (or more) versus two (or more) with a goal or target (2v2)	General space Depth in defense Areas Personal space Levels and lanes Pathways/ patterns of play	• Width in attack: give and go, one or two passes away • Covering space: to the goal, to the ball • Defense area, midfield, scoring area • Width and depth: ball-side, help-side, support • Shooting space: penetration of space • Dangerous space around the goal: clear from or attack goal • Open/free space: for cutting, for scoring, for receiving the ball • Covered/blocked space • Passing, shooting, defending, helping • Triangle of attack and defense, give and go, picks, zones

strength of the learners. Teachers may increase the size of the playing area or goal to provide an advantage for the offense.

The rules and conditions governing the game can be manipulated to match learner expertise and experience. Rules that prohibit checking or tackling an attacker with the ball can be imposed to account for beginners' skills and safety. Teachers may place conditions on the game to elicit certain tactical behaviors or to emphasize particular elements and skills within the game. For instance, to encourage a multipronged offense, a teacher could alter game conditions by changing the boundaries of the playing area from long and narrow to short and wide. Variations to meet the needs of the learners may be implemented

> *Teachers may place conditions on the game to elicit certain tactical behaviors or to emphasize particular elements and skills within the game.*

as well. Scoring could be changed so that learners have more success in the early stages. For example, players on defense can be given points for intercepting or regaining possession from a ground ball or rebound. Equipment can be varied to accommodate different skill levels and strengths.

The following examples demonstrate how to use the model to teach team passing in invasion games. The examples focus on developing the concept of space in order to promote a better understanding of the tactical concept of maintaining possession. After all, as Mitchell (2005) points out, "if you don't have the ball, you cannot score!" A player who understands the concept of space will be able to view the tactical problem of maintaining possession in a creative and thoughtful way (Howarth, 2001). Each game example has been chosen with the assumption that the players are in the early stages of skill, cognitive understanding, and social awareness. The questions about learners in table 14.1 can be used to determine players' level. Therefore, game shaping for these players (table 14.3) should involve small numbers and small areas to give optimum success with little or no defensive pressure. The game examples include at least two concepts related to space that teachers will need to explain through the example game. The design of the following games demonstrates how movement concepts are integrated using the overarching tactical concept. The examples start with large and broad concepts and skills, and then become progressively smaller and more specific.

Examples for Elementary or Beginning Players

The first three tactical and movement concepts explained here are developmentally appropriate for elementary or beginning players.

Table 14.3   Games Shaping

Numbers	Playing area	Rules and conditions	Variations
Number of players?	Size of area?	Primary rules?	Scoring variations?
Even number in teams?	Shape of area?	Secondary rules?	Playing time?
Odd numbers in teams?	The goal?	Conditions of play?	Equipment modifications?

Example 1: Movement Concepts—
Personal Space, General Space, and Directions

The tactical concept illustrated here is maintaining possession of the ball.

Lesson focus: Give-and-go passing triangle with two players

1. Throw the ball and then move into a new space to catch.
2. Throw to a space in front of a moving player.

Space concepts: Instructions to students

1. *New space.* "You are here. Now run somewhere else. That's a *new space*."
2. *Space in front.* "Point in front of you. Point to the side and then behind you. In which direction can you run fastest? That's where the ball needs to go."
3. *Personal space.* "What can you do from where you are now? Move forward? Move to the side? Help pass the ball to an open player?"

Example 2: Movement Concepts—
Personal Space and Pathways

The tactical concept illustrated here is maintaining possession of the ball.

Lesson focus: Protect the object. Win points by dodging past an opponent (2 players - 1v1).

1. Protect the object in a safe space.
2. Run in a zigzag pathway.

Space concepts: Instructions to students

1. *Safe space.* "What do you need to do within your personal space to keep the ball safe? Hold the ball away from a defender. Can they touch it? No? Then that's a safe space!"
2. *Zigzag pathway.* "Draw a Z in the air. Now do one on the floor with your feet. See the straight lines going in different directions? Can you do lots of them? Would it be difficult for me follow you? Why? Let's see if you can get away from someone else, just like the game of tag."

Example 3: Movement Concepts—
Personal and General Space, Directions, and Levels

The tactical concept illustrated here is maintaining possession of the ball.

Lesson focus: Throw to a free player in open space.
Three attackers maintain possession against one defender (3v1).

1. Look for the player who is in an open space and is not marked by a defender.

2. Throw to teammates who signal that they are in open space.

3. Throw to a player who signals and runs to an open space.

Space concepts

1. *Open space.* Ask one child to stand behind you. Can the other players see her? No. What if she waves her hand out to the side? Can they see her hand? Yes. What if she follows her hand and runs away from you? Can they see her now? Yes. She is now in an *open* or *general space.*

2. *Personal space.* What can players do in their *personal space* to help create an open space? Can receivers point to an open space, pivot, and run into the clear? Can ball handlers protect the ball by shifting it from one side of the body to the other? Does that enable them to pass safely?

3. *Signaling.* How do we know when a school bus is going to stop? How do we know when a train is coming through the station? Signals provide this information. How can we let each other know that we are ready to catch the pass? With a hand signal? With our voices?

4. *Levels.* What level (high, medium, or low) of signal can be used to indicate a safe passing lane to teammates?

Examples for Middle- and High-School Players

The model for teaching tactical and movement concepts can also be implemented at the middle- and high-school levels (for students aged 11 through 18). The following three examples align with the elementary (beginning) level outlined previously, but are developmentally appropriate for middle school (secondary) or novice (intermediate) players.

Example 1: Movement Concepts— Personal Space, General Space, and Directions

The tactical concept illustrated here is maintaining possession of the ball.

Lesson focus: Give-and-go passing in a 3v3 game

1. Throw the ball and then move into a new space to catch.

2. Throw to a space in front of a moving player.

Space concepts: Instructions for students

1. *New space.* "You see that your classmate or teammate, who has the ball, is positioned diagonally across from you and is being defended. That person needs to pass the ball to an open player.

Where do you need to move to be in position to receive the ball safely? Go to an open space to create a passing lane."

2. *Space to the side of you.* "In which direction can you run to get to an open space? Is there another player to the left or right of you? Are you being defended? Should you run to a space where there is another player or one where there is no player? Run to the space that is open."

Example 2: Movement Concepts— Personal Space and Pathways

The tactical concept illustrated here is maintaining possession of the ball.

Lesson focus: Protect the object. Win a point by dodging past an opponent (2v2).

1. Protect the object in a safe space.
2. Run in a V-cut pathway.

Space concepts: Instructions to students

1. *Safe space.* "If you have the ball, is it in a space that allows the defense to take possession of it? What do you need to do to protect the ball? How do you move yourself or the ball to a safe space away from defenders?"

2. *V-cut pathway.* "Your teammate needs to pass the ball to an open player. You are being defended and need to move away from the defender to get into an open space (to create a passing lane). How will you move to create that open space? Can you change directions (V-cut) to move into open space and lose your defender?"

Example 3: Movement Concepts— Personal and General Space, Directions, and Levels

The tactical concept illustrated here is maintaining possession of the ball.

Lesson focus: Throw to a free player in open space in a 3v3 game

1. Look for the player who is in an open space and is unmarked.
2. Throw to a teammate who signals to an open space.
3. Throw to a player who signals and runs to an open space.

Space concepts: Instructions to students

1. *Open space.* "Can your teammate see you when you are in front of or behind the defender? If the ball handler cannot see you, how can they get the ball to you? What can you do in your personal space to help create an open space (as a receiver and as a ball handler)?

How much time will that open space be available before a defender covers the space? What does the ball handler need to do to get the ball to the open space as a teammate moves toward it?"

2. *Signaling.* "If either the receiver or ball handler is being defended, how can you let one another know that you are ready to catch the pass? With a hand signal? With your voice? Can you fake and then signal a move to open space?"

3. *Levels and directions.* "What levels (high, medium, or low) and directions (forward, backward, or sideways) can you use to signal a safe passing lane?"

Conclusion

The model for teaching tactical and movement concepts is our first attempt to integrate movement concepts with tactical problems across game categories. Competent games players combine mature forms of both skills and movement concepts. To develop competent players, movement concepts need to be made more explicit and intentional in games education. This goal can be accomplished by threading movement concepts throughout preschool-grade 12 curriculums (for students aged 4 to 18). Examples provided for the elementary and intermediate (secondary) levels emphasized the movement concept of space within invasion games. Teachers should also develop progressions for the other movement concepts (body, effort, and relationships). We look forward to further discussion of learner-centered curriculum, and unit and lesson objectives that incorporate movement concepts with tactical concepts in games education.

Discussion Questions

1. Describe briefly the four movement concepts of body awareness, space awareness, effort and relationship. Explain how the use of these concepts adds to the development of tactical understanding.

2. Choose a tactical concept, such as attacking the goal or defending space. Design your own example of a lesson focus and movement concepts which would help your students explore and understand the tactical concept.

3. Give examples of how the following movement concepts could be explored to help students become more competent games players using an invasion game of your choice.

   a. The effort concepts of fast and slow

   b. The relationship concepts of in front, to the side, and behind

      c. The effort concepts of strong and light force

      d. The relationship concepts of near and far

References

Graham, G., Holt/Hale, S., & Parker, M. (2004). *Children moving: A reflective approach to teaching physical education* (6th ed.). Boston: McGraw Hill.

Howarth, K. (2001). Space, the final frontier: Space as a key concept in the teaching of invasion games. *Teaching Elementary Physical Education, 12,* 8-11.

Howarth, K., & Bailey, J. (2009). Game shaping: A tool for teachers. *Strategies: A Journal for Physical and Sport Educators,* 14-19.

Kirk, D., Brooker, R., & Braiuka, S. (2000, April). *Teaching games for understanding: A situated perspective on student learning.* Paper presented at the annual meeting of the American Educational Research Association, New Orleans, LA.

Laban, R. (1963). *Modern educational dance* (2nd ed.). New York: Frederick A. Praeger Publishers.

Light, R. (2005). Making sense out of chaos: Australian coaches talk about game sense. In L. Griffin & J. Butler (Eds.), *Teaching games for understanding: Theory, research, and practice* (pp. 169-181). Champaign, IL: Human Kinetics.

Mitchell, S. (2005). Teaching and learning games at the elementary level. In L. Griffin & J. Butler (Eds.), *Teaching games for understanding: Theory, research, and practice* (pp. 55-69). Champaign, IL: Human Kinetics.

Mitchell, S., Oslin, J., & Griffin, L.L. (2003). *Sport foundations for elementary physical education: A tactical games approach.* Champaign, IL: Human Kinetics.

Mitchell, S., Oslin, J., & Griffin, L.L. (2006). *Teaching sport concepts and skills: A tactical games approach* (2nd ed.). Champaign, IL: Human Kinetics.

Rovegno, I. (2008, May). *Teaching games to elementary school children: Children's understanding of game structures and tactics.* Paper presented at the fourth international TGfU, Vancouver, BC, Canada.

Siedentop, D. (1990). *Introduction to physical education, fitness and sport.* Mountain View, CA: Mayfield.

Index

Note: The italicized *f* and *t* following page numbers refer to figures and tables, respectively.

About the Contributors

Len Almond is the director of Physical Education and foundation director of the BHF National Centre for Physical Activity and Health at Loughborough University. He is currently a visiting professor at St. Mary's University College in London. He chairs the BHF National Advisory Group for Early Years, and he is a member of the Department of Health National Guidelines Expert Group preparing the first United Kingdom physical activity guidelines for children under age 5. Len has a long interest in curriculum development and has challenged teachers to rethink and develop physical education. He recognized the need to generate change from teachers' real love—games. As a result, he was part of the original team with Rod Thorpe and David Bunker to develop Teaching Games for Understanding. As editor of the *Bulletin of Physical Education,* he devoted a whole edition to articles on TGfU, which provided the first opportunity for TGfU to reach a wider audience beyond Loughborough University. He received his MEd from Manchester University and his doctorate from Loughborough.

Photo courtesy of Len Almond.

David Bunker, who was awarded the Loughborough University Medal, qualified as a teacher of physical education and geography at Loughborough College of Education (now Loughborough University) in 1964. He served as head of department of Alleyn's School in Dulwich, England for three years before attending the University of Iowa for postgraduate study. After heading back to the UK in 1968, he taught at an inner-London primary school for one year and at Brighton Grammar School (Sussex) for four years as head of the Department of Physical Education. While teaching, Bunker completed an advanced diploma in the psychology of education at Sussex University, which led to his arrival as a lecturer at Loughborough University in 1973. He and Rod Thorpe jointly developed a different approach to the teaching of games (TGfU) and revamped the undergraduate

Photo courtesy of David Bunker.

program for 9 programs and 900 students during David's term as director of undergraduate studies in the School of Sport and Exercise Sciences. David was awarded the Loughborough University medal after 30 years of a distinguished career in teaching, curriculum innovation and change, service, and administration. He received his honorary doctorate from Loughborough.

Joy I. Butler, EdD, (Associate Professor) is the coordinator of undergraduate studies and physical-education teacher education (PETE) graduate and undergraduate programs in the Department of Curriculum and Pedagogy at the University of British Columbia (UBC). She is also active in the international scholarship, organization, and advocacy for Teaching Games for Understanding (TGfU). Dr. Butler's research and teaching, which have developed around constructivist-learning theory, focus on research and practice in curriculum and pedagogy. She was the director of the first international TGfU conference in 2001 in New Hampshire, United States, and the fourth conference in 2008 at UBC in Vancouver, Canada. She founded the TGfU international task force in 2002 and chaired it until 2009. She is the coeditor of three books on TGfU and has authored many articles in the areas of physical-education learning and teaching, curriculum innovations, and teacher education. In July 2009, she convened the first M.Ed. cohort of physical educators at UBC.

Connie S. Collier, PhD, is an associate professor in the School of Exercise, Leisure, and Sport at Kent State University. She joined the faculty at Kent State University in 1997, having previously taught three years at Miami University and nine years in public schools in Ohio. She received her BS from Defiance College and her MA and PhD from The Ohio State University. Connie's scholarship focus is the preparation and professional development of physical-education teachers, with an emphasis on the development of pedagogical practices and curricula that are responsive to issues of social justice. Her recent research examines and critiques innovative curricular approaches in physical education, particularly games teaching and sport education.

Photo courtesy of Connie S. Collier.

John Corlett, PhD, is a professor of physical education and kinesiology and the dean of the Faculty of Applied Health Sciences at Brock University in St. Catharines, Ontario, Canada. Before coming to Brock in 2002, he held academic appointments at the University of Windsor in Canada and the University of Botswana in southern Africa. His area of teaching and research is sport philosophy with a focus on the philosophical foundations of education and health professions. He also has extensive coaching experience, primarily in the sport of basketball. He has been very active in international education for many years, traveling to more than 70 countries during his academic career. Since 2005, his primary scholarly focus has been on the development of physical education in El Salvador.

Photo courtesy of John Corlett.

Brent Davis, PhD, is professor and David Robitaille chair in mathematics, science, and technology education at the University of Calgary. His research focuses on the educational relevance of developments in the cognitive and complexity sciences, and he teaches courses at the undergraduate and graduate levels in curriculum studies, mathematics education, and educational change. Davis has published books and articles in the areas of mathematics learning and teaching, curriculum theory, teacher education, epistemology, and action research. His most recent book is *Engaging Minds: Changing Teaching in Complex Times* (2nd edition, 2008; coauthored with Dennis Sumara and Rebecca Luce-Kapler).

Photo courtesy of Brent Davis.

Adriano De Souza, MA, is a native of Sao Paulo, Brazil. He has been coaching for 15 years both in Brazil and in the United States. Currently working at Illinois State University in the Department of Intercollegiate Athletics, he has a licensure degree in physical education, a bachelor's degree in sports coaching from the State University of Campinas (Brazil), and, most recently, a master's degree with an emphasis in sport pedagogy from Kent State University. He enjoys studying topics such as practice design within the TGfU approach, player-centered approaches to coaching, game-intelligence development, empowerment coaching, and performance assessment. Adriano believes that a player-centered approach to coaching

Photo courtesy of Dennis Banks.

can enhance game performance by helping players solve problems more effectively.

Jennifer L. Fisette, EdD, is an assistant professor of sport pedagogy at Kent State University. She received her undergraduate degree in physical education from Rhode Island College, her master's degree in sport pedagogy at Ithaca College, and her doctoral degree in physical-education teacher education at the University of Massachusetts in Amherst. Prior to her graduate work, she taught physical education and health in the Middletown public-school system located in Rhode Island. Her current research interests explore  the complexities (such as power relations) of students' experiences with physical activity and physical education through student voice and activist initiatives. She is a member of numerous professional organizations, including AAHPERD, AERA, and OAHPERD.

Linda L. Griffin, PhD, received her doctorate in physical-education teacher education from Ohio State University. As a physical educator and coach since 1976, Dr. Griffin has conducted extensive research, published nearly 50 articles and book chapters, and given numerous presentations on the tactical approach. She served on the planning committee for the first TGfU Conference in New Hampshire in 2001 and was a keynote speaker at the Australia conference in 2003. A former volleyball player and coach,  she is a professor and associate dean of the School of Education at the University of Massachusetts in Amherst.

David Gutierrez, PhD, is a titular professor at Universidad de Castilla la Mancha, with expertise in sport pedagogy and games teaching. He studied at the Instituto Nacional de Educacion Fisicia in Madrid from 1992 to 1997, and received his PhD from the Universidad de Castilla la Mancha in 2008. His PhD research focused on the development of tactical knowledge in school-aged children. As part of his PhD studies, David was invited to Kent State University, where he served one semester as a visiting professor. He has  taught physical education at secondary-school and university levels for

11 years and has conducted several TGfU workshops. He has coauthored a book focusing on the games-centered approach (GCA) in net/wall games. As part of a research group, David continues to investigate and promote GCA and sport education. He was the coorganizer of the first seminar for GCA experts in Spain, April 2009.

Tim Hopper, PhD, is an associate professor and faculty member in the School of Exercise Science, Physical and Health Education, and the Faculty of Education at the University of Victoria. He received his master's degree and PhD from the University of Alberta. Dr. Hopper's research focuses on physical-education teacher education, particularly conceptual approaches to teaching, such as TGfU and movement education. Dr. Hopper has taught at all levels of the school curriculum, both in Canada and the

Photo courtesy of Tim Hopper.

United Kingdom. He maintains strong links with local schools through a teacher-education approach known as school-integrated teacher education (SITE) where, observed and assisted by his student teachers, he teaches physical education to classes of children with the eventual goal of training the student teachers to take over the process. His recent research focuses on program-wide development of electronic portfolios and the complexities of teaching from situated-learning experiences. Working with his student teachers, Dr. Hopper has created a continuously expanding Web site of units of instruction on TGfU (www.educ.uvic.ca/faculty/thopper/index.htm).

Kath Howarth, PhD, is a professor in Physical Education at SUNY Cortland, and has been involved in teacher education for most of her career both in England and in the United States. Her interest in TGfU began in England when Bunker and Thorpe first created the idea and has continued to the present time. She has contributed to several texts about TGfU and is particularly interested in the way tactical concepts can be introduced to the elementary-school age

Photo courtesy of Dawn Van Hall.

group. Her sports involvement was in women's lacrosse as a player for England and as an assistant coach for England in two events for the World Cup.

Lynn Kidman, PhD, is a coach educator at the University of Worcester in England. During the 2006-2007 academic year, Lynn was a senior advisor to Sport Recreation New Zealand (SPARC), coordinating the writing and implementation of a coach-development system that is philosophically guided by athlete-centered coaching. As part of SPARC's philosophy, TGfU is embedded into all coaching communities within the coach-development program. Lynn is the author and editor of *Athlete-Centred Coaching: Developing Inspired and Inspiring People* and three other books. She was on the TGfU task force and advocates that the approach is humanistic (athlete-centered), enabling awareness and learning for athletes. Lynn has coached many teams, mostly secondary-school age, in the sports of basketball, swimming, softball, and volleyball. Her most recent coaching experience was as a player manager, consulting with the coach, who used an athlete-centered approach and TGfU to enable athlete ownership and to encourage lifelong values.

Photo courtesy of Robert Kidman.

Raymond Liu Yuk-kwong, PhD, is an associate professor of the Department of Creative Arts and Physical Education at the Hong Kong Institute of Education in Hong Kong. He completed a MS and a PhD at the Loughborough University, UK, in 1990 and 1997. He was the head of the Department of Physical Education and Sports Science from 2000 to 2005. He is a pioneer in promoting TGfU in Hong Kong and mainland China. His current research investigates the implementation of education reform and TGfU. He has published extensively in the areas of TGfU, implementation of education reform, and physical-education curriculum. Dr. Raymond Liu Yuk-kwong was the chair of the organizing committee for the third international TGfU conference and is a former member of the TGfU task force and AIESEP.

Photo courtesy of Atease Production, Eric Yan Chi Liu.

Rebecca J. Lloyd, PhD, is an assistant professor in the Faculty of Education at the University of Ottawa in Canada who promotes interdisciplinarity in health and physical education by combining principles of pedagogy, sport psychology, and curriculum understanding. In collaboration with Stephen Smith, she has developed a motion-sensitive phenomenological approach to research and has explored the experience of flow in exercise pedagogy and the presence of vitality in physical education. Currently, Stephen and Rebecca are developing a model for physical mindfulness that fleshes out kinesthetic pathways toward experiencing enhanced flow and vitality in physical education, physical activity, and sport performance.

Photo courtesy of Gary Kuiper.

Bennett J. Lombardo, EdD, is a native of New York City and is a professor of health and physical education in the Feinstein School of Education and Human Development at Rhode Island College in Providence, Rhode Island. After teaching physical education and coaching in public schools for five years, he moved on to graduate school at Boston University. He served as department chairman for 12 years. His professional interests include pedagogy, specifically teaching and coaching behavior. He has published several works on alternative leadership styles in sport, with a specific focus on the humanistic educational models applied to coaching. He currently resides in Warwick, Rhode Island with his wife, Angela, who is also an educator.

Photo courtesy of Bennett J. Lombardo.

James Mandigo, PhD, is an associate professor at Brock University in the Department of Physical Education and Kinesiology. He is also the co-director for the Centre for Healthy Development at Brock University. His current research and development activities focus on how TGfU can foster physical literacy, positive youth development, and peace education. James has worked extensively with local teachers and school boards within Canada and throughout the Caribbean and El Salvador. His research and development activities in this area have been funded by the Canadian Social Science and Humanities Research Council and Scotiabank International.

Photo courtesy of James Mandigo.

Daniel Memmert, PhD, is a professor and chair of the Department of Movement Science for Team and Racket Sports at German Sport University Cologne in Cologne, Germany. He studied for high-school teaching (physical education, math, sports, and ethics) and has trainer licences in soccer, tennis, snowboarding, and skiing. Memmert received his PhD (basic tactics in team sports) and habilitation (creativity in team sports) in sport science from the University of Heidelberg. His special research areas of interests are cognition, attention, and motivation. He has 12 years of experience in teaching and coaching and has authored or coauthored more than 20 impact-factor publications and five books. He is also an ad-hoc reviewer for several international sport psychology journals. In addition, he has given more than 40 invited talks, 60 scientific talks at conferences, and 70 teaching courses for physical-education teachers and trainers. He collaborates with researchers from the US, Canada, Brazil, and Spain.

Photo courtesy of Institute of Sport and Sport Science, University of Heidelberg.

Steve Mitchell, PhD, is a professor of sport pedagogy in the School of Exercise, Leisure and Sport at Kent State University. He is in his 17th year at Kent State, having previously completed doctoral work at Syracuse University and master's and bachelor's degrees at Loughborough University, England. Steve has authored numerous articles and book chapters related to standards-based teaching in physical education. He has also coauthored two textbooks related to TGfU within public-school physical education, including one that is now in its second edition. Steve teaches undergraduate and postgraduate teacher education and also coaches high school soccer in Kent. His recent undertakings include curriculum and assessment projects with several school districts in northeast Ohio, membership on the curriculum writing team for state physical-education standards, and involvement with the Healthy Kids 4321 project in collaboration with Portage County schools.

Photo courtesy of Eve Dalton.

Judy Oslin, PhD, is professor emerita in the School of Exercise, Leisure, and Sport at Kent State University. Prior to her 16-year tenure at Kent State, Judy was an assistant professor at the University of Alabama, Tuscaloosa, for two years, served as an instructor and graduate-teaching assistant for seven years, and taught middle-school physical education for nine years. She received her BS and MA from Kent State University and her PhD from Ohio State University. Currently, she is working with clinical faculty to enhance professional networks and increase availability of professional development experiences. Besides golfing, working out, remodeling, and volunteering, Judy continues to present PIPEline (NASPE) workshops and promote tactical-games teaching at state, national, and international venues.

Photo courtesy of Judy Oslin.

Jean-François Richard, PhD, is a professor and dean of education at l'Université de Moncton in Moncton, New Brunswick, Canada. Having received a doctoral degree in physical education and educational assessment from l'Université Laval (Québec City, Canada), Jean-François specializes in the fields of curriculum planning and classroom assessment. To his credit, Jean-François has been a regular contributor to the growing body of knowledge in relation to physical education and pedagogy as a whole. Since 1996, most of his work pertaining to physical education has been centered on different aspects of learning and on assessment issues related to games education. This work has led to no less than 30 publications, including contributions to three books related to various issues of games education. Most of Dr. Richard's work has been funded by the Social Sciences and Humanities Research Council of Canada (SSHRC) and by other granting organizations in public and private sectors. The Canadian Association for Health, Physical Education, Recreation, and Dance (CAHPERD) acknowledged Jean-François's contributions to physical education by naming him young professional of the year for the province of New Brunswick in 1999 and CAHPERD scholar in 2007.

Photo courtesy of Jean-François Richard.

Judith Rink, PhD, is a professor in the Department of Physical Education at the University of South Carolina, Columbia. She has published numerous books, research, and articles related to effective teaching of physical education and the effectiveness of state policy on physical-education programs. She has been an editor of the major research journals in her field, including the *Journal of Teaching in Physical Education,* and a section editor for pedagogy of the *Research Quarterly for Exercise and Sport Science.* She is currently on the board of *Quest.* She was the chairperson of the committee to develop the first national content standards for physical education and has been the recipient of many national awards for her scholarship, teaching, leadership, and service to the field. She is currently the program director of the South Carolina Physical-Education Assessment Program.

Photo courtesy of Judith Rink.

Daniel Rodriguez, MA, received his master's degree in physical education at Kent State University. An avid games player and licensed coach, he has applied his educational knowledge to coaching basketball and baseball at local high schools for the past three years. A former college baseball player, Daniel now enjoys softball, running, golf, and fishing. He is a member of the Ohio Association for Health, Physical Education, Recreation, and Dance (OAHPERD). Daniel and his wife, Faith, currently reside in Kent, Ohio.

Photo courtesy of Daniel Rodriguez.

Inez Rovegno, PhD, is a professor in the College of Education at the University of Alabama. She has focused on the development of pedagogical content knowledge for teachers and preservice teachers, constructivist and situated curricular and instructional approaches for elementary physical education, and children's development of basic game understanding and tactics. She has published elementary physical-education curriculum work and research in a range of journals. She also serves on the editorial boards of the *Journal of Teaching in Physical Education* and *Physical Education and Sport Pedagogy.*

Photo courtesy of Inez Rovegno.

Kath Sanford, EdD, is the associate dean of teacher education in the Faculty of Education at the University of Victoria. She is currently the president of the Canadian Society for the Study of Education (CSSE). Her research interests include gender and literacy, alternative literacies, popular culture, and teacher education. She is currently working on one funded research project (CCL) entitled *Literacy Learning through Video Games,* and has two funded SSHRC projects involving gender and literacy learning through video games and E-portfolios in teacher education for individual and programmatic development. These projects have provided the foundation for a variety of recent publications, including *Gendered Literacy Experiences: The Effect of Expectation and Opportunity for Boys' and Girls' Learning* (2006), *Democracy in a Globalized World: Children's Art Exchange From a School/University Partnership* (2006), *Representing Multiple Views of Self-as-Teacher: Integrating Teacher-Education Courses and Self-Study* (2004), and an edited book entitled *Boys and Girls and the Myths of Literacies and Learning* (2008, Canadian Scholars Press).

Photo courtesy of Kath Sanford.

Stephen Smith, PhD, is associate professor and director of Professional Programs at Simon Fraser University. He is responsible for the administration of preservice-teacher-education programs, which cover K-12 schooling across all curriculum areas and include programs in French and indigenous and first nations, as well as international programs in China, Trinidad, Tibet, Jamaica, and Mexico. His scholarly work pertains to curricular and instructional practices in physical education, health education, and teacher education. His illustrative publications include the 1997 book, *Risk and Our Pedagogical Relation to Children: On the Playground and Beyond*, and the 2004 book, *The Bearing of Inquiry in Teacher Education*. His recent work addresses vitality and physical mindfulness as overarching concepts of physical education and, more broadly, a somatic approach to teacher education. His work is published in a range of journals, including the *International Journal of Qualitative Health Research*, the *Indo-Pacific Journal of Phenomenology*, and *Phenomenology and Practice*.

Brian Storey, MA, PhD (in progress), is currently the Chair of the Sport Science department at Douglas College in New Westminster, BC, Canada. He is also a PhD student in the Curriculum Theory and Implementation program at Simon Fraser University. He holds prior degrees in human kinetics, elementary education, and educational psychology from the University of British Columbia. His work has spanned from being a full-time athlete, culminating in representing Canada at the 1996 Olympic Games, to being a full-time elementary-school teacher. The common threads in his work can be characterized by a high degree of attention to the learning environment, attention to the efficacy of learning tasks, and an openness to pedagogical possibility as opposed to curricular constraints.

Photo courtesy of Brian Storey.

Dennis Sumara, PhD, is professor and dean of education at the University of Calgary, Canada. His research explores how imaginative identifications with literary characters and their situations become productive sites of learning, both in school classrooms and in informal learning contexts. Professor Sumara is author of several books, including *Why Reading Literature in School Still Matters: Interpretation, Imagination, Insight,* which won the Ed Fry Book Award at the 2003 national reading conference in the United States. He has also published many research papers and essays in journals, such as *Harvard Educational Review, Educational Theory, Journal of Curriculum Studies, Journal of Literacy Research, International Journal of Qualitative Research in Education,* and *International Journal of Educational Action Research.*

Photo courtesy of Dennis Sumara.

Michele Sweeney, EdD, is an associate professor and coordinator for undergraduate physical education in the Department of Sport and Movement Science at Salem State College in Salem, Massachusetts. She received her master's degree from Ithaca College and her doctorate degree from Boston University. Dr. Sweeney has 30 years of experience teaching physical education and coaching field hockey, soccer, softball, and basketball at K-12 and college levels. She has presented numerous papers and workshops on TGfU and has fully integrated the model into the sport-and-movement-science

Photo courtesy of Michele Sweeney.

curriculum for Salem State College. She is a member of the American Alliance for Health, Physical Education, Recreation, and Dance (AAHPERD), the Association of Supervision and Curriculum Development (ASCD), and the TGfU special-interest group.

Rod Thorpe, DUniv (Doctor of the University), has served Loughborough University sport for 33 years as a lecturer in sports psychology and coaching studies in the Department of Physical Education, Sports Science, and Recreation Management, and since 1997 as the director of the Sports Development Centre. He coached rugby at Loughborough for more than 10 years and has coached and developed tennis for 27 years. He is a coach, author, and lecturer of international renown, particularly in methods of teaching and

Photo courtesy of Rod Thorpe.

coaching games. He was one of the first tutors for the National Coaching Foundation, and was integral to the development of the East Midlands Regional Coaching Centre at Loughborough University as well as the recent evolution of Loughborough's reputation for sport and sports development. Rod Thorpe is currently central to the development of the English Institute of Sport and to the contribution of the Loughborough University site. In 1997, his international contribution to sport, particularly to developments in coaching, was recognized by the International Olympic Committee when he was inaugurated into the UK coaching Hall of Fame. He received the Munrow Award for his services to University Sport in the United Kingdom. Finally, in 2006 he was awarded an honorary doctorate by Loughborough for his contribution to the development of teaching and coaching of young people and to the development of a world-class training facility at the University.

You'll find other outstanding
physical education resources at
www.HumanKinetics.com

In the U.S. call 1.800.747.4457
Australia 08 8372 0999
Canada. 1.800.465.7301
Europe . . . . .+44 (0) 113 255 5665
New Zealand 0800 222 062